CryENGINE 3 Game Development Beginner's Guide

Discover how to use the CryENGINE 3 free SDK, the next-generation, real-time game development tool

Sean Tracy

Paul Reindell

BIRMINGHAM - MUMBAI

CryENGINE 3 Game Development Beginner's Guide

First published: September 2012

Production Reference: 1140912

Published by Packt Publishing Ltd.
Livery Place
35 Livery Street
Birmingham B3 2PB, UK.

ISBN 978-1-84969-200-7

www.packtpub.com

Cover Image by Hazel Denise Karunungan (denise@crytek.com)

Credits

Authors

Sean Tracy

Paul Reindell

Reviewers

Marcieb Balisacan

Michelle M. Fernandez

Christos Gatzidis

Sascha Hoba

Robertson Holt

Lee Chiu Yi Joanna

Adam Johnson

Morgan Kita

Acquisition Editor

Robin de Jongh

Lead Technical Editor

Dayan Hyames

Technical Editors

Sharvari Baet

Manmeet Singh Vasir

Jalasha D'costa

Copy Editors

Insiya Morbiwala

Laxmi Subramanian

Project Coordinator

Leena Purkait

Proofreader

Clyde Jenkins

Indexer

Monica Ajmera Mehta

Graphics

Valentina D'silva

Aditi Gajjar

Production Coordinators

Nitesh Thakur

Manu Joseph

Cover Work

Nitesh Thakur

About the Authors

Sean Tracy is Crytek's Senior Field Application Engineer for the award-winning CryENGINE. He is responsible for adapting the engine and its features to individual licensees, as well as developing full technical and "vertical slice" demos for prospective and existing clients. Describing himself as a "generalizing specialist", he also gives support directly to CryENGINE licensees while designing and maintaining their workflows, pipelines, and development techniques.

Sean was recruited by Crytek in 2008 after working as an electronics technician for the Canadian military. He was recruited due to his role in founding and leading development on the award-winning total conversion project—MechWarrior: Living Legends. Since then, he has been featured in numerous gaming magazines and has been invited to speak at many game-related trade shows, conferences, and seminars. He is an avid gamer with extensive modding experience on titles, including Never Winter Nights, Battlefield, Doom, and Quake.

This is Sean's second book.

I would first like to thank my beautiful wife, Kristy, for her love and support throughout the process of writing this book and for her ongoing support allowing me to do what I truly enjoy for a living. I also want to thank her for giving us a gorgeous baby girl who is the light of my life. I would also like to thank my colleagues for taking the time to review the book with me, as it's a pleasure to work with people with the same love for real-time technology as I have. Finally, I'd like to thank Crytek and Packt for their support in allowing me to write this book and for making one of the best game engines on the market.

Paul Reindell has been an Engine Programmer in the SDK team since June 2010. He is responsible for UI programming, next-generation features, and the development of new tools for the CryENGINE 3 Sandbox, as well as for forum support for CryENGINE licensees. He has also worked on projects for licensees and evaluators.

During his diploma thesis, Paul started as an Intern at Crytek in March 2010. He finished his diploma theses successfully in June and started directly as a Junior Programmer in the SDK team. During his academic studies, he created a mod prototype with CryENGINE 2 (GarbageWarz); and during his diploma thesis, he was able to connect CryENGINE 3 successfully with a Head tracking API. Before working at Crytek, he worked for three years as a programmer at DENSO Germany besides his studies.

I would like to thank my family, who have been positive and unconditional supporters. I would also like to thank my girlfriend, who always encourages me more than anyone else.

I would also like to thank my colleagues, who have provided invaluable opportunities for me to expand my knowledge and shape my career.

About the Reviewers

Marcieb Balisacan is a game programmer, designer, and producer working in the Philippines. Being from a computer science and multimedia background, he has released several games for mobile devices and social networks on the Web since 2006. His passion for game development is equaled only by his passion for music and storytelling, all of which he uses to share his love for the art of creation.

> I would like to acknowledge my newborn daughter, Nikita Lyric, who during the time of this review, kept me awake and inspired me to move ahead.

Michelle M. Fernandez is a mobile game developer for iOS/Android platforms, and co-founder of MobiDojo (`http://www.mobidojo.com`), which is based out of San Diego, California. MobiDojo has released apps in the marketplace for iOS, Android, Nook, and Kindle. Michelle has had numerous years working in the game industry, in the development and e-commerce environment. She is a mentor for aspiring artists and programmers trying to break into the industry. She also extends her expertise as a panelist at the University of California, San Diego Extension—DAC and The Art Institute of California, San Diego—by participating in sessions relating to game production, design, and marketing.

Michelle is the author of *Corona SDK Mobile Game Development: Beginner's Guide*, which was published by *Packt Publishing*. She has also written an article called *How to Create a Mini-Game in Corona SDK* for Game Coder Magazine. You can also view her personal website at `http://www.michellefernandez.com`.

Dr Christos Gatzidis is a Senior Lecturer in Creative Technology at Bournemouth University, UK at the School of Design, Engineering, and Computing. He has a PhD from City University London, UK and an MSc in Computer Animation from Teesside University, UK; he has also previously published work in a number of academically edited books, conferences, and journals. He is also the framework leader for the Creative Technology collection of degrees at Bournemouth University (which includes the BSc in Games Technology and the MSc in Computer Games Technology courses). Christos teaches a variety of units on these courses and uses game engines (such as Epic's Unreal Development Kit) across all years of the undergraduate course, to cover topics ranging from basic-level design fundamentals to more advanced scripting.

I would like to thank the authors of this book and also the great people at Packt for producing this excellent guide in one of the most engaging game development tools around today.

Sascha Hoba is an Engine Programmer for Crytek's award-winning CryENGINE. He is responsible for implementing new features, improving existing ones, and keeping the engine up-to-date with improvements made across all Crytek teams to increase the overall quality of the engine. He also gives direct support to CryENGINE licensees around the world, guiding them on how to use CryENGINE from a programmer's perspective and trying to find possible solutions for special requests made by licensees.

Sascha was recruited by Crytek back in 2010 after studying IT—Information Technology—at university. He was recruited due to his experience in working with all the revisions of CryENGINE since CryENGINE 1, back in 2004. He gained his experience as an active member of the FarCry and Crysis modding communities, where he always tried to push the engine to its limits and solve individual problems on how to implement certain features with the available CryENGINE SDK.

I would like to thank Sean Tracy and Paul Reindell for giving me the opportunity to review this book, which has been quite an interesting experience.

Robertson Holt is a polymath autodidact with a formal education. He is the founder of http://www.headshrinkerstudio.com/ and http://www.anatomicrecords.com/. When Robertson is not engaged with these activities, he's goofing off with his two little pugs, living his fun-loving life in downtown Toronto.

I would like to thank Bob Edward Wilson and Yog Sothoth.

Lee Chiu Yi Joanna is an experienced game developer. She started her game development career in game programming. She has programmed for an action game, KengoZero on the Xbox360, and for a Massively Multiplayer Online Game (MMOG), Otherland, on the PC. She is now also a game designer and has a collection of game designs/writings. Her interest in the mobile/web has led her to develop apps and games for these popular platforms as well. Do keep a look out for her apps/games when they are launched! She is also currently translating and reviewing another book about another interesting topic, Unified Communications. Just a note, she is not just a tech mouse; she also loves food, traveling, taking photos, and spending time with family and friends.

I would like to thank my family and friends for letting me take time away from them to review this book.

Morgan Kita is an AI Engineer working at Crytek in Frankfurt, Germany. He has a background in Computer Science and Genetics. He started his career in the biotech industry and later moved over to the games industry. He has experience in various aspects of the software industry, from databases and tools development, to multiple aspects of games development, such as artificial intelligence and multiplayer networking.

I would like to thank my mother and my brother for encouraging me to follow my passion.

www.PacktPub.com

Support files, eBooks, discount offers and more

You might want to visit www.PacktPub.com for support files and downloads related to your book.

Did you know that Packt offers eBook versions of every book published, with PDF and ePub files available? You can upgrade to the eBook version at www.PacktPub.com and as a print book customer, you are entitled to a discount on the eBook copy. Get in touch with us at service@packtpub.com for more details.

At www.PacktPub.com, you can also read a collection of free technical articles, sign up for a range of free newsletters and receive exclusive discounts and offers on Packt books and eBooks.

http://PacktLib.PacktPub.com

Do you need instant solutions to your IT questions? PacktLib is Packts online digital book library. Here, you can access, read and search across Packt's entire library of books.

Why Subscribe?

- ◆ Fully searchable across every book published by Packt
- ◆ Copy and paste, print and bookmark content
- ◆ On demand and accessible via web browser

Free Access for Packt account holders

If you have an account with Packt at www.PacktPub.com, you can use this to access PacktLib today and view nine entirely free books. Simply use your login credentials for immediate access.

Table of Contents

Preface

The complexity and difficulty involved in making current generation games is increasing. Even the games industry itself is becoming a more competitive and demanding industry to work, than it has been in the past. Project budgets are smaller, production times are shorter, and milestones seem to come more often, especially when working with a publisher. With the increased time and expertise required to engineer these games, many professional and hobbyist developers alike have turned to middleware game engines, such as the CryENGINE, to save them time, money, and frustration, while manifesting their ideas into releasable games.

The CryENGINE is a comfortable fit for most developers, because it allows users to create their content quickly, iterate on that content, and to finalize it without leaving the comfort of the CryENGINE's Sandbox Editor. I often refer to the CryENGINE as a force multiplier, since its tools make it possible for smaller teams to accomplish what used to take an entire development studio, full of people. This book is an introduction to the CryENGINE technology, and is comprised of achievable, small-scale examples, which can be applied in almost any game genre. This book is not designed to cover exhaustively every feature and function in the CryENGINE, but rather is designed to give you the knowledge and tools needed to get you of to a smooth and painless start when making your own games with the CryENGINE 3.

What this book covers

Chapter 1, Introducing the CryENGINE 3 Free SDK, covers the beginning to developing your own games of any scale by learning to harness the power of the award-winning CryENGINE® 3 game engine. In this chapter, you will learn to navigate and interface within the CryENGINE® 3 Sandbox, the tool used to create AAA games, such as Crysis 1 and 2, as well as the soon to be released Crysis 3.

Chapter 2, Breaking Ground with Sandbox, covers building your game worlds in real time with CryENGINE® 3 Sandbox, as we share insights into some of the tools and features useable right out of the box. In this chapter, you will learn how to create your own worlds by following straightforward examples that use some of the important fundamental features available to developers of the CryENGINE®. This includes tools and techniques related to sculpting, molding the terrain, and placing vegetation.

Chapter 3, Playable Levels in No Time, covers more advanced level design tools, which are discussed in the chapter, as well as simple modeling techniques using the integrated CryENGINE solids system.

Chapter 4, I'm a Scripter, Not a Coder, covers learning the method of visual scripting used to create amazingly complex scripted events.

Chapter 5, C++ and Compiling Your Own Game Code, follows along with in-depth C++ programming examples, designed to expose powerful game customization opportunities available to game programmers.

Chapter 6, User Interface and HUD Creation with Flash, covers how to use Autodesk Scaleform in conjunction with the CryENGINE® 3 to create high fidelity 3D heads up displays and menus for the player.

Chapter 7, Creating Assets for the CryENGINE 3, covers how to create your own custom characters and objects for use within the examples.

Chapter 8, Creating Real-time Cutscenes and Cinematic Events, covers how to create your own cutscenes, animations, and videos using the power of the CryENGINE 3 engine to maximize the output.

Chapter 9, Immersion through Audio Design, covers how to use the FMOD designer along with the CryENGINE 3, to add sound and music to your game.

Chapter 10, Preparing to Share Your Content, helps you explore some of the key performance and optimization strategies for levels, and helps you learn to share your content with others.

What you need for this book

- ◆ CryENGINE 3 Free SDK v 3.4
- ◆ Autodesk 3D Studio Max 2010
- ◆ Adobe Photoshop CS4
- ◆ Notepad++

- Visual Studio Express 2010
- Adobe Flash CS 5.5

Who this book is for

This book has been written with the beginner and casual developer in mind. That being said, however, the professional developer will still find valuable knowledge related to other specialties within the examples of this book. For some of the examples in this book, the reader should have some fundamental knowledge of some Digital Content Creation tools, which include Photoshop and 3D Studio Max. Though not a fundamental requirement, having some basic knowledge of real-time graphics software and, consequently, the terminology used, will make the goal of these tutorials more clear. The freely available version of the CryENGINE® 3 has been used for all the examples in this book, and *Chapter 1, Introducing the CryENGINE 3 Free SDK* will guide the reader to download and install the CryENGINE® 3 Free SDK.

Conventions

In this book, you will find several headings appearing frequently.

To give clear instructions of how to complete a procedure or task, we use:

Time for action – heading

1. Action 1
2. Action 2
3. Action 3

Instructions often need some extra explanation so that they make sense, so they are followed with:

What just happened?

This heading explains the working of tasks or instructions that you have just completed.

You will also find some other learning aids in the book, including:

Pop quiz – heading

These are short multiple choice questions intended to help you test your own understanding

Have a go hero – heading

These set practical challenges and give you ideas for experimenting with what you have learned.

You will also find a number of styles of text that distinguish between different kinds of information. Here are some examples of these styles, and an explanation of their meaning.

Code words in text are shown as follows: " If you now navigate to the level directory using Windows Explorer, you will notice a new folder called Layers. Inside that folder, you will see a file named SpawnPoints.lyr."

A block of code is set as follows:

```
<Constraints>
    <Align mode="fixed" />
    <Position top="100" left="100" width="800" height="600" />
</Constraints>
```

New terms and **important words** are shown in bold. Words that you see on the screen, in menus or dialog boxes for example, appear in the text like this: "Look in the **UI:Functons:MainMenu:AddButton** node of the **mm_main** UI Action that creates the button with the **@ui_SoundSettings** caption".

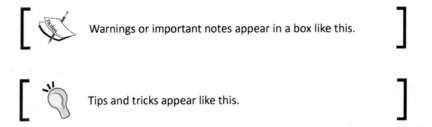

Warnings or important notes appear in a box like this.

Tips and tricks appear like this.

Reader feedback

Feedback from our readers is always welcome. Let us know what you think about this book—what you liked or may have disliked. Reader feedback is important for us to develop titles that you really get the most out of.

To send us general feedback, simply send an e-mail to `feedback@packtpub.com`, and mention the book title through the subject of your message.

If there is a topic that you have expertise in and you are interested in either writing or contributing to a book, see our author guide on `www.packtpub.com/authors`.

Customer support

Now that you are the proud owner of a Packt book, we have a number of things to help you to get the most from your purchase.

Downloading the example code

You can download the example code files for all Packt books you have purchased from your account at `http://www.packtpub.com`. If you purchased this book elsewhere, you can visit `http://www.packtpub.com/support` and register to have the files e-mailed directly to you.

Downloading the color images of this book

We also provide you a PDF file that has color images of the screenshots/diagrams used in this book. The color images will help you better understand the changes in the output.

You can download this file from `http://www.packtpub.com/sites/default/files/downloads/2007_graphics.pdf`.

Errata

Although we have taken every care to ensure the accuracy of our content, mistakes do happen. If you find a mistake in one of our books—maybe a mistake in the text or the code—we would be grateful if you would report this to us. By doing so, you can save other readers from frustration and help us improve subsequent versions of this book. If you find any errata, please report them by visiting `http://www.packtpub.com/support`, selecting your book, clicking on the **errata submission form** link, and entering the details of your errata. Once your errata are verified, your submission will be accepted and the errata will be uploaded to our website, or added to any list of existing errata, under the Errata section of that title.

Piracy

Piracy of copyright material on the Internet is an ongoing problem across all media. At Packt, we take the protection of our copyright and licenses very seriously. If you come across any illegal copies of our works, in any form, on the Internet, please provide us with the location address or website name immediately so that we can pursue a remedy.

Please contact us at copyright@packtpub.com with a link to the suspected pirated material.

We appreciate your help in protecting our authors, and our ability to bring you valuable content.

Questions

You can contact us at questions@packtpub.com if you are having a problem with any aspect of the book, and we will do our best to address it.

1

Introducing the CryENGINE 3 Free SDK

The CryENGINE 3 Software Development Kit (SDK) comes from a pedigree of high fidelity, real-time game engines. It is now freely available for non-commercial use, which allows anyone to leverage the power of the CryENGINE 3 to make their own games and simulations.

In this chapter we will be:

- Joining the development community on `http://www.crydev.net`
- Downloading and installing the CryENGINE 3 SDK
- Reviewing past and present games created using past and present iterations of the CryENGINE
- Exploring some of the latest features available in CryENGINE 3 SDK
- Running the sample content in the `launcher.exe` application
- Analyzing the typical roles that developers undertake to create a game on the CryENGINE, and establishing where we fit in
- Installing the 3D Studio Max exporter tools and acquiring the sample source asset package
- Installing the Adobe Photoshop CryTif plugin
- Opening the Forest map in the CryENGINE 3 Sandbox application
- Interacting with objects and entities in the CryENGINE 3 Sandbox application

What is the CryENGINE?

Not every new computer game needs to start from scratch. A technique that's becoming increasingly common for most developers is to reuse existing game engines. This is where the CryENGINE 3 SDK comes in. The **CryENGINE 3 SDK** is a game engine which drives the visual actions taking place on the screen. Within this engine are the rules that dictate the way the game world works, and how objects and characters should behave within it. Due to the fact that creating the underlying code for the variety of systems within a game engine is usually very expensive and time consuming, the starting point of working with a game engine thus makes excellent financial sense for most developers. Throughout this book, and for all intents and purposes, we will be referring to the CryENGINE 3 SDK as **the engine**.

The CryENGINE has been developed over the past 10 years by the award winning independent developer, Crytek. Crytek has made major iterations to the original CryENGINE over a number of years and is currently on the third iteration, which is why we refer to this version of CryENGINE as the CryENGINE 3.

Arguably, the most prominent tool provided by a game engine is the level, or **World Editor**. The editor used with CryENGINE is known as the **CryENGINE Sandbox**, and it contains a whole suite of tools and sub-editors for developing games.

You can think of the CryENGINE Sandbox as a game compositing tool that acts similarly to any digital video compositing software such as Sony Vegas, Adobe Premiere, and even Windows Movie Maker. However, as opposed to inserting video and audio clips, the developer inserts art, design, and code that will all eventually come together to create a game.

Applying your vision

Many people will have their own ideas for games. The first step on the path to manifesting that idea into reality is to undertake some basic research in order to expand the idea into a robust proposal, or "pitch" as it's in the game industry. There are simple considerations that a game designer can make in order to take their loosely defined idea into a solid concept. It might be tempting for some of us to jump straight into designing levels, characters, icons, and other fine details but as the saying goes, "the devil is in the details". It is best to avoid getting caught by this. If the basic premise of the game changes in the early development stages, much of the work on these small details will be wasted. A good practice is to spend a relatively short but valuable amount of time at the outset making sure the idea has the potential for development.

There are some genres that are inherently easier to achieve in CryENGINE simply due to the nature of its underlying design. Developers should consider that the CryENGINE has historically been used to create realistic and highly interactive experiences.

Creating a game that uses the first-person or third-person perspectives is relatively easy compared to creating something as a full scale real-time strategy game. To get some inspiration, let's explore the pedigree of the CryENGINE and what other visions have been achieved using it. As you browse through these games, remember that none of these were created in a day! These games were built with large teams over a number of years and thus, we should be realistic with ourselves about what we can achieve and how long it will take.

Far Cry by Crytek – first-person shooter

Far Cry, launched in 2004, sporting the first version of the CryENGINE used the technology that changed the face of gaming.

Far Cry was the first full game developed on CryENGINE. It can be argued which came first, the engine or the game; but so as to not commit to either side, I would like to say the vision and requirements that were put forth for the game drove the technology, or the engine, into what would finally be known as CryENGINE 1.

This critically acclaimed game put to use the technology that allowed for a level of graphical fidelity, never seen before in games, such as huge view distances, high precision HDR lighting, and even more importantly, the game introduced a toolset for development that expressed the **what you see is what you play (WYSIWYP)** philosophy. This philosophy describes how Far Cry was created as the designers were able to enter in and out of game mode instantly using a shortcut key without having to wait for any saving, compiling, or baking. Designers were thus able to try as many iterations as it would take to create a particular aspect of gameplay in far less time than it would take in other game engines.

The game was truly a Sandbox first-person shooter. To be more precise, it was designed so that the player is directed to achieve certain goals, but the way in which they can accomplish these goal is completely up to him or her. The developer decides to give the player certain tools, which they can use or combine for a unique experience while accomplishing these goals. To be able to do this requires technology to be able to support huge maps and thousands of game entities.

Aion by NCsoft – massively online role-playing game

First released in Korea in 2008, Aion redefined the standard for the quality of art and rendering achievable in such a massive world, populated by thousands of players at once.

Aion was developed by NCsoft on the CryENGINE 1, with a significant amount of customization done to the engine to support the complex database and server requirements of a massively multiplayer online role-player game. It also demonstrated some unique gameplay features never before seen in an MMO. For example, the ability to fly and glide with your character's wings to travel in the world.

Expecting to create Aion in our spare time is largely beyond the scope of this book and likely also beyond the scope of any small development team. Aion was created by a large team and required developers who were experienced in creating MMO games.

This is a good example demonstrating how the engine is easier to adapt to certain genres than others. Of course, Sandbox and the CryENGINE can be used to achieve this; but it requires significantly more customization and innovation than a first-person shooter would.

Crysis by Crytek – first-person shooter

Crysis truly drove the next generational leap for the CryENGINE. Crysis, upon its launch in 2007, exceeded all expectations and set the new standard for real-time PC gaming.

CryENGINE 2 was made available for licensing shortly after the release of Crysis, due to popular demand of many developers in the industry.

The big technological jump for CryENGINE 2 was in sheer rendering fidelity and hyper-interactivity of its physical worlds.

This leap made it even more ideal for developing open-world Sandbox games. Though Crysis was a first-person shooter, the engine lent itself well to third-person adventure games and even vehicle simulations. In addition, visualization with CryENGINE 2 expanded as artists discovered the ability to create photorealistic scenes in comparatively less time than was considered possible at that point in time.

Crysis Warhead by Crytek – first-person shooter

CryENGINE 2 was further updated, in tandem, with the release of Crysis Warhead in 2008. This expansion took the player back to experience the same timeline of events from the original Crysis, but from a different protagonist's perspective.

In terms of technology, the engine's performance was further optimized to allow for a truly cinematic experience. It was designed to be a faster, more intense an experience than the original and it achieved its goal.

At this time, it was recognized by Crytek that to remain competitive, games must be able to run on the Xbox 360 and PS3, as such, development began in earnest of the console-friendly future generation CryENGINE 3.

Crysis 2 by Crytek – first-person shooter

Finally, we end our nostalgic journey at the current generation of CryENGINE 3.

Crysis 2 was released in March 2011 on Xbox 360, PS3, and PC. This was a huge milestone for CryENGINE, as it demonstrated that CryENGINE could achieve its historic rendering quality on this generation of gaming consoles, namely, Xbox 360 and PS3. Finally, the console users were able to experience the level of fidelity demanded by Crytek games, and other developers began actively pursuing their own AAA games using CryENGINE 3.

CryENGINE 3 Free SDK

This brings us to the present as the package that you will be soon downloading and running, is the freely available CryENGINE 3 SDK, initially released in August 2011. It gives anyone with an Internet connection access to the CryENGINE 3 game engine. It continues to be updated to keep it in line with the same features and tools Crytek uses internally, bringing a huge advantage to anyone wanting to make high quality games and simulations.

The following screenshot is a depiction of a CryENGINE 3 creation:

What's in it for me?

Having seen some of the games that have been released on CryENGINE, you may have dreams and visions of creating huge open world online role-playing games, or AAA first-person shooters. This is quite normal, as the most aspiring and even veteran game developer's bite off more than they can chew in their initial designs. Creative and passionate people typically have big ideas, and this is great! I say that, with my fingers crossed behind my back, as there is one caveat to this, that it's ok as long as you practice a very important skill, which is, to be able to temper those huge ideas and split them up into smaller, more achievable goals. Achieving smaller victories while approaching such a vast and complex piece of technology will keep you far more motivated and will build confidence so that eventually you will be able to solve creatively just about any problem that you are faced with while creating your game.

Do I need a full team to develop with the CryENGINE?

As we mentioned before, the previous games we explored were created by huge teams, and you might think it's impossible then to create a game by yourself or even with a small group. I have some good news though! In the examples to come, you will not require an entire team. We will create some customizable elements, which are useable in games through a set of understandable examples. Working as a team, however, is becoming increasingly common even among hobbyist game developers. When working in a team you should recognize that there can be generalists and specialists in every field. Typical teams break down to the following groups. It should be noted that there are a variety of subcategories within each group, and the following breakdown doesn't claim to describe them all:

- **Programming**: The entire gaming industry was created by programmers. Without programmers this industry simply wouldn't exist! They are the specialists who take the expectations and designs of everybody else and are tasked with finding a way to make them a reality. They are tasked with everything from creating and modifying the game engine to developing tools, and implementing game mechanics. If there are bugs or important changes to be made usually it's the programmer who must work late to fix or implement changes. There are a variety of subcategories of programming, which include physics, rendering, shaders, animation, sound, tools, and so on.

- **Art**: Artists have become increasingly important in the production of high-quality games. Having truly talented artists can take a bland game created using teasingly named, programmer art to an AAA photorealistic experience. There are many subdisciplines within art as there are in programming, some of which include concept, environment, character, technical, lighting, and visual effects.

- **Animation**: Animators are the ones that perform the role of providing life to otherwise static games. This is just as essential to a game's immersion as the texture or geometry of any model. There are a few subcategories to animation which include riggers, facial animators, technical animators, cinematic animators, and others.

- **Design**: I really think designers can come from anywhere within all the disciplines and roles! They are typically people who excel at combining mechanics to make fun! Creating fun, as strange as that may sound, is the main goal of the designer within any game production. During my career, I have personally seen a trend in the industry where designers are often undertaking the role of what I would term **game compositors**. Game compositors take all the different aspects of a game's production, including art, animation, code, cinematics, and so on, and combine them all together in creative ways that challenge and reward the player. For this reason, being a designer can be a demanding, yet rewarding role, as it allows you to generalize in many areas. One thing I have personally found as a designer is that the more you know about each area of the technology with which you are working, the more tools you will have at your disposal while creating interesting puzzles, challenges, and adventures for your players.

- **Sound**: The sound group consists of sound engineers and musicians. Sound engineers are typically skilled at designing sound into games. This may sound abstract, but it's the skill of being able to amplify emotions throughout different areas of the game. For example, if you had a creepy cave with no sound, it would be less realistic. The immersion and believability could be greatly improved by adding ambient wind sounds and the sound of dripping water echoing off the walls. Musicians add unique soundtracks, which have vaulted games to high popularity and are sometimes the most memorable parts of some of your own gaming experiences! This is a difficult role as you must depend on sound engineers to implement your creations into the game and accurately represent the mood and intensity of the piece.

◆ **Quality Assurance** (play tester): Quality assurance plays a huge role in any production that you wish to release to an audience, especially when the audience is large. Games that go to market with mistakes and bugs in their code, art, or design have potentially disastrous consequences for game development teams and companies. A typical entry-level point into quality assurance is that of a play tester. They will play and replay levels, repeat and document certain circumstances, however obscure they might be, the same with levels that crash or interfere with the game.

◆ **Producer** (project manager): In game development companies, the producer plays a major role and will most likely have a good deal of experience at varying levels of the gaming industry. The producer is responsible for all sorts of things and can be seen as a shield for the team against the business of a game. One of the other critical roles for a producer is to make sure that the development schedule meets all of its milestones and is finished on time.

With large projects or titles, such as the ones we discussed earlier, it's essential to recruit these specialists to your team or if all else fails become one yourself.

This book is written in a way that will explore each role in a lightweight and exploratory manner. My personal experience comes from being a generalist technical designer. Thus, each example will concentrate on getting game features to function using some tools and techniques from art, design, sound, and code.

If you are already a specialist in one or more of these roles, you will still be able to follow these examples to add additional tools to your repertoire of skills and techniques for creating games.

Learning by example

The best way, in my opinion, to go about learning to use CryENGINE 3 SDK is by actually using it to create a variety of achievable genre-specific mini games or prototypes. These examples will then become the stepping stone that will give you the ability to create more complex games using the same skills and functions explored in simplified examples. You should be aware that these examples most likely won't make you millions of dollars, but will rather teach you the tools and techniques required to make your own successful game, should you have the passion and desire to do so.

The relatively straightforward examples in this book will give you a focus to concentrate your efforts as you learn CryENGINE 3 SDK, since attempting to master the engine all at once would be an extremely difficult and a time-consuming task for anyone.

This book will mainly focus on what you can do within Sandbox, but we will still explore the occasional need for external applications, such as 3ds Max and Photoshop. There are countless resources available to learn these applications.

Once you have gone through these examples, you will understand and even feel empowered by being able to create your very own game worlds within CryENGINE 3 SDK.

Time for action – installing the CryENGINE 3 Free SDK

Before we dive in, we must ensure that our computer system meets the requirements for development with the CryENGINE 3 SDK. As opposed to some reports, it does not take a super computer to run the CryENGINE 3 SDK. It should be noted that the system requirements for a developer do differ from that of a player, otherwise known as the end user.

The CryENGINE 3 SDK is designed to scale reliably on a variety of systems with varying amounts of video and computational processing power.

The system requirements for a developer are as follows:

♦ Supported Operating Systems: Windows XP SP2, Windows Vista SP1, Windows 7.

♦ Processor: Intel Core 2 Duo 2 GHz, AMD Athlon 64 X2 2 GHz, or better.

♦ Memory: 2 to 4 GigaBytes of RAM.

♦ Video card: NVIDIA 8800GT 512 MB RAM, AMD 3850HD 512 MB RAM, or better. Shader Model 3 is the minimum.

A multi-core processor is strongly recommended for development, as subsystems in CryENGINE 3 SDK can make use of multiple cores.

The system requirements for end users are as follows:

♦ Supported Operating Systems: Windows XP SP2, Windows Vista SP1, or Windows 7.

♦ Processor: Intel Core 2 Duo 2 GHz, AMD Athlon 64 X2 2GHz, or better.

♦ Memory: 1 GigaByte of RAM is the minimum, however, 2 GigaBytes is strongly recommended.

♦ Video card: NVIDIA 8800GT 512 MB RAM, AMD 3850HD 512 MB RAM, or better.

To get our hands dirty, we are going to need to download and install CryENGINE 3 SDK. This will allow us to create and run new games and the included sample content. Following are the steps to download and install CryENGINE 3 SDK:

1. Go to `http://www.crydev.net`.

2. Register yourself to create a unique login, which we will soon use to run CryENGINE 3 SDK.

3. Once registered, download the CryENGINE 3 Free SDK package.

4. Extract the content of the downloaded package to your desired directory. For this book, create a new directory on your `C:`, and name it `Crytek`. Then, create a new folder in the `Crytek` folder, and name it `cryengine3_sdk`. You should end up with all files from the archive in the directory `C:/Crytek/cryengine3_sdk`.

What just happened?

In the previous section, we took our first and very important step on our way to becoming a CryENGINE developer.

Now that you've installed the CryENGINE 3 Free SDK, you can run and view the sample content. Now, you can also interact with the rest of the CryENGINE 3 developers, post screenshots, ask advice, or even download other developer's creations on `http://www.crydev.net`.

Come in...stay awhile

Now, we can go to explore the sample level. This sample map should give you a good idea of the fidelity of rendering and interaction that can be achieved with the currently available generation of the technology.

Time for action – load the sample map in the launcher

Let's rev it up! Let's see what the example level would look like from the end user or what we can call the player's perspective.

1. Navigate to the `Bin32` or `Bin64` folders in your installation of the SDK. For this book, the root directory is `C:/Crytek/cryengine3_sdk` The `Bin32` folder is where the 32-bit binaries are stored and the `Bin64` folder stores the 64-bit versions.

2. Run the `launcher.exe` application in either 32 bit or 64 bit.

3. When prompted, enter your CryDev login information created in the previous *Time for action – installing the CryENGINE 3 Free SDK*.

4. Once the launcher has opened, you will be presented with a start screen and menu.

5. Select **Single player** from the menu, and then select **Forest**. This will load the forest sample map for you to explore.

6. Move your player character through the level using the *W, A, S,* and *D* keys; you can also press the Space bar to jump.

7. A nice path has been kindly laid by the developers, thus making this level easy to explore. Follow the river all the way down to the coastal village.

8. Experiment interacting with different objects by firing your weapon at them, or by pressing the *F* key to initiate actions like opening doors. Go ahead and explore the sample interactions that are available in the level.

9. Once you are done exploring and interacting with the level, you can close the launcher.

10. To close the launcher, you can simply close the window if in windowed mode, or press the *Esc* key, and select **Exit game**.

What just happened?

Having loaded and explored the sample content, you sho ld now have a pretty good idea of the overall quality you can achieve with the engine and how a first-person shooter might look like when built on it. Up to this point, you have experienced CryENGINE as a user or player would. Let's now get into some of the different tools we can use to edit this experience so that we can call ourselves *developers*.

Visual Studio Express and C++ game code

As discussed earlier, programmers basically rule the world when it comes to game development. For this reason, having C++ game code released in the Free SDK for the CryENGINE is an invaluable tool. I encourage everyone to download the freely available **Visual Studio Express** to at the very least explore the provided game code. This game code is designed to be a template to create your own games and has a huge array of possible functions.

Later examples in this book will delve into how we can use the game code to make our games truly unique and explain how to download and install Visual Studio.

Acquiring the sample source assets

Crytek provides a downloadable file containing sample assets on `http://www.crydev.net`. These assets are in the form of uncompressed textures and source 3ds Max or Maya scene files. For many, it is valuable to use these to learn how to use complex asset features or to customize them to create your own amazing piece of interactive game art.

The examples in this book will exclusively use 3ds Max. However, the process for many asset creation procedures for Maya can be found online in the provided documentation at CryDev site.

Time for action – installation of the 3ds Max exporter Plugin

The examples in this book will all use 3ds Max and Adobe Photoshop as the primary digital content creation tools, otherwise known as **DCC tools**. Since we will use 3D Studio Max for this book, let's install the tools we will need to open and export the sample models to the engine. The steps to do so are as follows:

1. Explore to the `\Tools\CryMaxTools\` directory in the root directory of your build.

Locate and run `copytoMax.bat`, which will copy the required tools to your 3ds max installation directory. For whatever reason, should the automatic installation of the exporter tools fail, you can install the files manually. Follow these steps to either manually copy or to simply verify that the tools have been installed correctly.

2. Locate the `.dlu` file that is matched to the 3D Studio Max version you will be using. The following files are found in the `/tools` directory of your build:

   ❑ 3ds Max 9 32 bit use `CryExport9.dlu`

   ❑ 3ds Max 9 64 bit use `CryExport9_64.dlu`

   ❑ 3ds Max 2008 32 Bit use `CryExport10.dlu`

   ❑ 3ds Max 2008 64 Bit use `CryExport10_64.dlu`

   ❑ 3ds Max 2009 32 Bit use `CryExport11.dlu`

   ❑ 3ds Max 2009 64 Bit use `CryExport11_64.dlu`

   ❑ 3ds Max 2010 32 Bit use `CryExport12.dlu`

   ❑ 3ds Max 2010 64 Bit use `CryExport12_64.dlu`

3. Once you have located the `.dlu` file that is associated to your installation of 3ds Max, copy this file to the `/plugins` directory of your 3ds Max installation.

4. Finally, we need to install the 3ds Max Cry Tools Max Scripts. To install them, simply copy the `LoadCryTools.ms` located under the `/tools/CryMaxTools` folder to the `/Scripts/Startup` folder of the 3ds Max installation.

What just happened?

The tools that we have just installed are used by 3D artists and some multi-role designers to create models and other content for use within games. These tools are essential because, later on in this book, we will want to make some custom assets for use within CryENGINE.

Time for action – downloading and opening the sample assets

Having installed the required tools, let's now download and open the source sample assets and to do so we will perform the following steps:

1. Download the sample assets from the following web location `http://www.crydev.net/dm_eds/files/General_Downloads/CryENGINE_FreeSDK_v3_3_5_Sample_Assets.zip`.

2. Extract the contents of this package to the `/game` folder of your root directory.

3. Browse to any 3ds Max scene within these samples and open it to ensure it works.

What just happened?

The source sample assets are provided as examples by Crytek. They are very useful as a learning tool and can also be used within your project. There are full characters, vehicles, and vegetation samples that can be used directly or simply as reference to verify the setup of your own assets.

Time for action – installing the Adobe Photoshop plugin-CryTif

The textures we will create throughout the course of this book will be created or edited using Adobe Photoshop. **CryTIF** is a Photoshop plugin developed by Crytek that can load and save merged Photoshop images as TIF files. It's important to realize though that the `.TIF` format images are not used when rendered in the launcher or even the editor, but they are rather converted to a more optimized format, in this case from a `.TIF` file to a `.DDS`. The following steps show how to install the plugin and save files in the `.TIF` format:

1. Copy the following files to the root Photoshop directory:

   - `Bin32\zlib1.dll`
   - `Bin32\jpeg62.dll`
   - `Bin32\libtiff3.dll`

2. Copy the file that enables support for the CryTif format `Tools\CryTIFPlugin.8bi` to the root Photoshop `/Plugins` folder.

3. Test whether the installation is functioning by first starting Photoshop.

4. Create a new image with dimensions 512 x 512.

5. Create a simple pattern or import your own texture.

 If your texture has an alpha channel on it, the CryTIF plugin will detect this and change its conversion process automatically.

6. Next, select **File | Save As** in Photoshop.

7. Save this file as a CryTIF (`.TIF`) file type. This format should now be available as a file format in the Photoshop file dialog.

8. Create a `textures` directory in your game folder and save this texture in your game under `game/textures/test_pattern.tif`.

What just happened?

In the previous section, we installed the very important CryTif plugin, which is essential while creating any textures for the CryENGINE. When saving a `.TIF` file, the CryTif plugin displays a dialog to the user where the compression settings may be selected. The settings that get chosen in the dialog are stored as metadata on the TIF file.

We have finally installed all the tools required for us to make an amazing amount of content from code, to textures, to models, and animation! Having done this, we are now ready to find out how to start putting everything together!

CryENGINE 3 Sandbox

The CryENGINE 3 Sandbox is the level compositing tool built for CryENGINE, which is used to create and edit the majority of the content for games, visualizations, and simulations. It is likely, if you are developing a game based on CryENGINE—whether you are an artist, programmer, animator, or designer—you will have to use it at some point of time. As such, you should have a basic understanding of the CryENGINE 3 sandbox and some of the subsystems contained within. Fortunately, you'll find it to be an extremely powerful tool with a deep assortment of subsystems available to just about anyone involved in a game's development process.

Time for action – starting Sandbox and WYSIWYP

Let's open the editor so that we can see the sample level from a developer's perspective. Perform the following steps:

1. Navigate to the `Bin32` or `Bin64` folder in your installation of the CryENGINE 3 Free SDK.

2. Run the `editor.exe` application in either 32 bit or 64 bit.

3. Login with your CryDev account when prompted.

4. Once the editor is open, go to **File | Open**.

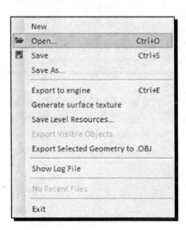

5. Browse to the `Forest.cry` file contained in the folder `/game/levels/ Singleplayer/forest/`, and select **Open**.

6. The editor application will then load the example map forest for us with which to experiment.

7. Once the level is open, the first thing to try is to hit the shortcut **Ctrl + G**, or go to the **Game** menu, and choose **Switch to Game**.

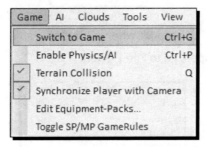

Upon switching to game, you will be able to instantly play as if you had loaded the level in the `launcher.exe` application, as you can see in the following screenshot:

Using this feature, you are able to play the sample map the same way in the editor as you would in the launcher. This fact proves invaluable for iteration, because you can modify the majority of the game without having to restart the editor. It should be understood, however, that this is the emulated version of the game and doesn't fairly represent performance in the launcher as there is added overhead to running the Sandbox Editor and various debug modes.

8. To go back to editing mode, press the Escape key at any time.

What just happened?

We have just learned how to launch and run a level in the editor and also how to simulate playing in the launcher. We will explore the interface to Sandbox in the next chapter of this book and do not be alarmed if the interface is a bit foreign to you.

Getting around in the Sandbox Editor

Now that we have run the two principal applications of the engine, we should take some time to learn the interface to the development application CryENGINE Sandbox. The ability to navigate levels is a basic skill with which all developers should be familiar. Thankfully, this interface is quite intuitive to anyone who is already familiar with the WASD control scheme popular in most first-person shooter games developed on the PC.

Time for action – manipulating the perspective camera

1. If not already done, open the Forest.cry sample level with the editor.exe application.

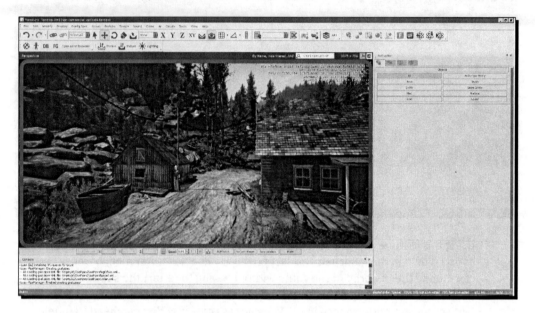

The window highlighted in the previous screenshot is the perspective viewport; this is where you can see the level. The perspective viewport is used as the main window to view and navigate and even edit your levels. This is where a large majority of your level will be created and common tasks such as object placement, terrain editing, and in-editor play testing will be performed.

Sandbox is designed to be ergonomic for both left-handed and right-handed users. For this example, we will use the WASD control scheme, but it should be noted that the arrows keys are also supported for movement of the camera.

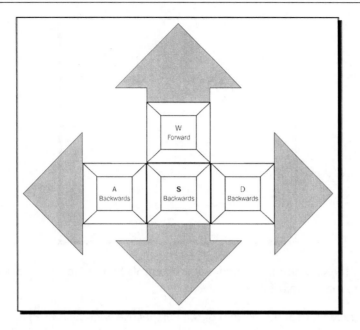

2. Press **W** to move forward.

3. Then press **S** to move backward.

4. Press **A** to move or strafe towards the left.

5. Press **D** to move or strafe towards the right.

Now that you have learned to move the camera on its main primary axis, it's time to adjust the rotation of the camera. The following steps will indicate the same:

1. When the viewport is the active window, hold down the right mouse button, and move the mouse pointer to turn the view.

   You can also hold down the middle mouse button, and move the mouse pointer to pan the view.

2. Roll the middle mouse button wheel to move the view forward or backward.

3. Finally, you can hold down *Shift* to double the speed of the viewport movements.

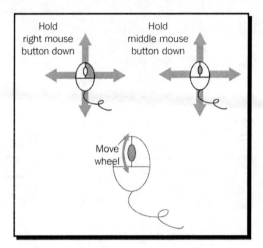

4. Adjust the Viewport Movement Speed Controls to find the speed with which you are most comfortable.

The **Speed** input at the bottom of the Perspective window is used to increase or decrease the movement speed of the camera as you move in the main Perspective Viewport.

What just happened?

The **Viewport** allows for a huge diversity of views and layouts which you can use to view your levels. The Perspective view is just one of the many. This view also renders a view of the level using the standard camera perspective, showing all level geometry, lighting, and effects.

Handling level objects

Levels in the CryENGINE Sandbox are composed of any number of entities, brushes, and other objects. These will each be explained later in this book, but for now we need to know how to manipulate and adapt these objects to our desires.

Time for action – selecting and browsing objects

The following steps will help you to select and browse through objects:

1. If not already done, open the `Forest.cry` sample map in the CryENGINE 3 Free SDK.

2. Enable or Disable object helpers using the shortcut *Shift* + Space bar or use the toggle in the viewport shown in the following screenshot:

3. You can now simply point and click on objects to select them, or if you'd like to be more accurate, you can hold the Space bar to get a small box selection helper around the object's pivot.

4. Select an object.

You should now see your gizmo attached to the object's pivot point also known as origin. The gizmo represents the three dimensions of space used within the world otherwise known as **axis**. Most game engines use Cartesian coordinates which consist of three axes *X*, *Y*, and *Z*.

- *X* is red and represents left and right in the CryENGINE
- *Y* is green and represents front and back
- *Z* is blue and it represents up and down

5. Click-and-drag on any of the axes to move the object along that axis.

> You can switch between the move, scale, and rotate tools by using their toolbar icons or the shortcut keys, which are 1, 2, and 3 respectively.

6. Change the direction in which you are able to move the object using the constrain to axis tools in the main toolbar. There are six settings; the first three correspond to each axis, and the fourth *XY* will lock the object so it will not move up or down. The final two are the snap to terrain and snap to terrain and objects.

7. Experiment by changing these values. To finalize the placement of the object you selected, it will likely be easiest to use snap to terrain highlighted in the following screenshot:

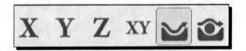

An extremely powerful yet underused snapping ability is the shortcut *Ctrl + Shift + click*. This will snap the object to the first physical surface under the mouse cursor.

8. Try this by holding *Ctrl + Shift*, and then click in the Viewport where you would like to snap the object.

Notice that when you selected the object, particular properties appeared in the **RollupBar**. The **RollupBar** is where entity parameters, settings, and controls are listed and accessed. These parameters will depend on the type of objects you have selected, but it should be known that this is the primary way to adjust any aspect of entities within the Sandbox.

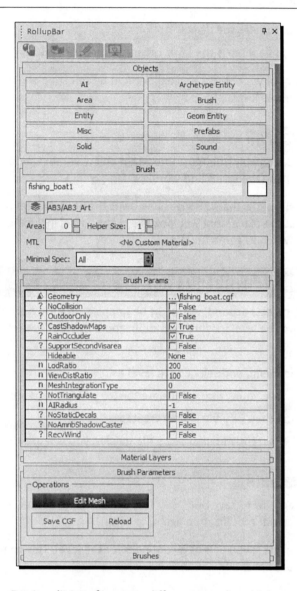

The top of the **RollupBar** is split into four very different panels, which are accessed from their corresponding tabs. They are as follows:

- The first tab contains the object and entity creation tools for the editor, as well as being the tab that will display all entity-specific information and dialogs.

- The second tab is the overall environmental, vegetation, and terrain editing tools. It should be noted that these tools are usually used to modify the specific level you have loaded in Sandbox.

- The third tab contains the display options.
- The fourth and final tab is the layer organizational tool tab.

Finalize the placement of your object and experiment by selecting and moving different entities within the sample level.

What just happened?

You have just learned, arguably, the most important ability within Sandbox and that is the ability to move and shape the levels and worlds.

One of the greatest strengths that this gives us now is the ability to iterate quickly and with a full preview of what the placement will look like in the game, including full physics and gameplay using the switch to game function.

Time for action – saving our work

Having moved some objects around, we might be happier with the new placement of them, or simply want to save the level for further modification. In order to do that, perform the following steps:

1. Go to the **File** menu, and select **Save level as**.
2. You will now save your `.cry` file. Name the `.cry` file as `forest_myedit.cry`.
3. Click **Save**, and the `.cry` file will be created.
4. To save to the currently loaded `.cry` file quickly, you can use the shortcut *Ctrl + S*.

What just happened?

We have just reviewed how to save our `.cry` file, which will, of course, be required if we wish to be able to load our modification again.

The `.cry` file that we just saved acts as a container for the level. This container can only be accessed by the editor application.

Have a go hero – free your mind

Already with just a few examples, we know enough to be all powerful within CryENGINE 3. As some of the greatest ideas have come about from experimentation, challenge yourself by trying a few things, for example:

- Use the rotate and scale tools on various entities. Access them using the shortcut keys *2* and *3*.

- Create a prototype platforming game using just dock objects. If you place a series of them at different angles, varying heights, and distances, you can get some rudimentary platforming gameplay.
- Alternate between moving objects and then switching to game mode to try to jump from one object to the other. This is where the true power of the Sandbox toolset is shown and that's in speed of iteration. You can test your game play in full scale instantly after editing it.

Summary

We've come a long way in just a few pages! We can now open, edit, and save levels, giving us access to some of the most important tools to create games. The next chapter will take us deeper into Sandbox and will expose how we can use the interface to perform a enormous variety of modifications to our level.

We have learned a good deal already about the CryENGINE 3 SDK and how we can use the application within. We took our first few steps by opening a level in the launcher and in the editor, as well as installing some of the tools we will need in the later chapters.

Now that we are dangerous enough to load the sample level in the editor, we're ready to begin ravaging the example map and to learn a few of the useful functions available within the CryENGINE 3 Sandbox. In the next chapter, we will use some of the tools within the CryENGINE Sandbox to create our own levels and environment. It will guide through creating your own heightmap and terrain textures in addition to distributing vegetation and setting a time of day.

2
Breaking Ground with Sandbox

You may now be asking yourself, "I've downloaded the CryENGINE 3 SDK. Now how do I start making games with it?" Such a question has far-reaching implications and is awfully difficult to answer! So in my attempt to answer this question, let's create our own game together, in a short amount of time, using some of the functions and entities that the CryENGINE 3 SDK gives to us straight out of the box.

In this chapter, we will be:

- Beginning with our first example using out of the box features of the engine
- Creating and sculpting terrain for a new level, from scratch
- Creating and using terrain texture layers
- Creating vegetation groups and applying them to your level
- Creating and setting a basic time of day to light our level

What makes a game?

In the previous chapter, we saw that majority of the games created on the CryENGINE SDK have historically been first-person shooters containing a mix of sandbox and directed gameplay. If you have gone so far as to purchase a book on the use of the CryENGINE 3 SDK, then I am certain that you have had some kind of idea for a game, or even improvements to existing games, that you might want to make. It has been my experience professionally that should you have any of these ideas and want to share or sell them, the ideas that are presented in a playable format, even in early prototype form, are far more effective and convincing than any PowerPoint presentation or 100-page design document.

Reducing, reusing, recycling

Good practice when creating prototypes and smaller scale games, especially if you lack the expertise in creating certain assets and code, is to reduce, reuse, and recycle. To break down what I mean:

- Reduce the amount of new assets and new code you need to make
- Reuse existing assets and code in new and unique ways
- Recycle the sample assets and code provided, and then convert them for your own uses

Developing out of the box

As mentioned earlier, the CryENGINE 3 SDK has a huge amount of out-of-the-box features for creating games.

Let's begin by following a few simple steps to make our first game world.

Before proceeding with this example, it's important to understand the features it is displaying; the level we will have created by the end of this chapter will not be a full, playable game, but rather a unique creation of yours, which will be constructed using the first major features we will need in our game. It will provide an environment in to which we can design gameplay.

With the ultimate goal of this chapter being to create our own level with the core features immediately available to us, we must keep in mind that these examples are orientated to compliment a first-person shooter and not other genres. The first-person shooter genre is quite well defined as new games come out every year within this genre. So, it should be fairly easy for any developer to follow these examples.

In my career, I have seen that you can indeed accomplish a good cross section of different games with the CryENGINE 3 SDK. However, the third- and first-person genres are significantly easier to create, immediately with the example content and features available right out of the box.

For the designers

This chapter is truly a must-have for designers working with the engine. Though, I would highly recommend that all users of sandbox know how to use these features, as they are the principal features typically used within most levels of the different types of games in the CryENGINE.

Time for action - creating a new level

Let's follow a few simple steps to create our own level:

1. Start the **Editor.exe** application.

2. Select **File | New**. This will present you with a **New Level** dialog box that allows you to do the adjustments of some principal properties of your masterpiece to come. The following screenshot shows the properties available in **New Level**:

3. Name this **New Level**, as Book_Example_1. The name that you choose here will identify this level for loading later as well as creating a folder and .cry file of the same name.

4. In the **Terrain** section of the dialog box, set **Heightmap Resolution** to **1024x1024**, and **Meters Per Unit** to **1**.

5. Click on **OK** and your **New Level** will begin to load. This should occur relatively fast, but will depend on your computer's specifications.

6. You will know the level has been loaded when you see **Ready** in the status bar. You will also see an ocean stretching out infinitely and some terrain slightly underneath the water.

7. Maneuver your camera so that you have a good, overall view of the map you will create, as seen in the following screenshot:

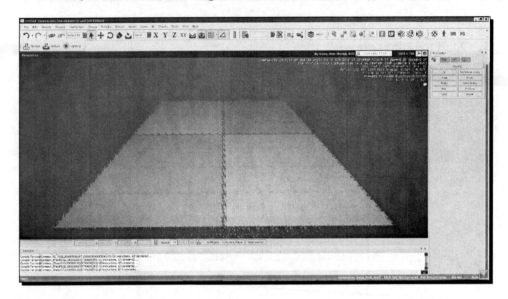

What just happened?

Congratulations! You now have an empty level to mold and modify at your will.

Before moving on, let's talk a little about the properties that we just set, as they are fundamental properties of the levels within CryENGINE. It is important to understand these, as depending on the type of game you are creating, you may need bigger or smaller maps, or you may not even need terrain at all.

Using the right Heightmap Resolution

When we created the **New Level**, we chose a **Heightmap Resolution** of **1024x1024**. To explain this further, each pixel on the heightmap has a certain grey level. This pixel then gets applied to the terrain polygons, and depending on the level of grey, will move the polygon on the terrain to a certain height. This is called displacement. Heightmaps always have varying values from full white to full black, where full white is maximum displacement and full black is minimum or no displacement.

The higher the resolution of the heightmap, the more the pixels that are available to represent different features on said heightmap. You can thus achieve more definition and a more accurate geometrical representation of your heightmap using higher resolutions.

The settings can range from the smallest resolution of **128x128**, all the way to the largest supported resolution of **8192x8192**. The following screenshot shows the difference between high resolution and low resolution heightmaps:

Scaling your level with Meters Per Unit

If the **Heightmap Resolution** parameter is examined in terms of pixel size, then this dialog box can be viewed also as the **Meters Per Pixel** parameter. This means that each pixel of the heightmap will be represented by so many meters.

For example, if a heightmap's resolution has 4 **Meters Per Unit**, then each pixel on the generated heightmap will measure to be 4 meters in length and width on the level.

Even though **Meters Per Unit** can be used to increase the size of your level, it will decrease the fidelity of the heightmap. You will notice that attempting to smoothen out the terrain may be difficult, since there will be a wider, minimum triangle size set by this value.

Keep in mind that you can adjust the unit size even after the map has been created. This is done through the terrain editor, which we will discuss shortly.

Calculating the real-world size of the terrain

The expected size of the terrain can easily be calculated before making the map, because the equation is not so complicated. The real-world size of the terrain can be calculated as:

(**Heightmap Resolution**) x **Meters Per Unit** = Final Terrain Dimensions. For example:

- (128x128) x 2m = 256x256m
- (512x512) x 8m = 4096x4096m
- (1024x1024) x 2m = 2048x2048m

Using or not using terrain

In most cases, levels in CryENGINE will use some amount of the terrain. The terrain itself is a highly optimized system that has levels of dynamic tessellation, which adjusts the density of polygons depending on the distance from the camera to the player. Dynamic tessellation is used to make the more defined areas of the terrain closer to the camera and the less defined ones further away, as the amount of terrain polygons on the screen will have a significant impact on the performance of the level.

In some cases, however, the terrain can be expensive in terms of performance, and if the game is made in an environment like space or interior corridors and rooms, then it might make sense to disable the terrain. Disabling the terrain in these cases will save an immense amount of memory, and speed up level loading and runtime performance.

In this particular example, we will use the terrain, but should you wish to disable it, simply go to the second tab in the **RollupBar** (usually called the environment tab) and set the **ShowTerrainSurface** parameter to **false**, as shown in the following screenshot:

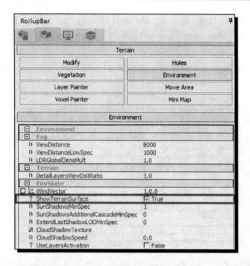

Time for action - creating your own heightmap

You must have created a new map to follow this example.

Having sufficiently beaten the terrain system to death through explanation, let's get on with what we are most interested in, which is creating our own heightmap to use for our game:

1. As discussed in the previous example, you should now see a flat plane of terrain slightly submerged beneath the ocean.

2. At the top of the **Sandbox** interface in the main toolbar, you will find a menu selection called **Terrain**; open this. The following screenshot shows the options available in the **Terrain** menu.

3. As we want to adjust the terrain, we will select the **Edit Terrain** option. This will open the **Terrain Editor** window, which is shown in the following screenshot:

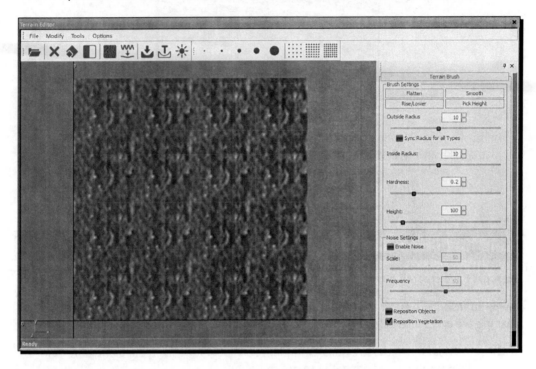

4. You can zoom in and pan this window to further inspect areas within the map. Click-and-drag using the right mouse button to pan the view and use the mouse wheel to zoom in and zoom out.

5. The **Terrain Editor** window has a multitude of options, which can be used to manipulate the heightmap of your level. Before we start painting anything, we should first set the maximum height of the map to something more manageable:

　1. Click on **Modify**.

　2. Click on **Set Max Height**.

　3. Set your **Max Terrain Height** to **256**. Note that the terrain height is measured in meters.

6. Having now set the **Max Height** parameter, we are ready to paint!

Using a second monitor

This is a good time to take advantage of a second monitor should you have one, as you can leave the perspective view on your primary monitor and view the changes made in the **Terrain Editor** on your second monitor, in real time.

7. On the right-hand side of the **Terrain Editor**, you will see a rollout menu named **Terrain Brush**. We will first use this to flatten a section of the level.

8. Change the **Brush Settings** to **Flatten**, and set the following values:

- ❑ **Outside Radius** = 100
- ❑ **Inside Radius** = 100
- ❑ **Hardness** = 1
- ❑ **Height** = 20

 NOTE: You can sample the terrain height in the **Terrain Editor** or the view port using the shortcut *Control* when the flatten brush is selected.

9. Now paint over the top half of the map. This will flatten the entire upper half of the terrain to **20** meters in height. You will end up with the following screenshot, where the dark portion represents the terrain, and since it is relatively low compared to our max height, it will appear black:

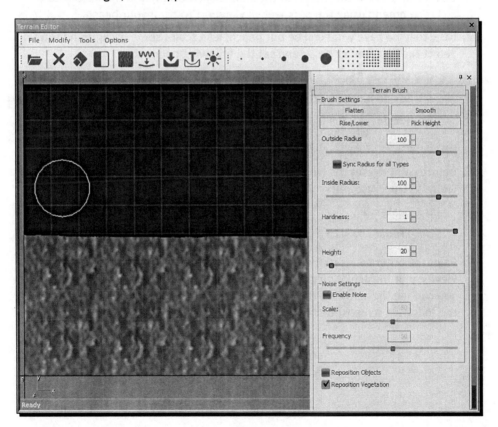

Note that, by default, the water is set to a height of 16 meters. Since we flattened our terrain to a height of **20** meters, we have a 4-meter difference from the terrain to the water in the center of the map. In the perspective viewport, this will look like a steep cliff going into the water.

10. At the location where the terrain meets the water, it would make sense to turn this into a beach, as it's the most natural way to combine terrain and water. To do this, we will smoothen the hard edge of the terrain along the water. As this is to become our beach area, let's now use the smooth tools to make it passable by the player:

    ❑ Change the **Type** of brush to **Smooth** and set the following parameters:

    Outside Radius = 50

    Hardness = 1

I find it significantly easier to gauge the effects of the smooth brush in the perspective viewport.

11. Paint the southern edge of the terrain, which will become our beach. It might be difficult to view the effects of the smooth brush simply in the terrain editor, so I recommend using the perspective viewport to paint your beach.

12. Now that we have what will be our beach, let's sculpt some background terrain. Select the **Rise/Lower** brush and set the following parameters:

    ❑ **Outside Radius = 75**
    ❑ **Inside Radius = 50**
    ❑ **Hardness = 0.8**
    ❑ **Height = 1**

13. Before painting, set the **Noise Settings** for the brush; to do so, check **Enable Noise** to **true**. Also set:

    ❑ **Scale = 5**
    ❑ **Frequency = 25**

14. Paint the outer edges of the terrain while keeping an eye on the perspective viewport at the actual height of the mountain type structure that this creates. You can see the results in the **Terrain Editor** and perspective view, as seen in the following screenshots:

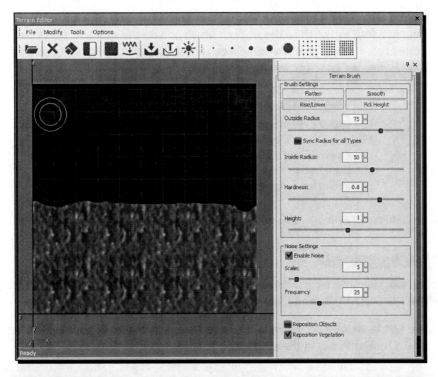

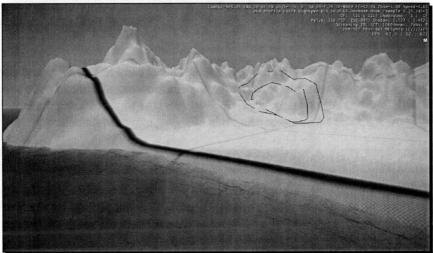

15. It is a good time to use the shortcut to switch to smooth brush while painting the terrain.

❑ While in perspective view, switch to the smooth brush using the *Shift* shortcut.

A good technique is to use the **Rise/Lower** brush and only click a few times, and then use *Shift* to switch to the smooth brush and do this multiple times on the same area. This will give you some nice terrain variation, which will serve us nicely when we go to texture it.

Don't forget the player's perspective

Remember to switch to game mode periodically to inspect your terrain from the players level. It is often the case that we get caught up in the appearance of a map by looking at it from our point of view while building it, rather than from the point of view of the player, which is paramount for our game to be enjoyable to anyone playing it.

16. Save this map as `Book_Example_1_no_color.cry`.

What just happened?

In this particular example, we used one of the three different techniques to create height maps within the CryENGINE sandbox:

1. The first technique, which we performed here, was manually painting the heightmap with a brush directly in the sandbox.
2. The second technique, which we will explore later, is generating **procedural** terrain using the tools provided in sandbox.
3. Finally, the third technique is to import a previously created heightmap from another program.

You now have a level with some terrain that looks somewhat like a beach, a flat land area, and some mountains. This is a great place to start for any outdoor map as it allows us to use some powerful out of the box engine features like the water and the terrain. Having the mountains surrounding the map also encourages the illusion of having more terrain behind it.

Have a go hero – using additional brush settings

With the settings we just explored, try to add some more terrain variation into the map to customize it further, as per your game's needs. Try using different settings for the brushes we explored previously. You could try adding some islands out in the water off the coast of your beach or some hills on the flat portion of the map.

Use the **Inside Radius** and **Outside Radius**, which have a falloff of the brushes settings from the inner area having the strongest effect and the outer having the least.

To create steeper hills or mountains, set the **Inside Radius** and **Outside Radius** to be relatively similar in size. To get a shallower and smoother hill set the **Inside Radius** and **Outside Radius** further apart.

Finally, try using the **Hardness**, which acts like the pressure applied to a brush by a painter on canvas. A good way to explain this is that if the **Hardness** is set to **1**, then within one click you will have the desired height. If set to **0.01**, then it will take 100 clicks to achieve an identical result.

You can save these variations into different `.cry` files should you wish to do so.

Using alternative ways for creating terrain

There are still two other methods we have not yet explored for creating terrain. Before experimenting with either of these, I recommend that you create a new level.

Generating procedural terrain

Use the **Tools** menu in the **Terrain Editor** and click on **Generate Terrain**; you can modify many parameters when generating new terrain procedurally like this:

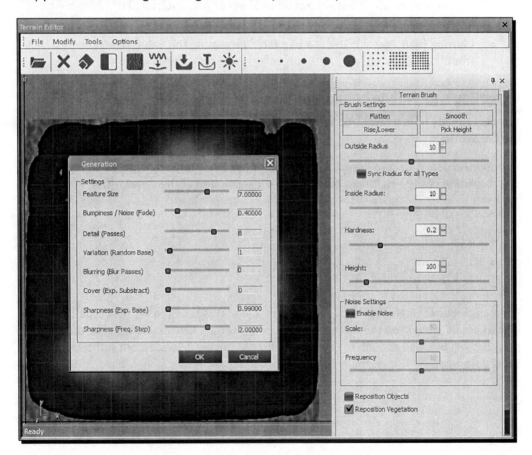

Have a go hero – generating procedural terrain

Try adjusting some of the automatic generation parameters like:

- **Feature Size**: This value handles the general height manipulations within the seed and the size of each mound within the seed. Since the size of the feature depends greatly on rounded numbers, it is easy to end up with a perfectly rounded island. This is not realistic, so it is best to leave this value to around 7.

- **Bumpiness / Noise (Fade)**: This is a noise filter for the level. The greater the value, the more the noise that will appear on the heightmap.

- **Detail (Passes)**: This value controls how detailed the slopes will become. By default, this value is very high so that you can see the individual bumps on the slopes, and it gives a better impression of a rougher surface. Reducing this value will decrease the amount of detail/roughness in the slopes seen.

- **Variation**: This controls the seed number used in the overall generation of the terrain heightmap. There are a total of 33 seeds ranging from 0 to 32 from which to choose, as the starting base for a basic heightmap.

- **Blurring (Blur Passes)**: This is a blur filter. Increasing this value yields progressively smoother slopes.

Importing a pre-made heightmap

You may already have a heightmap prepared, or you may even have exported one from the CryENGINE.

To import/export your own grayscale heightmaps use **File | Import/Export Heightmap**. The resolution of the heightmap must match the resolution of the terrain.

The supported formats are:

- 8-bit BMP
- 16-bit PGM
- 16-bit RAW

For maps requiring high detail close to the player, it makes sense to set the resolution as high as possible but keep the meters per unit of the terrain low. In this way, the terrain polygons will be small enough to represent accurate terrain displacement sufficiently at short distances.

Pop quiz – level size and scale

1. What is the largest supported resolution for a heightmap within CryENGINE?

    a. 128 x 128

    b. 2048 x 2048

    c. 8192 x 8192

2. If you wanted to make a map that measured 2 km x 2 km and still wanted to use the highest resolution possible at that size, what combination of heightmap and **Meters Per Unit** would you use from the following?

    a. 512 x 512 at 8 meters per unit

    b. 1024 x 1024 at 2 meters per unit

    c. 2048 x 2048 at 1 meter per unit

    d. 8192 x 8192 at 2 meters per unit

3. If a developer doesn't require terrain for their level, which property can be set to `false` to remove it?

    a. ShowTerrainSurface

    b. Displayground

    c. Character Editor

    d. Database View

Creating terrain textures

Up until now we've been using the default **terrain texture**, and since real life doesn't look like a checker or grid pattern, it is imperative that we paint some textures onto this terrain. We can do this with sandbox relatively easily, and it allows us to leverage the power of the advanced shading features of the CryENGINE3 quickly.

Terrain textures are split up into multiple layers and are painted manually, directly in the viewport onto the terrain. Each **Terrain layer** consists of a **Surface texture** and a **Detail material**. The various components of the **Terrain layer** are shown in the figure below:

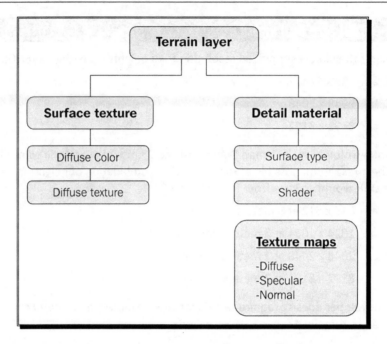

The **Surface texture** will be the surface the player can see from a long range. It is also blended together, when viewed close up, with the **Detail material**. This is done to provide a higher quality of shading and realism around the player where needed. As seen in the preceding figure, it is made up of a **Diffuse color** and a **Diffuse texture**.

The **Detail material** is what a player will see when they are close. It is similar to other materials in CryENGINE as it is comprised of a particular **Shader**, **Surface type**, and textures. The **Surface type** of the material defines how the layer reacts to physics and other systems such as sound and particles.

Time for action - creating some basic terrain texture layers

Applying a good set of terrain layers depends heavily on the environment in which you wish to create your map. In this particular example, we will use a somewhat straightforward setup of rocks, forest, grass, mud, sand, and underwater.

1. Create a new map and generate some terrain, or open `Book_Example_1_no_color.cry` because we need to have some terrain loaded for us to paint onto like a blank canvas.

2. Open the **Terrain Texture Layers** window found in the main sandbox toolbar under **Terrain | Texture**.

3. In this window we want to create some new layers because, as we can see, it has only a single layer at present.

4. Create a new layer using the **Add Layer** command, as shown in the following screenshot:

5. Rename the new layer **grass**.

6. Next, change the **Surface texture** of this layer.

7. Use the **Change Layer Texture** command shown in the following figure, and navigate to `Book_Chapter_2_Assets\low_detail_terrain_textures\directory` and select the **grass.tif** texture. In this case, this texture is a small, 256-pixel, green image with some variations in it, which will work well tiled across our grasslands.

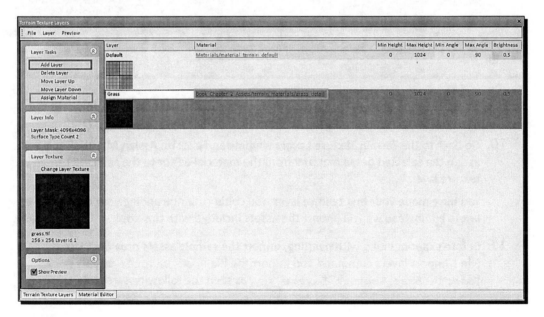

8. Next, change the **Detail Texture** by using the **Material** hotlink path in the grass layer; click on the link, and the material file `Materials/material_terrain_default.mat` will open in the **Material Editor**.

By default, the terrain materials contained in the SDK are located in `materials\terrain`. Terrain material can be identified as they must always use the **Terrain. Layer Shader**, as seen in the following screenshot:

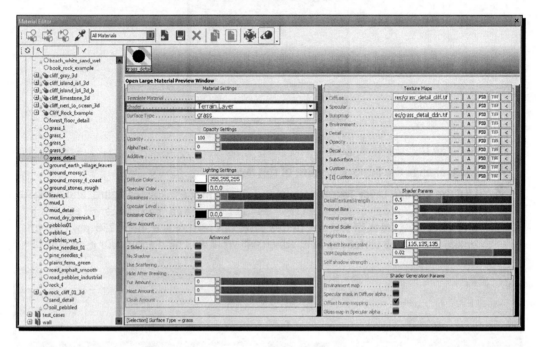

9. Navigate to the `Book_Chapter_2_Assets\terrain_materials\` folder in the **Material Editor**, and select the **grass_detail** material.

10. Go back to the **Terrain Texture Layers** window and click on **Assign Material**; this will assign the selected detail material from the material editor to the selected terrain texture layer.

You have made your first texture layer. You could continue adding your own texture layers but instead we will import the assets included with this book.

11. Before experimenting with painting, import the sample assets provided. Use the **File | Import layers** command and import the file `Book_Chapter_2_Assets/Example_Base_Terrain_Layers.lay`, as seen the following screenshot:

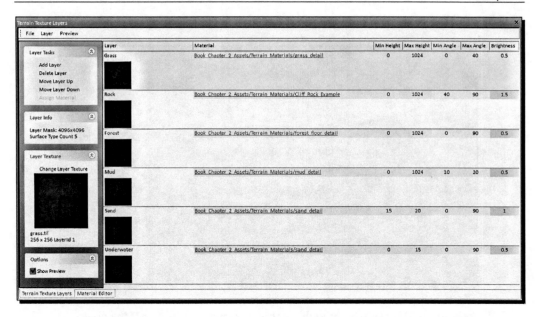

Having loaded a base set of texture layers into our level, we can now get to the fun part of painting them!

12. As the layers are already set up with basic values, you can switch immediately to the layer painter under the **Environment** tab of the **Rollupbar**.

13. Once in the layer painter dialog box, you can select the layers and paint them by clicking and dragging them in the viewport on the terrain. The selected layer will be painted using the **Radius** and **Hardness** settings within the layer painter.

14. After experimenting with painting a layer onto your map, scroll down in the layer painter rollout to where you see the **Tile Resolution** along with the button **Change**.

15. Click on **Change** and turn your brush into a terrain sector selection tool with which you can adjust the overall resolution of your terrain textures in certain sectors. It is recommended to maintain a **1024X1024** resolution or more in gameplay areas and where you expect the player to be, and setting exterior sectors or non-playable areas to a lower resolution.

16. In our case, we have a relatively small map, so setting this to the maximum of **2048X2048** will produce the best results. To disable the **Tile Resolution** tool, simply click on the **Change** icon a second time.

17. In the layer painter, select the grass material and set the Min/Max angle setting to **Min:0** and **Max:40**. This will paint grass on any terrain that has an angle less than 40 degrees.

18. Paint the grass layer onto the terrain as seen in the following screenshot:

19. You can use this same technique for the rock layer. Set its **Min/Max angle** setting to **Min 40** and **Max 90**, which will effectively fill up the rest of the terrain.

20. Paint the rock layer onto the terrain as seen in the following screenshot:

21. Don't forget the terrain under water! There is some terrain that can still be seen from above the water and as such we should enhance its color. Use the **Min/Max Height** to achieve this. Set the **Min/Max height** of the underwater layer to **Min 0 Max 16**. Note that the height we set exactly matches the water level; who said math isn't fun.

22. Finally, painting sand or a beach can be done quite quickly by clicking and dragging a fairly large brush manually, and it will allow you to blend the texture to your liking into the grass and rocks.

23. Paint the beach section of the level as in the following screenshot:

24. The other two layers can later be used when painting vegetation objects as they will compliment the objects nicely.

25. Once you have finished painting, you must compress the texture and generate a surface texture for the engine.

26. Do this by going to **File | Generate Surface Texture**.

27. Select a resolution and click on **OK**.

Generating surface texture at a high quality

A higher resolution will result in better, overall quality. The optional high quality setting creates an additional way over the textures to bake in further detail while keeping the same memory footprint.

It should be noted that once the `terraintexture.pak` is generated, it will appear on all `.cry` files stored within that directory, should it contain the corresponding, terrain texture layers.

28. When you are happy with the terrain textures, save your level.

What just happened?

Congratulations! You are well on your way to becoming a terrain painting master. Now, our level is starting to take shape. It's so colorful now!

Let's further explain some of the layers that this example uses:

◆ **Grass**: This layer attempts to match a natural color tone while using some variations of bright colors to break up the tiling.

◆ **Rock**: Using this for cliffs and other steep terrain will be ideal. It utilizes a 3D material to aid in an attempt to avoid obvious tiling.

◆ **Forest**: Use this layer for the vegetation layers, which we will import later, to blend them into the environment better. It is slightly brownish, to match the color of dead leaves.

◆ **Mud**: This layer has some specular and wet qualities, and uses small stones and a few different types of vegetation that blends best with the terrain.

◆ **Sand**: This layer uses some variations in bright textures to break up the tiling on the beach or in other sandy areas.

◆ **Underwater**: This layer uses a darker blue color to enhance the depth of the water when seen from above or below the surface. You can lighten this layer if you desire to achieve a coral reef-type effect.

This gives us a ton of possibilities for various types of terrain.

Adding altitude and slope

As we saw, these parameters can be set per layer, allowing you to paint that layer within the altitude measured in meters or the slope measured in degrees. This is especially useful for cliff-like layers (for example, 55 degrees to 90 degrees).

Adjusting the tile resolution

A tile's resolution affects how many terrain tiles there are in each terrain sector. The higher the resolution, the higher the amount of tiles used, which leads to better layer blending, as well as softer transitions in the high detail textures. It can be set from as low as 64x64 to as high as 2048x2048; this tiling resolution is an important factor when it comes to optimization, as well as high quality terrain. A good technique is to utilize only higher resolution tiles within the gameplay area of a level, and to use lower resolution tiles on the surrounding terrain for performance and memory considerations.

Pop Quiz – terrain texture layers

1. A **Terrain Layer** consists of 2 main components. What are they?

    a. Surface Texture and Detail Material

    b. Surface Type and Detail Bump map

    c. Shader and Material

2. What constraints can be set for a terrain texture layer to only appear in certain areas?

    a. Min/Max Height and Min/Max Angle

    b. Min/Max polygons

    c. Brightness and Contrast

3. What shader is used for all the terrain texture layers?

    a. Glass

    b. Illum

    c. Water

    d. Terrain.Layer

Creating vegetation

The vegetation system in CryENGINE is powerful, you can utilize a small amount of assets and use procedural placement to make their placement look quite natural.

The interface for vegetation painter is similar to painting terrain textures. They are both based on a brush-like interface where you can click-and-drag directly on the terrain as if you were painting. Both the terrain painter and the vegetation painter support the same altitude and angle properties, and can be used together to achieve very realistic results.

It is important to understand though, that quite differently than painting terrain textures, painting vegetation is a placement of geometry. This geometry is then instanced, a technique used to increase performance, since the objects that are being drawn are already in memory for the entire map.

Placing geometry as vegetation allows us to use the vegetation system to its full potential, as applying the vegetation shader to these geometry objects allows for realistic physics such as touch bending simulation (where the player can physically bend branches) and also wind bending.

Time for action - creating some flora for your level

Without further ado, let's bring some life to the map we have been working on.

1. Open `Example_Level_2.cry` or your own, already textured level.

2. From the **RollupBar**, open the **Terrain** tab and click on the **Vegetation** button as shown in the following screenshot:

Before we can paint the vegetation, we first must add in some objects that we want to use. The first vegetation we will place will be some trees.

3. Click on the icon called **Add Vegetation Category**, as shown in the following screenshot:

4. Name the new category **Trees**.

5. Select the newly created **Trees** category.

6. Click on the **add vegetation object** icon as shown in the following screenshot.

7. Navigate to `.../Objects/Natural/vegetation/rocky_ravines/` and select **a_spruce_a.cgf**, then click on **Open**.

You can hold *Control* and click on multiple objects in a category at once.

8. All of the highlighted trees have now been placed in this category. You can now start painting with a few of the selected trees or select the entire category to paint.

9. Paint the objects into the level, making sure to use a brush size larger than zero; you can quickly remove them by using the remove shortcut, which is the *control* key, when painting.

10. You can remove the category you just created, or leave it and carry on importing the preset vegetation sets.

Having seen how we can create our own categories, let's see how we can import the preset vegetation sets.

11. Click the **import vegetation** icon seen in the following screenshot, and browse to
`Book_Chapter_2_Assets\vegetation_categories\forest_trees.veg`
and click on **OK**. Also, import `forest_ground_mixed.veg`.

You will now have two categories one of trees and one of detail objects detail objects with some preset parameters with which to work, as seen in the following screenshot:

You can immediately start to paint these categories and experiment with the parameters at the bottom of the rollup bar while the vegetation tool is active.

Changing the vegetation properties after they've been placed

The properties of a vegetation object are only applied while painting, so if you want to change the properties after the vegetation has been placed, you will need to repaint it. Some properties such as random rotation use terrain color, and properties such as wind bending will update to the currently placed vegetation objects.

12. First, let's set the brush radius to 50 percent and then select the category **Forest_Trees**.

 You will notice a number beside each object within the vegetation category, which is meant to be a quick reference to the number of instances, which a current object has, within the level.

13. Next, click on the **Paint Objects** button seen here:

14. A good technique to create good vegetation with a brush is to just click a few times, rather than actually painting by clicking and dragging.

15. Next, paint the second category **forest_ground_mixed** in the same places where you have placed trees. These two categories are meant to work well together.

16. After painting some fairly dense areas, use the remove tool at 1020 percent width to erase a path through the forest, as you can see in the following screenshot:

Remember that you can quickly switch between painting and erasing by using the *control* key. We can also customize these landscapes using the individual selection mode available.

17. Select individual objects by toggling the paint mode off and by holding the *Space bar*. This will display a small selection helper at the base of the object.

18. Select an individual vegetation object.

19. Hold *Alt*, and click-and-drag this vegetation object to adjust its scale.

20. Hold *Alt* and *Ctrl*, then click-and-drag the vegetation object to rotate it.

21. Finally, hold *Shift*, and click anywhere on the terrain to create the selected object.

22. A good technique is to select certain instances of vegetation individually to adjust their placement, rather than trying to get the perfect, painting settings.

Note that in one of the vegetation groups, a stone is used. Not usually considered vegetation, it is a good example of demonstrating that you can use any sort of model as vegetation, but it should be noted that they will be typically restricted to terrain. Another good use of the vegetation system could be small, rubble pieces, twigs, and so on.

What just happened ?

Congratulations! You have just become accustomed with one of the most powerful tools the CryENGINE has to offer for creating realistic forests and environments containing massive amounts of vegetation.

In this example, we used the vegetation painter and some of its parameters to create and sculpt the flora for our level.

Time for action - setting up time of day and its basic parameters

Now, the time has come to adjust the overall lighting of our level. The fastest and easiest way to achieve a huge variety of atmospheres and settings is by using the **Time of day** feature in CryENGINE.

The sun in CryENGINE is approximated by a colored, directional light without distance attenuation. This is important to understand as its properties are similar to that of a regular light, and properties such as color and specular level can be adjusted. There is an important distinction, however, to the sun and other lights in CryENGINE, as the sun uses a technology called cascaded shadow maps.

1. Open the **Time Of Day** dialog box from **Terrain | Time Of Day**.

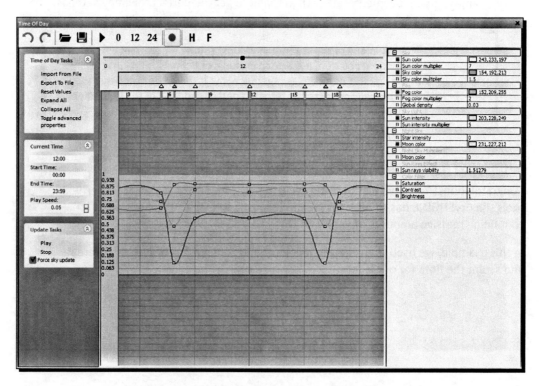

Note that when you highlight any of the basic parameters in the time of day dialog, there are **key frames** set already represented by the small, yellow squares on the timeline in the preceding screenshot.

This timeline is represented by a 24-hour slider at the top of the **Time Of Day** interface.

Since the best way to learn to manipulate the **Time Of Day** editor is to create your own. So, let's reset all the values before starting.

2. To do this, click **Reset Values** in the **Time of day** tasks window, which will give you a blank **Time Of Day** as shown in the following screenshot:

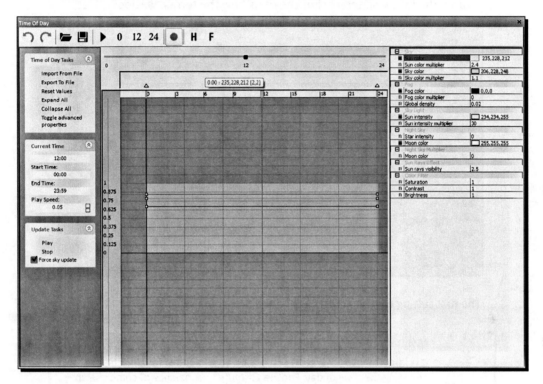

This will effectively remove all the key frames outside of the default values of 0000 and 2400.

3. Before we adjust the parameters to suit our needs, set **Force Sky Update** to **true** and ensure that the **record** button is highlighted.

    Next, let's set the **Current Time** value in the level and camera so that we can see the sun clearly.

4. To do this, click-and-drag the arrow on the slider to late afternoon. If you have difficulty getting the **Current Time** value accurate, you can type in the time you desire.

5. Set the **Current Time** value to 0700. At 0700, the sun should be fairly low in the sky and the shadows on the vegetation in our level will be quite long. You can of course use whatever time you like, however, for this example we will use 0700.

Having the sun intersect some geometry will allow the sunrays to be shown more clearly. The following screenshot shows us how the terrain will look:

The first setting we will adjust, will be the **Sun color**.

Monitor settings and calibration

It is important to have good settings on your monitor for color before adjusting the time of day. For the absolute best balance of color, use an external monitor calibrator.

The sun in CryENGINE3 has an advanced, dynamic light. Adjusting the **Sun color**, in simple terms, will adjust the diffuse color for this light.

6. To adjust the overall color, first click on the **Color** sampler box and then click-and-drag the black target to your preferred value. In our case, let's take a realistic approach to lighting this level and set the sun color to a warm, yellow tone of RGB **235,230,190**. We choose a warm yellow as the sun scattering in the atmosphere has the effect of becoming slightly yellow.

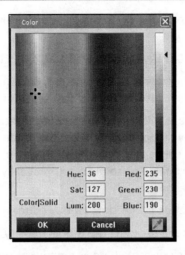

After clicking on **OK**, you will see that new key frames have now been created on the timeline. You can see the interpolation of the values from 0000 to 2400, which will be used in the case where you have an animated time of day.

The next parameter we will adjust will be the multiplier for the **Sun color** we previously set.

7. Set the **Sun color multiplier** to a level of **8**.

Next, we will set the **Sky color**.

Though the setting is called **Sky color**, it is more accurately the ambient lighting color for the entire level.

To observe the effects of changing this color, simply look anywhere, where there is no sun affection on objects from the sun lighting, otherwise known as indirect lighting.

Let's set the **Color** to the currently visible color of the sky.

8. To do this, click on the **Color** sampler box for the **Sky Color** parameter and click on the sample tool. The sample tool icon is shown in the following screenshot:

9. Next, click somewhere on the sky in the perspective viewport that will sample its color.

10. For this tutorial, set your **Sky Color** to RGB 150,200,210.

11. The **Sky Color** multiplier works as the ambient, color multiplier. Since we are going for a more realistic-looking time of day, set this to **0.8**.

> **Sky light** parameters are solely used to compute the atmospheric appearance of a dynamic sky. They do not directly affect the rendering of objects in the world (for example, lighting colors and intensities). However, they are used by the engine to compute an approximate **Fog color** to automatically fog the entire scene in appropriate colors.
>
> Next is the **Fog** subsection of the **Time Of Day** editor.
>
> In our case, we only need to adjust the **Global density** value.
>
> When using a dynamic sky, some haze is already calculated by the sky model. The fog specified by the **Fog color** gets added to that haze. In many cases, the haze may be enough to get properly colored fog for a given period of time.

12. As we do not require a high amount of fog for a pleasant, realistic scene, let's set the global density to a value of **0.02**.

> The next setting we will adjust will be the **Sky Light** Parameters.

13. Adjust the **Sun Intensity Multiplier** to a value higher than normal, to give a volumetric look to the fog. For this, try to use a multiplier of **50**.

> For the time being, we will not be setting any parameters for the **Night Sky** and **Night Sky Multiplier**, as we will discuss that later.
>
> The next setting is **Sun rays visibility**, in which we will adjust what our basic time of day will be.

14. This value controls the visibility of the sunrays. Higher values will cause brighter rays to appear around the sun, and lower values are a bit less stylized but more akin to a realistic look. Set this to **2.0**.

> Finally, to put a nice final touch on the lighting for this environment, we will enable some **High Dynamic Range** (**HDR**) lighting.

15. Toggle the display of the advanced parameters in the time of day dialog.

16. Locate, at the very top of the dialog, the HDR Dynamic Factor and set this to between 2 and 3. This will brighten the overall image and increase the variance in some of the color.

You should end up with something like the following screenshot.

What just happened?

Having now set some of the basic **Time Of Day** settings, we have added some important aspects to our level. Not so much in terms of gameplay, but rather in theme and atmosphere.

Our level now has some **Fog**, a good **Sun color**, some contrast on the ground between shadows and light, as well as a fairly intense sun with sunrays.

An important point to realize is that there is truly no single, correct or perfect setting for the time of day; this will depend greatly upon your taste and your overall needs for different environments. Be sure to experiment with the values, and try to create some dramatically different atmospheres. When using the **Time Of Day** feature, it is recommended to not have the sun perfectly at the highest position. The **Time Of Day** dialog box has a huge variety of settings for simulating realistic and surrealistic lighting effects. Having completed setting up the basic parameters will make it substantially easier to adjust the advanced effects that time of day allows you to adjust, to achieve photorealistic-looking, outdoor lighting.

Have a go hero – moving the sun

For truly precise lighting, you can supplement the time of day using the **Lighting tool**.

1. Open the terrain **Lighting tool** by clicking on the **Terrain** section of the main toolbar and then on **lighting**. A **Lighting Tool** dialog box will be opened, as seen in the following screenshot:

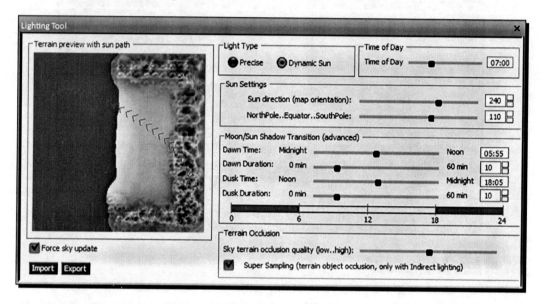

2. Under the **Sun Settings** section, there are two sliders. Adjust the first slider named **Sun direction** to the centermost point on the slider. This aligns the sun, so that it rises in the east and sets in the west.

North is assumed to be on the Y positive axis (y+) in the CryENGINE.

3. Next, adjust the second slider named **NorthPole..Equator..SouthPole** to its centermost position.

   This will change the *tilt* of the sun when set at the center; setting the **Current Time** to 1200 will cause the sun to be directly above you. Adding a *tilt* in either direction will infer that your level's location, in reality, is closer to either pole of the planet.

4. Adjust the tilt slightly towards the North Pole as this particular environment looks to be in the northern hemisphere.

5. Click on **OK** to save your modifications.

Do not point the sun straight down on your level

It is good to have some rotation on the sun so that the shadows are not aligned with the world direction and thus objects that may be aligned. This is all done to make man-made buildings and other level objects look better because they are often world aligned and built straight up.

Adding Atmosphere

As with film and television, atmospheric effects play an essential role in a level's environmental design. As you saw in the previous examples, adding atmospheric effects using the time of day tool can change the look and feel of your level drastically. An old building can look perfectly harmless in the bright sunshine, but in the fog it can take on a sinister appearance, which hints at underlying drama yet to unfold!

Summary

In this chapter, we've found out that gameplay needs an environment in order to take place, and so the creation and design of a level's environment is a critical factor in developing top-quality games. The level's environment is just as important as character design and presents several unique challenges to designers.

Designing levels breaks down into two distinct parts. The first of which is the look and feel of the level's environment, which we've gone over in a good amount of detail in this chapter. The second, which we will explore in the next chapter, is the design and challenge of the play space itself. The whole purpose to this chapter was to provide the space and ambience to host the various challenges of **AI** enemies, puzzles, and trials within our game.

Having made an interesting environment, let's fill it with some gameplay, using entities and objects essential to making our first game example!

3
Playable Levels in No Time

The most critical time for any level is in the beginning. The method in which the level is initially built will determine how the rest of the level will evolve. As levels are becoming increasingly complex within games, speed and efficiency are highly valued traits for designers. Putting the essential objects in place to rapidly prototype a level within the CryENGINE will be the focus of this chapter.

In this chapter, we will explore:

- Creating a road to give some direction to our player
- Placing a spawn point entity into the world to give our player somewhere to start
- Utilizing layers for organizing our level objects
- Using the asset browser to place brushes
- Creating **Constructive Solid Geometry (CSG)**
- Placing a basic **Artificial Intelligence (AI)** entity
- Creating an entity archetype
- Generating AI navigation and exporting it to the engine

Building levels with entities and objects

In the previous chapter, we saw how to create a relatively simple environment as a foundation in which we can build our first examples of gameplay. Levels within the CryENGINE SDK always consist of collections of static and dynamic objects, which include all manner of things that you might require in your game, from simple geometric objects to full dynamic AI entities.

In this chapter, we will learn to use some essential game objects to rapidly make our level playable within the CryENGINE launcher.

Starting a level

If you asked most designers about how they begin their levels, their answers would vary. One designer may transcribe his idea, and write it into an exhaustive and detailed design document. Others may plan the important elements in their head and prototype the key elements relatively quickly, by making them playable as soon as possible. There might, however, be situations where mixes of both the techniques are used, or if you are working within a team environment, more or less of the design might need to be communicated. For this chapter, we will concentrate on getting a playable level together, and then iterating on it by adding and modifying various gameplay objects.

Creating a spawn point

The spawn point entity is easily the most important entity for a level to be considered playable within the CryENGINE SDK. The spawn point dictates the starting location and view for your player as soon as the level is started.

Time for action - creating a spawn point

The CryENGINE acts out of the box, as you would expect the real world to act, with gravity and physics affecting the human player. For this reason, it is best to place the spawn points where the player can physically stand when they are started within the level:

1. Open the level `example_4` inside the **Editor.exe** application.
2. In the **RollupBar**, select the **Objects** tab and click on **Entity** option.
3. Open the **Multiplayer** folder in the **Entity List** window.
4. Click-and-drag the **SpawnPoint** entity into the perspective viewport, and then release the mouse button.
5. Finalize the initial placement by clicking on it again.
6. Move the **SpawnPoint** entity to the location you wish to spawn the player.
7. Note that the direction of the **SpawnPoint** entity helper icon represents the direction the player will face when spawned, as seen in the following screenshot:

For this example, a suitable location to start our player is along the surface of the terrain. As you place the **Spawn Point** entity, you will want to test it, and this can be done by quickly running the test from within the editor.

8. Click on the **Switch to Game** mode, and press *F2* on the keyboard to instantly spawn at the **SpawnPoint** entity.

9. Save the `.cry` file.

10. Under the **File** menu, select the **Export to Engine** option.

This will send a command to the CryENGINE application to package and compress the information within the level into an optimized format, which can be run from the launcher application. As a reminder, the launcher application should always be considered as the end user application, which means that our players will use this to play our game and its levels. See the *Exporting to engine* section of this chapter for further information on this process.

11. For now, close the sandbox editor and open the **launcher.exe** application.

12. Launch the `example_4` map using the map's **Console** command or by selecting from the list of maps in the menu.

Note that this first **SpawnPoint** entity will automatically function as the default spawn location for your map in the launcher application.

 You can quickly cycle between multiple spawn points in the editor and pure game by repeatedly pressing the *F2* keyboard shortcut.

What just happened?

You have now created a **SpawnPoint** from where the player can begin his/her journey into your level.

Though we did not use multiple **SpawnPoint** objects in the previous example, it is important to realize that some level configurations may require multiple **SpawnPoint** objects. Using multiple **SpawnPoint** objects can be useful if you want to spawn two opposing teams of players in different locations, in multiplayer. However, when using multiple **SpawnPoint** objects in multiplayer, it is good practice to not place them in identical locations, as this will potentially pose a problem if two players are spawned concurrently.

Multiple **SpawnPoint** objects could even be used in single player mode, as checkpoint or save locations, to allow the player or designers to skip portions of the levels.

Landmarks to guide the player

Our player will use landmarks to help navigate them through the level. Within most games, almost nothing is placed completely randomly, not even natural landmarks such as rocks and trees. In the game world, there should always be a certain amount of reasoning behind the position, angle, and size of the objects. Landmarks can be just about anything—large or small—that stands out in some way. They can be big objects, such as roads, buildings, and terrain formations; or they can be small, such as markings on walls or even unique objects such as vehicles.

An important consideration when placing landmarks is that they are very useful to help the player to not only navigate in the world, but to also get a feel for the sense of scale in the level.

Using roads in levels

Roads are a very useful landmark within levels, just as in the real world. The **Road** tool within sandbox can be used to create paths, which direct the player within a level. You can also use the **Road** tool to sculpt the terrain into path-like shapes, for example, a ledge on the side of a huge cliff.

Time for action - creating a road object

In this example, we will explore the basic uses of the **Road** tool and learn how to create paths, which are easy for the player to recognize and traverse:

1. Open the level `example_4`, or the level you saved in the previous chapter, with the **Editor.exe** application.

2. In the **RollupBar**, open the **Objects** tab.

3. Select the **Misc** button.

4. From the **Object Type** section, select **Road**, as seen in the following screenshot:

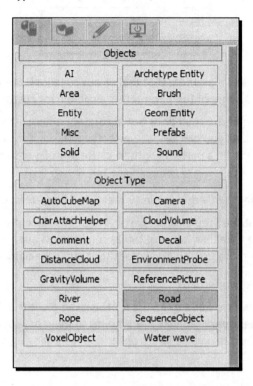

5. Set your alignment tools to the **Align to Terrain** icon, as seen in the following screenshot:

6. Click on the **Terrain** object to create five or six points along the curved line, representing the **Road** entity.

7. Double-click to finalize the shape of the **Road**.

   By default, **Road** does not have material applied to it yet. So, let's apply a suitable material.

8. Open the **Material Editor** using the keyboard shortcut *M*, or open it by using the **Open View Pane** menu.

9. Browse to the material, **Materials | Roads | forest_trail_mud**, and assign it to the road using the assign material to selected object function highlighted in the following screenshot:

Having now applied a material that makes our road look like a muddy, driven-on path, let's adjust some of the parameters available for customizing the road.

The default scale of the road does not accurately reflect in the particular material we have applied. As you can see, the material has, what looks to be, worn tire tracks, which must be a certain width to cause our player to believe a car has driven on it.

10. To rectify this, set the **Width** property measured in meters to 6.5.

Next, let's adjust the **Step Size** property. A high **Step Size** property yields physically bigger tiles, and a smaller value will yield smaller tiles but more polygons. Thus it will appear as a more precise and smoother road, especially at curves.

11. Set the **Step Size** property to 2.

The last value that we need to adjust for this example is the **Tile Length** property. The **Tile Length** property adjusts the amount of tiling or repetition of the material on the road. Adjust this value while observing the changing appearance of the road's material.

12. Set the **Tile Length** property to 6.5.

Matching the **Tile Length** and **Width** properties will give us a perfectly square material and thus no texture stretching or squashing; this is not a rule, but is useful to keep in mind.

You should now have ended up with something similar to the following screenshot:

What just happened?

Roads, as you can see, are a very fast and useful tool when it comes to directing our player to certain places or simply along certain paths within levels. The Z axis makes little difference in the way the road material is projected onto the terrain; however, it is still good practice to keep the road close to the terrain surface.

Remember that using other features such as vegetation, as seen in *Chapter 2, Breaking Ground with Sandbox*, in conjunction with roads will require some iteration. When you refer to the real world, you will see that usually when a road is created there is a natural boundary that is created between the road and the environment surrounding it. So, it doesn't make any sense to have a tree or a large bush growing in the middle of a concrete road. Iteration is the key here, thus some time will be spent switching back to your vegetation tools to remove or add certain pieces of vegetation where it makes sense.

Have a go hero – mastering roads

Let's try to use some of the more advanced features available using the **Road** tool, to further customize it for our needs:

1. You are able to modify any preexisting road by selecting it. Click on the **Edit** icon from the **Shape Editing** menu.

2. Press *Ctrl* and click on the road to add additional control points.

3. Change the angle at which the projection of the road is casted. Do this by adjusting the **Angle** parameter for the individual points. Valid angles range from -25 to +25.

4. Turn off the **Default width** option, which will enable you to adjust the width of the individual points in the road.

5. Use the **Align Heightmap** tool to align the terrain's heightmap to the Z locations of the points on the road quickly. This is an excellent method for also making **Ramps**, as you can simply adjust the Z position of any point and click on **Align Heightmap**, and the terrain will adjust to the road. This process is depicted in the following two screenshots:

This tool is extremely useful for any designer who wishes to sculpt ramps, paths, or any simple shape into the terrain that might not be as easily achieved through the use of the heightmap modification brushes.

Utilizing layers to organize level objects

In the following example, we will learn how to use the layer system for the organization of our object, as layers are a very useful way of hiding and freezing whole groups of objects quickly and easily within sandbox. Layers also serve two other important functions. The first of which is that they can be made external, which means that they can be saved as a separate file, independent of the level, to allow a collaboration with other developers on the same level. The second is that entire layers full of objects can be streamed in and out during game play, by using triggers and scripting to help performance.

Time for action - creating and managing layers

Until now, we have placed all our objects onto the layer created by default upon starting any new level, which is known as the main layer. We will now create some custom layers:

1. Open `Example_5` inside the **Editor.exe** application.

2. Create a new **Layer** by clicking on the add layer icon, as seen in the following screenshot:

A **New Layer** dialog box will appear.

3. In the **New Layer** section, enter the following parameters:

    ❑ **Name = Spawnpoint**

    ❑ **Visible = True**

    ❑ **External = True**

    ❑ **Frozen = False**

    ❑ **Export To Game = True**

4. Select the **SpawnPoint** entity and **Road** created earlier, and switch to the **Objects** tab within the **RollupBar**, as seen in the following screenshot:

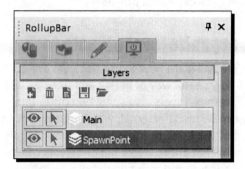

In the entity properties, you will see a button for layers as seen in the following screenshot, which at present is set as **Main**, as both the objects exist on the main layer:

5. Click on the **Layers** button, which will reveal a list of the other layers available to place objects onto.

6. Click again on the **SpawnPoint** layer, which will move the **SpawnPoint** and **Road** entities placed earlier to that layer.

7. Finally, save the level by clicking on **File | Save**.

If you now navigate to the level directory using Windows Explorer, you will notice a new folder called Layers. Inside that folder, you will see a file named SpawnPoints.lyr.

What just happened?

You have just created a new layer and learned how to move objects between them. You can now create new layers to easily manage multiple objects and entities that we will place into levels in later examples.

Even though any entity or object you place in your level can be placed into an external layer, it is important to note that there is some type of level data that cannot be placed inside of these layers. Following is a quick list of the commonly used, level data types that are exclusively stored by the .cry file and cannot be stored in layers:

- **Terrain** data

- **Heightmap** data

- **Unit Size** setting

- **Max Terrain Height** setting

- Terrain **Holes**

- Terrain **Textures**

- **Vegetation** objects and categories

- **Environment** settings including **Ocean Height** and **Time Of Day**

- Generated AI Navigation

Have a go hero – utilizing layers for multiple developer collaboration

Try using the layer system for collaborating with other developers.

Commit your level's layer directory to a Tortoise SVN or GitHub repository.

After doing so, you may now have your other developer make changes to that layer by moving objects to different locations. Once they have modified the layer, have them save the map, which then writes the changes to the external .lyr file.

Have them then commit only the changes they have made to the layer file you committed. You can then retrieve it from the repository. Upon retrieving the file, you will notice that whatever objects were moved, added, or modified, will be updated within the level.

Setting layers to external is the key to this whole process.

Once a .cry file has been saved to reference an external layer, it will access the data inside of those layers upon loading the level in sandbox.

It is good practice to assign an "owner", who will be responsible for the data types associated only with the .cry file. Since this is the master file, only one person should be in charge of maintaining it and creating new layers if necessary.

Adding objects using the asset browser

The **Asset Browser** in sandbox is a very useful tool for anyone placing models into sandbox. It can even be used to place sounds and review textures. In the following example, we will add some art to our level using some of the assets immediately available to us.

Time for action - adding brushes to the level

We will use **Asset Browser** to add some natural objects to the level. Natural objects such as trees and rocks should be placed in such a way that a balance is kept between a completely artificial look or being placed too randomly. Considering how these objects typically appear together in real life is a good way to achieve this:

1. Open the `example_5.cry` file.

2. Then, open **Asset Browser** by clicking on **View | Open View pane | Asset Browser**.

3. By default, **Asset Browser** is set to display **Sounds**, **Models**, and **Textures**.

4. Use the database filter to display only **Models** by removing the check marks beside **Sounds** and **Textures**, as seen in the following screenshot:

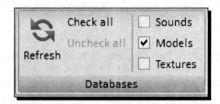

The **Asset Browser** window contains a search function, which can be used to include only those objects that are used in a specific level, or with specific properties.

5. We can **Search** with the name of the file or the path to the file. Type `rock` in the **Search** text field. In the thumbs browser, you can scroll through all the **Models** window with `rock` in their name or path.

The thumbs browser shows a preview of objects with a certain size, defined by the **Thumb size** setting. Each object can be rotated within the assets window by clicking and holding the left mouse button. You can zoom in and out as well, using the mouse wheel.

The size of the thumbnail can be adjusted from 16 x 16 pixels up to 1024 x 1024 pixels.

6. Select a model by clicking on it; in this example, we will use `cliff_rock_a_med.cgf`. The view of **Asset Brower** is seen in the following screenshot:

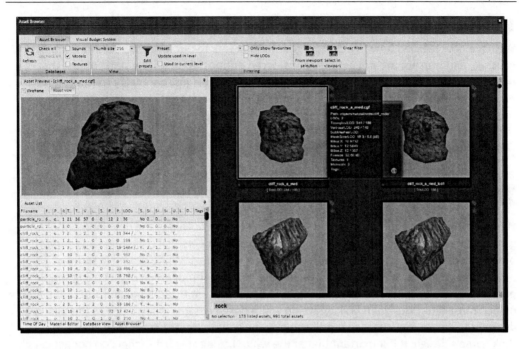

7. Now that we have selected the asset we want to add, click-and-drag `cliff_rock_a_med.cgf` from the thumbnails browser into your level.

It is highly recommended to use the **Align to Terrain** tool when placing brushes into the world, as seen in the following image:

Experiment by dragging and dropping multiple rocks and even other assets, which add to the overall composition of your level.

One important feature of brushes (which is the type of geometry we are placing) is that they can be either scaled, rotated, or both. When placing multiple brushes, it is good practice to ensure that the objects don't have identical rotation or even scale, as this will break the believability of their placement. So, make sure to adjust the scale and rotation of the objects, as well as their position, for optimal placement.

What just happened?

We have now learned how to add new geometry assets to our level; we call these objects brushes, and brushes are not actually considered entities. A **brush** is a static object that does not require entity identification, because the object is just geometry to the engine beyond the visual and physical characteristics. The player will only interact with these brushes in simple ways. An important consideration later on will be that what this really means, in most cases, is that brushes cannot be directly used in any prescribed events, which we will see later in the book.

White boxing

White boxing is not a common term if you haven't been involved in the development of a game before. The history of the term actually comes from personal computers and server boxes that do not have a name brand, thus being a white box. White boxing in terms of game development is in spirit a similar concept, where a designer models an object using simple primitives, such as spheres, boxes, and cylinders to represent the volume and size of the final object. Most often, designers will iterate on white boxed designs many times as this allows a designer to create, remove, and modify quickly the geometric structures they create to suit their game's design. It is important that at the white boxing stage, designers do not get caught up in the details or even cosmetics of the objects, but rather get the level to a playable state as fast as possible.

White boxing using Constructive Solid Geometry (CSG)

To expedite white boxing, there is an important tool within the sandbox editor application, and it is called the **Solid** tool. As previously discussed, this tool can be regarded as a very simplistic, shape creator. To reiterate a previous point, some designers will prefer to create their floor plan and design on paper first, before moving onto actually doing it with the technology they will use. In our case, we will instead go straight into the application, and since the **Solid** tool is so fast to use, it's sometimes just as fast to layout your design in real time versus going through a long, planning process.

Time for action - creating constructive solid geometry

CSG or solids allow you to create a multitude of different shapes, all of which have their own physics properties tied to them; you can thus have your player collide into them, shoot them, or even walk on them. You can use these shapes to form complicated objects and merge them together, and later save and export these objects for use within other 3D art packages, such as 3D studio max or Maya.

On that note, let's get right into modeling some structures for us to use in our level. Before we begin, you must have Sandbox 3 open to any level:

1. In the **RollupBar**, click on the **Solid** button.

2. Ensure that the alignment tool is set to **Follow Terrain** and that the **Grid snap** value is set to the default **1** meter snapping.

3. Click-and-drag anywhere on the terrain, in the level, and you will see a two-dimensional form starting to take shape. Once you release the mouse button, the width and length of the shape will be set.

4. Next, note that when you drag your mouse up-and-down, you will see that this is adjusting the height of the **Solid** object. Clicking on the left mouse button a second time will finalize its placement.

5. Create a **20x20x20** meter cube by reading the size (in meters) displayed on each axis of the solid as you create it. You should end up with something like the following screenshot:

As you can see, the **Solid** tool is a very basic geometry creation tool within the editor, which is very easy to use.

Try experimenting with some of the different properties that are available. Create other shapes, such as cones, spheres, and cylinders.

 The **Num Sides** parameter is used to define how many sides you want your solid to have. This parameter only changes the initial number of sides, the shape will have, for the cones, spheres, and cylinders.

6. Select the **Solid** object you just created, and click on the **Editing Mode** button in the **Solid Parameters** tab, as seen in the following screenshot:

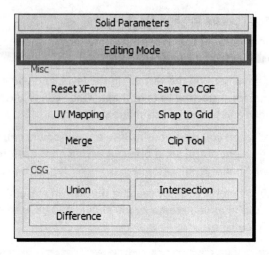

7. For those who are familiar with DCC tools such as 3DS Max or Maya, **Editing Mode** should look very familiar. It allows you to modify the shape of the solid by changing the location of the vertices, edges, faces, and polygons.

Let's now turn our cube into a very simplistic, house-like structure, keeping in mind that the goal is simply to make it suitable for the white boxed level art.

8. Change **Selection Type** to **Polygon** as seen in the following screenshot:

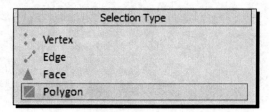

9. Select the top of the **Polygon** on the cube by clicking on the face; you will know it's selected when the face is highlighted in red, as seen in the following screenshot:

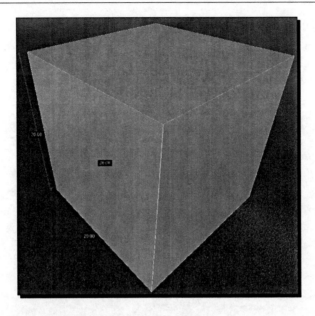

10. Under the **Sub Object Edit** rollout, select **Face | Split**.

11. Now change your **Selection Type** from **Polygon** to **Vertex**.

12. Select the top center of **Vertex**, which will have been created when the face was split in the previous step.

13. Drag this **Vertex** slightly upwards, on the Z Axis, so that the total height of the **Solid** object is now around 30 meters; you will now have something akin to the following screenshot:

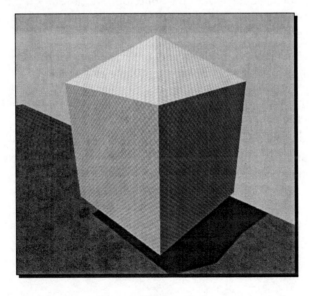

14. Change your **Sub Object | Selection Type** back to **Polygon**.

15. Now, select the bottom of the **Polygon** object and move it upwards to reduce the overall height of the body of the white boxed house. The final height should end up around 20 meters and look similar to the following screenshot:

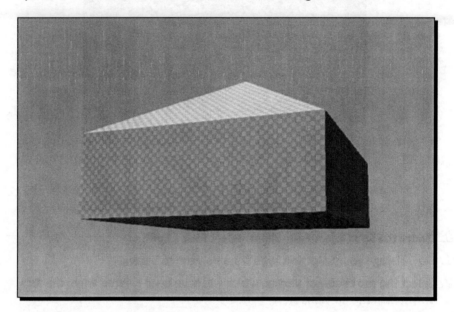

16. Exit the **Editing Mode** window by pressing the *Esc* key and then move the entire object itself down to the terrain.

When constructing objects with the **Solid** tool, we can stack multiple, primitive shapes together to form the groups of shapes required for an object or even to form quite elaborate structures over time.

Let's create one now by making a very basic chimney for the white box *house* we created, to make it a bit more recognizable as a house.

17. Using the methods learned in the previous steps, create a new **Solid** shaped as a box, with the dimensions of 5x7x10 meters.

18. With the new box selected, move it to the roof of the house and place it where a chimney would make sense. Again, refer to real life houses to get the positioning correct.

 Shift + click on the roof to move the object to that physical surface.

Once completed, you should have something similar to the following screenshot:

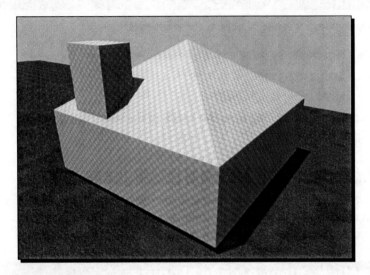

19. Select both the **Solid** objects you have created by holding the *Ctrl* key and clicking on them both.

20. In the **Solid Parameters** rollout, click on the **Merge** button.

You now have combined **Solid** objects that can be managed as a single object.

21. To export the newly merged solid from the editor, click on **File | Export Selected Geometry to .OBJ**.

22. Set the name that you wish to save the .obj file as, and select the location in which to save it.

You can now either send this file to a 3D artist or open it yourself in a DCC tool, such as 3D Studio Max or Maya, to further polish and finalize the asset.

What just happened?

Congratulations! You have made your first white box model. This is just a simple example, and you can easily use the skills learned in it, to create just about any kind of creative mean to show you some of the tools. You have just learned the basic of white boxing and CSG modelling within the CryENGINE SDK. A very important fact about creating these box-modelled structures is that they are not automatically combined into a single mesh. They are dealt with, currently, as two distinct objects. It is desirable to merge these objects into a single mesh for a few reasons, the first being that once combined into a single object, it can be easily copied and pasted throughout the level. Additionally, should you want to export these objects from the level into a format readable by external 3D applications, you will need to merge them together.

Have a go hero

Try to build a few different types of objects for your level:

- Create a skyscraper by using a single **Solid** object
- Create a bridge using merged objects
- Create a room using simple walls
- Try to build a dock coming from the beach to the water using various primitives shapes

Adding characters with Artificial Intelligence (AI)

In the following example, we will learn how you can place down a simple AI character. The entity is called **Grunt** and it represents a simple AI entity that packages extra properties, which can be customized. We will see these properties later in this chapter.

Time for action - place a basic AI entity

Let's now add one of the most advanced and dynamic entities available to us within the sandbox application:

1. In the **RollupBar**, click on the **Entity** button.
2. Under the **AI** folder, find the **Grunt** tab.
3. Click-and-drag the entity anywhere on your terrain within the perspective viewport.
4. Switch to game mode near their location, and the **Grunt** object will immediately attack you, if you are within range.

When selecting the **Grunt** object, you will be presented with a huge variety of properties that have been previously set in the `.lua` script in the **Entity Properties** section of the **RollupBar**. The default settings of the **Grunt** object will suffice for this example, but it is recommended that you experiment with some of the parameters available.

What just happened?

You have placed your first enemy and can now interact with them. Having characters to breathe some life into our story and game gives us tons of gameplay possibilities by simply placing them in progressive and interesting ways. A common mistake when dealing with AI placement is that the characters are placed without being given a task or without being hidden slightly from view. Consider the placement of AI carefully. As this example showed you the procedure of getting an AI entity into the world, it is worth noting that the use of advanced spawning and scripting actions can be achieved using the flow graph, which is explained in the next chapter.

Have a go hero

Try adjusting some of the properties of your AI to make it more or less challenging. Change the **attackrange** parameter to a lower value so that the AI doesn't react until you are very close, or set it very far so that they react to you sooner.

Use the **Faction** parameter to have the AI fight each other or aid the player by setting them to oppose **Faction** objects.

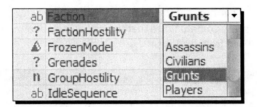

Create an archetype entity

Although not essential, it is very good practice, when creating games with a variety of enemies, to create different templates for the player to fight in. We call these templates archetypes. **Archetypes** store all the properties of their associated entity. For example, you can have archetypes of lights with certain settings, breakable objects with specific parameters, and finally AI entities with specific parameters. In the case of an AI archetype, some of the important parameters could be **attackrange**, **Field of Vision**, **Health** and some other properties.

The most important benefit of using archetype entities is when you consider trying to change every placed AI entities' properties across all levels. Without the archetype entities, you would have to physically go in and change all the instances of each character for it to reflect your changes. Using archetypes allows you to modify this once and affect every single instance across multiple levels at the same time.

Time for action - creating your own archetype

As we just discussed, archetypes are templates based on predefined script values. These parameters are exposed in the **Archetype Library** tab, which can be found in the **DataBase View** window.

In this example, we will create two opposing teams of **Grunt** objects using two archetypes:

1. Open the **DataBase View** window by selecting the **View** menu and then opening **View pane | DataBase View**.

2. In the **DataBase View** window, click on the create new library icon.

3. Name this new .xml library **Book_Example_5_Archetypes**.

4. Add an item to the library with the add item icon.

5. Name the group **Enemies** and the names of the enemy to **Grunt_1**.

6. Do the same for a second group called **Friendly**, and name the friend **Grunt_2**.

7. Set the **Faction** parameter of **Grunt_2** to **Players**, as seen in the following screenshot:

 You will notice that the parameter will be highlighted permanently to visually communicate that the highlighted parameter has been modified from its defaults.

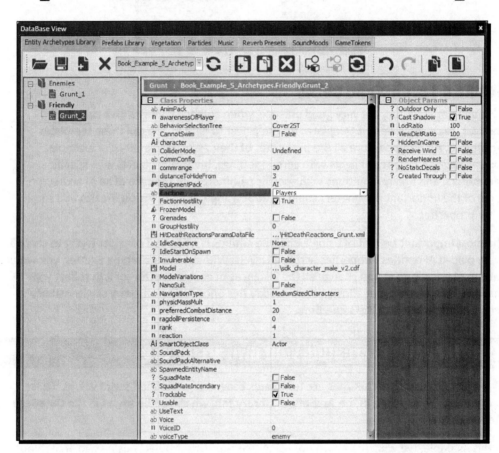

8. Drag **Grunt_1** and **Grunt_2** from the **DataBase View** and place them into your level.

9. Copy a few **Enemies** and place them throughout your level, making sure that their **attackrange** is set to a suitable value.

10. Copy a team of **Grunt_2** characters.

11. Once you switch to game mode, if the **Grunt_2** characters are in range of **Grunt_1** characters or vice versa, they will attack each other.

What just happened?

Using archetype entities is the best way to avoid the need to open every level across your game to change the settings of the AI. It is also highly useful when balancing and organizing your game entities.

Pop quiz – essential game objects

1. What is the main tool used within sandbox, for white boxing geometric design assets?

    a. Database view

    b. Solid tool

    c. Road tool

    d. Archetype entities

2. What is the entity used at the start of a level that set's where the player will be standing when a level is started?

    a. Smart object

    b. Grunt entity

    c. Tag point

    d. Spawn point entity

3. If you want to use multiple developer collaboration on a level, how would you accomplish this?

    a. Using external layers and version controlling them

    b. Ensuring that one designer works on the level at a time

    c. Dif-merging the `.cry` file

Exporting to engine

Now that we have some basic gameplay entities in place, we can proceed with saving and getting the level ready to be launched in the **launcher.exe** application.

Even though saving the level will create a `.cry` file, it is extremely important to know that the `.cry` cannot be accessed by the **launcher.exe** application. To export the level in a format that can be used by the launcher application, we will have to use the **Export to Engine** function, which even though we used in the first example, we will explore in a bit more detail.

Time for action - exporting your level to engine

This process will have to be used on any level, but for the sake of this example, you should have the `example_6.cry` file open inside sandbox:

1. Go to **File | Export to Engine**, or press *Ctrl + E*.

    This crucial step is required to convert all the raw data contained in the `.cry` file and its layers into a `level.pak` archive.

2. Close the **Editor.exe** application and run the **launcher.exe** application.

3. Open the map `example_6.cry`, and you will have spawned at the correct **SpawnPoint** and be forced into a fierce AI battle.

What just happened?

As the **launcher.exe** application is our target, this is important to do once in a while. Though sandbox supports the **Switch to Game Mode** function, it is not an accurate representation of the performance as the additional overhead of the editor and debugging tools can slow frame rates.

Have a go hero

It is possible to open `.pak` files and access the information stored inside of them by using third-party compression software such as WinZip and WinRar. However, it is not recommended to do this unless you are familiar with handling the files that you may wish to change. If you do change the files that are inside of these `.pak` files, you run the risk of damaging the `.pak` file and breaking your level for use within the launcher application. Corrupted `.pak` files should be deleted and reexported from the sandbox application.

There is no need to panic if, for whatever reason, any of your `.pak` files become corrupted and unusable in the launcher, as you can always delete them and generate a new one from your `example_6.cry` by repeating this example.

Summary

We've done it! We've created our first, simple, yet playable, game example, and have gone through a typical workflow of tools in designing objects and placing entities into our small level. We've also seen some of the immediate out of the box features available to us to create levels for our games in CryENGINE.

Specifically in this chapter, we explored how to create landmarks such as roads, and natural objects such as rocks and some other geometry. We've learned about some of the essential game objects, which include the **SpawnPoint** and AI entities. In the next chapter, we will explore visual scripting which is used to tell these entities how to react in particular ways, or to set up a prescripted event.

4
I'm a Scripter, Not a Coder

Scripting gives you the ability to code your game's major functionality without having to recompile the C++ game code. Some of the scriptable game components are Artificial Intelligence (AI), User Interface (UI), game events, save and load game functionality, and many others. Scripting also provides the vehicle for designers without deep technical knowledge or code training. It also gives the designers the ability to change a huge variety of gameplay functions quickly and easily, to facilitate balancing and tweaking. They sometimes do that so much that the game looks completely different, like a brand new game; and they did all that without touching or having the ability to touch the game engine source code.

This chapter will spend a good deal of time exploring the use of Flow Graph scripting. The Flow Graph is easily one of the most powerful tools within the CryENGINE Sandbox as it allows you to visually script triggers and events versus having to write them manually using programming knowledge.

In this chapter, we shall:

- Discuss game scripting and it's usage within CryENGINE 3
- Explore the Flow Graph—CryENGINE 3's visual scripting tool
- Create some examples of Flow Graph for various uses in our game examples
- Make a Flow Graph to spawn the player at a specific location
- Add a trigger to Flow Graph and monitor it's status
- Create a patrolling AI
- Debug the Flow Graph
- Add and remove breakpoints

Scripting and the CryENGINE 3

In game development, scripting languages are used primarily to reduce the iteration time of the compile, linking, and running of the executable. In CryENGINE 3, most scripts can be hot loaded during runtime. What this means, is that the property changes similarly to how the **Health** of an object can be changed without the need to relaunch the editor application.

A great advantage to scripting is that it allows developers from various disciplines such as design, animation, art to work on their particular piece of the game without having to rely on the C++ programmers to change small variables within a game's code. In previous chapters, you have actually already done basic scripting by changing some of the variables of the entities and objects you've placed into the world.

In the CryENGINE 3 SDK, there are principally two different methods of scripting. The first method uses the Lua script language, which will be explained in detail in the next chapter. The second method uses a visual scripting system called **Flow Graph**.

Lua usage in the CryENGINE 3

In CryENGINE 3, there are various types of predefined Lua entities. These entities can have, attached to them, a script proxy. This appears in the form of a table that can include data and functions. For example, the AI system has behaviors and goal pipes written in scripts. Additionally, several game systems such as the actor, item system, vehicle system, and game rules rely on scripting to extend their functionalities.

Various systems in the CryENGINE expose script bind functions, which allow Lua scripts to call existing code written in C++. Using Lua scripts and entities will be discussed and demonstrated in the next chapter. In this chapter, we will focus on the visual scripting element of the CryENGINE 3 SDK termed Flow Graph.

Visual scripting with Flow Graph

The Flow Graph is a visual scripting system embedded in the CryENGINE Sandbox editor. Visual scripting is a hugely powerful tool as it visually represents basic functions and their connections in a far more accessible way than a scripter would be able to represent in code. This means that developers really don't need to have any scripting or programming knowledge to use it! A huge library of node provides the user with everything needed to fully control the entities and AI in a level.

In addition to being the main tool used for creating mission logic in single player and, even recently, multiplayer levels, the Flow Graph can also be used to prototype gameplay, effects, and sound design. Levels can have multiple graphs performing different tasks at the same time, and we can even extend these Flow Graphs to change level or global variables called **game tokens**, making them consistent and useable over the entire game. In the following screenshot, you see an example of how a typical Flow Graph looks:

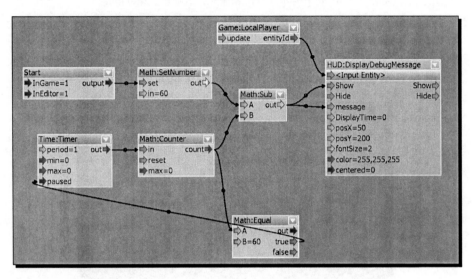

Scripted events

One common and design wise, important element of most games is scripted events. In game development, we refer to events that are singular situations or usually happen unexpectedly to help reduce gameplay repetitiveness, as scripted events. When games lack scripted events, they usually end up being stale and eventually very predictable. To really involve the player in your game or level, it's important that you always provide variations and exciting, unique moments to motivate your player to keep playing.

Scripted events can be just about anything! They can be as simple as an enemy suddenly bursting through a door or being dropped from a helicopter. They can also be complex events, such as an entire level being changed by the sudden collapse of a bridge or the explosion of a building, changing the course of the story or even the gameplay.

In the rest of the chapter, we will use the Flow Graph visual scripting tool within Sandbox to create a series of useful scripted events and to learn the overall use of the Flow Graph system.

Time for action - making a Flow Graph to spawn the player at a specific location

Let's get right to learning how to use Flow Graph to accomplish some basic game scripting:

1. Open the level from the previous chapter, or create a new level.

2. Drag-and-drop the **SpawnPoint** entity, from the **Entities | Multiplayer** section in the **RollupBar** tab, into the level.

3. Select the **SpawnPoint** entity and right-click to open the contextual menu. Select **Create Flow Graph** as seen in the following screenshot:

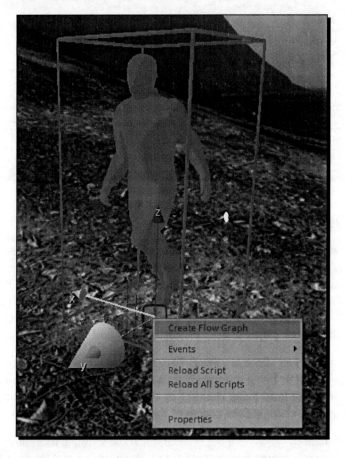

4. Name the created Flow Graph as `Player_Spawn` in the new Flow Graph dialog box.

The Flow Graph window will now be opened, as a new script is ready to be added to the **SpawnPoint** entity.

Flow Graphs created in this fashion are saved on the entity itself. This should be considered when copying and pasting any entity with a Flow Graph saved on it, as a Flow Graph will also be copied as part of the entity.

5. Select the **SpawnPoint** entity and right-click on any open space in the Flow Graph editor viewport.

6. A contextual window will be displayed upon right-clicking, click on the **Add Selected Entity** function.

   This now adds the entity and its corresponding logic block (otherwise known as a **Node**) to the Flow Graph. The inputs and outputs of this entity can now be used for various functions, as seen in the following screenshot:

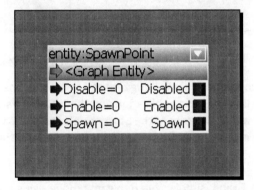

We have now added an entity node.

 There is a distinction between entity nodes and one other type of node called a component node, which we will discuss next.

7. We will now add our first component node. Easily, the most commonly used component node is the **MISC:START** node.

8. To add this component node, right-click in some empty space in the Flow Graph viewport, and from the contextual menu, select the **Add Start Node** option.

9. Next, we need to link the nodes together to create some logic. Click-and-drag a link from the **Start** node's **output** to the input named **Spawn** of the **SpawnPoint** node, as seen in the following screenshot:

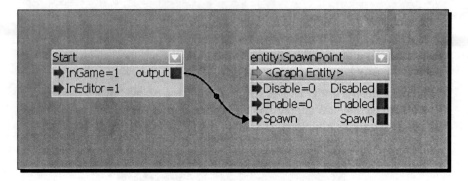

Having connected the two nodes, we can now test our Flow Graph.

10. There are two conditions that will trigger the **Start** node. The first is when the player is loaded in the **launcher.exe** application and the **InGame** parameter is set to **1**. The second condition that will trigger the **Start** node's **Output** is when it is detected that the Flow Graph is being used from the editor and the **InEditor** parameter is set to **1**.

Believe it or not, that's it! No saving, compiling, or waiting; we are ready to try it!

11. To test this Flow Graph, simply switch to game mode using the shortcut *Ctrl + G* or use the **Game | Switch to Game** option in the menu tab.

12. You will know the Flow Graph is functioning correctly if you are spawned at the **SpawnPoint** location upon entering the game mode.

13. Exit the game mode by pressing the *Esc* key.

14. Move the **SpawnPoint** entity to a new location.

15. Switch to game mode and you will see that regardless of the position of the **SpawnPoint** entity, you will be placed at that location.

Finally, save the level; we will use this as a starting point for examples further in the chapter. In the case of component nodes, you can use the quick search in the Flow Graph by pressing on *Q* in the Flow Graph viewport and by typing the name of the node you'd like to place.

What just happened?

We have now created a simple, but effective Flow Graph. The purpose of this Flow Graph is to spawn the player at the predefined location, whenever the level is loaded. This is useful for a variety of reasons, but most importantly for prescripted events, we know where the player will begin and can plan a design accordingly.

In the examples to come, we will build on this concept. We will also learn to use some of the more advanced features of the Flow Graph system.

Component and entity nodes

In the previous example, we used the two types of nodes available to the Flow Graph system. The **Start** node is a component node and the **SpawnPoint** entity is an entity node.

There is a distinction between these two. Component nodes are nodes that do not represent an actual entity, but rather perform a defined action or calculation. For some component nodes, there is a special input port at the top of the entity, which is used for setting the target entity of the node. You can also assign an entity directly to some component nodes by simply right-clicking the node and using the **Assign Selected Entity** function.

An **entity node** is a node that represents the actual entity in the level. The input and output ports depend on the events and ports defined directly in the entities script. Entity event nodes are triggered in the entity class `.lua` script. You can extend entity nodes with a bit of `.lua` knowledge, which we shall see in the next chapter.

Composition of flow nodes

The layouts of all flow nodes are somewhat standardized and are quite similar to each other. At the core, a node consists of two sides—inputs and outputs. The information transfer of the nodes is handled through these ports. Ports can either send or receive information. On the left-hand side of a node, you will find the input ports, which are used for connecting incoming links and logic. Links from other nodes are connected to these ports. The ports on the right-hand side of the node are called **output ports** and are activated depending on the behavior of the node.

Ports can have different data types, which can be determined by their color. A port can have one of the six different data types available, some of which are seen in the following screenshot:

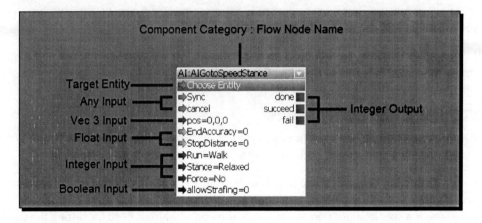

Let's see the different data types:

Data Type	Color	Function
Any	Green	Unspecified data type; any input can be applied into this port.
Boolean	Blue	A Boolean value can be either `true` or `false`.
Integer	Red	An integer is a whole number that can be either positive or negative.
Float	White	A floating point value data type.
Vec3	Purple	A data type consisting of three float values, representing a vector; it can be used for storing positions, angles, or color values.
String	Turquoise	A string is an array of characters that is used for storing text.

This might all seem very complex and hard to remember! However, flow nodes are quite forgiving, as when values are received whose type doesn't match the input port data type, they will be, if possible, automatically converted to match the type of the port they are connected to.

Any output port can be connected to any input port, no matter what type. An integer with the value 1 can be fed in a Boolean input port and will be converted to a `true` to match the data type of the port.

As previously mentioned, some component nodes have a special input port at the top of the entity, which can be used for setting the target entity of the node. In some cases, there are even two of these inputs, which are used by other systems such as animation, that might require two entities to interact in some way.

Have a go hero - experimenting with different flow nodes

Now that we understand the theory behind flow nodes, it is time to try some out! Here is a fast way of mapping certain key's to trigger individual nodes or whole graphs:

1. Add the **Input:Key** flow node to your Flow Graph.

2. Type the letter **p** into the **Key** as an input.

3. Use this to test a variety of other component nodes.

4. Link the **Pressed** output to the input of the spawn point created in this example, and to other entities.

5. A fun example of using the **Input:Key** flow node is adding an explosion entity under **Physics/Entities** to your level, which you can then trigger to explode on a key press, as seen in the following screenshot:

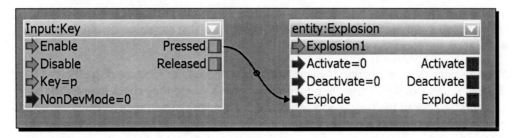

The **Input:Key** node is a very useful debug and testing tool as it outputs a signal on **Pressed** and **Released**. Use this node to trigger different component nodes found within the component node list. They can be dragged and dropped into any existing Flow Graph. The following screenshot shows the list of component nodes:

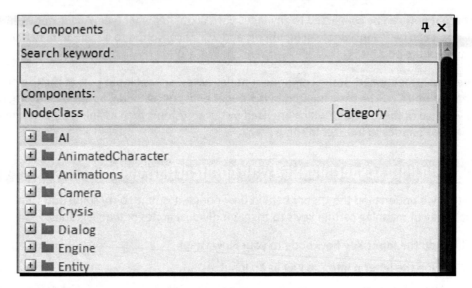

Using trigger entities with Flow Graph

A common technique for games is to use a combination of triggers and Flow Graphed logic, to force certain events to occur based on what the player is doing or has even done already. This is where you create the experience for the player. A reason why you want to implement scripted events with triggers is to introduce new traps, new gameplay elements, and other situations. If there is a new type of enemy or a very dangerous portion of the level coming up, a scripted event can be used as a powerful design tool that can communicate important information and focus the player.

When working on level's within the CryENGINE SDK, a designer has access to different types of triggers, some of which operate on a proximity basis where they check how far the player is from the center of the trigger, and some which are even simpler, such as checking whether the player enters or exits a certain area.

Time for action - adding a trigger to Flow Graph and outputting its status

We are going to add a trigger directly in front of the **SpawnPoint** entity in our level. We know where our player is starting from, and so we can add this trigger in front of the **SpawnPoint** entity so that our player will always have to enter it:

1. Open the level from the previous example.

   Ensure you have a **SpawnPoint** added, and a Flow Graph on the **SpawnPoint** entity to force the player to spawn at its location.

2. Place a **Proximity Trigger** entity into the level from the **Entity | Triggers** section of the **RollupBar** tab.

3. Align the **Proximity Trigger** entity so that the bottom is level with the terrain, and move the trigger slightly in front of the **SpawnPoint** entity placed earlier.

    Remember to use the shortcut *Shift + Space bar* to display the trigger helpers, which will show you the bounding area that is being monitored.

4. Ensuring that you can see the trigger bounds, let's now set the dimensions of the trigger. Set the dimensions in the trigger's entity properties in the **RollupBar** tab. Set them to the following:
   - **DimX = 10**
   - **DimY = 10**
   - **DimZ = 5**
   - **OnlyPlayer = True**

   Triggers are invisible volumes in the game mode, as we usually don't want our player to know where they are. We should thus add some solid geometry to show us clearly where our proximity trigger is, for development and testing purposes.

5. Create a new **Solid** white box to mark the area covered by the proximity trigger. You may want to refer back to the *White Boxing using Constructive Solid Geometry (CSG)* section in *Chapter 3, Playable levels in no time* for the example on creating white box solids.

6. Match the dimensions of the newly created **Solid** to that of the proximity trigger, except for the height. You will end up with a simple square on the ground measuring 10 x 10 x 1 meter, as in the following screenshot:

 Use the **Grid Snapping** tool and **Align to Object** tool to make the placement easier.

Now that we have our trigger set up in front of the **SpawnPoint**, let's use the trigger to kick off a scripted event using Flow Graph!

7. Right-click on the **Proximity Trigger** entity and select the **Create Flow Graph** option.

8. Next, add the **Proximity Trigger** as an entity node to the Flow Graph. As mentioned in the previous example, you can do this by selecting the **Proximity Trigger** entity and right-clicking in the graph and choosing **Add Selected Entity**.

9. The second node that we will use is the **HUD:DisplayTimedDebugMessage** component node. This component node's function is straightforward; it outputs the text directly to screen based on its inputs.

10. Add another component node to the graph called **String:SetString**. For this example, we will need three of these nodes.

11. In two of the **String:SetString** nodes, type in the inputs. Click on the **In** port and type **Entered** into one and **Exited** into the other.

12. Finally, add a **Logic:Any** node and hook up the links.

13. Add the third and final set string node and link it to the output of the **Logic:Any** node, as seen in the following screenshot:

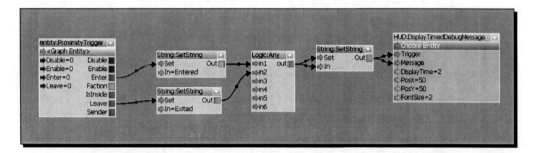

14. To test this graph, switch to game mode and walk into the area where we placed the **Proximity Trigger** entity earlier. You will know it's functioning properly when you observe the text in the top right-hand side of the screen, which will display **Entered** when you enter the trigger and **Exited** when you leave the trigger volume.

What just happened?

To break down the actual logic here, the functions of each of the nodes need to be explained. This Flow Graph begins when the **Proximity Trigger** node is **Entered** in or **Exited** by the player. When the **Enter** or **Leave** output is triggered, this then sets the **String:SetString** node. The **String:SetString** node operates in a way that, when the input **Set** is triggered, it sends the **In** string value to the **Out** port. Since we have hooked up the **Enter** output of the **Proximity Trigger** node to the **String:SetString** node that has the string **Entered** typed in it, this will then send the string **Entered** to the **Logic:Any** node. Once the **Logic:Any** node receives the input, it then outputs the string on its output. We then use this signal to set the string in the last **String:SetString** node and also trigger the **Set** input of the node. Finally, the string is fed into the **Message** and **Trigger** input of the **HUD:DisplayTimedDebugMessage** node to display what exactly was triggered from the **Proximity Trigger**, either **Entered** or **Exited/Leave**.

This example is meant to show how the output from a trigger can be used to trigger whichever other components or entity nodes you like. It also demonstrates how you can take advantage of the fact that a node will take any input and try to convert it to its required data type. We use this in the final link in the Flow Graph, where a string is used as a **Trigger** signal and as the data to be displayed. In this case, we simply output the events to screen text rather than triggering something else in our game world, as this is the next step in our examples.

Pop quiz - scripting

1. What are the two methods most commonly used when scripting in the CryENGINE 3?

    a. Character editor and animation graph

    b. Track view and database view

    c. C++ and C#

    d. Lua and Flow Graph

2. There are two principal types of flow nodes. What are they?

    a. Smart objects and character nodes

    b. Component and entity nodes

    c. Image nodes and game nodes

    d. Engine nodes and level nodes

3. What specific flow node is used to set a key press in Flow Graph?

    a. Controller: Input node

    b. Debug: Keyboard node

    c. Input: Key node

AI scripting with Flow Graph

Using Flow Graph to direct AI is one of the most used functions of Flow Graph. Simply exploring all the component nodes under the AI category will demonstrate this, as there are over 30 different nodes with varying functions.

It's typically required that some amount of scripting be set up when AI is to be used in the level. Flow Graph is perfect for this as it can be used to supplement and augment AI behaviors.

Time for action - creating a patrolling AI

An enemy that is guarding something, for example, does not just stand still. This would be very awkward and would break immersion. Usually, this can be solved by giving the AI entity some task or job in the world, which would give his presence much more sense and make him act more lifelike.

In this example, we will create an AI entity that will patrol between some predefined points. We will set this AI to start his patrol when the player enters a particular trigger:

1. To begin, open a new level where you'd like to place AI, or use the level created in the previous example.

2. Make sure you have generated the AI navigation for the level by using the **AI** menu and selecting **Generate All Navigation**.

3. Place a **SpawnPoint** and **Proximity Trigger** into the level, as we did in the previous examples.

4. Next, drag-and-drop a **Grunt** entity from the AI entities in the **RollupBar** tab.

   This **Grunt** will be our enemy AI.

5. Place a **TagPoint** in a location near the AI entity. **TagPoint** entities are under the AI button in the **RollupBar** tab.

   This **TagPoint** will act as our go-to point.

6. For this example, we will use our **Proximity Trigger** to store the Flow Graph, so create a new Flow Graph on the **Proximity Trigger** entity.

7. In the perspective viewport of the editor, select the **Proximity Trigger** entity and then press *Ctrl*, and also select the **TagPoint**.

8. Add both these entities to the new Flow Graph by right-clicking and selecting the **Add Selected Entities** entry from the context menu.

9. To command our AI character, we need one of the AI component nodes. Add the **AI:GotoSpeedStance** node.

10. Select the **Grunt1** from the perspective viewport.

11. Right-click on the **AI:GotoSpeedStance** node and select **Assign Selected Entity**.

    Most of the AI component nodes must be assigned to a particular AI entity; this is how the component nodes are told which AI they are to affect.

12. Link the **Enter** output from the **Proximity Trigger** entity to the **Sync** input of the **AI:GotoSpeedStance** node. Finally, link the **pos** output of the **TagPoint** to the **pos** input of the **AI:GotoSoeedStance** node.

Your Flow Graph should now be set similar to the screenshot below:

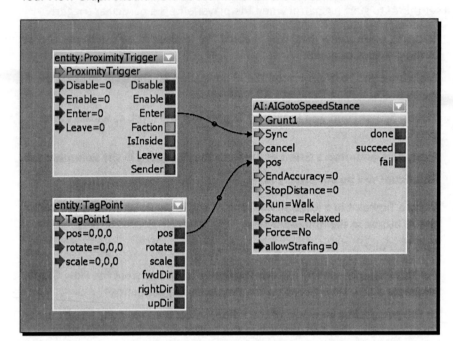

13. Test the first waypoint by switching to game mode and then walking into the trigger.

You may find that the AI immediately engages you and so does not walk to the position that we want. The reason for this is that the AI has a perception and attack range, which we might be in range of one or both. Let's adjust this.

14. The fastest way to rectify this issue without editing the AI's properties is to set the **AI:GotoSpeedStance** component node's **Force** input to **IgnoreAll**.

15. Upon changing the **Force** input, you should now, once you enter game mode and walk into the trigger, see the AI entity walk to the position of the **TagPoint** entity.

Let's now extend this graph to give the AI entity some more points to patrol.

16. Create three more **TagPoint** entities and three more **AI:AIGotoSpeedStance** nodes.

17. Finally, add a **Logic:Any** node.

18. Link them as shown in the following screenshot:

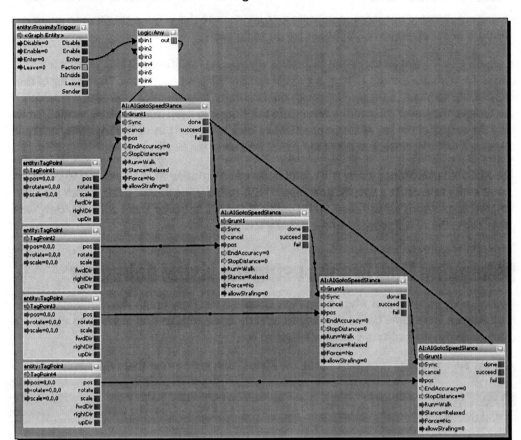

19. You will notice that we have created an endless loop using the **Logic:Any** node to loop back the **done** output from our last patrol leg to the **Sync** input of the first patrol leg.

20. This AI will infinitely patrol between these points until such a time that he is sent a new command or the player comes within the **attackrange** area of the particular AI. At this point, the AI behaviors take over and he will attack the player.

What just happened?

Having now created our scripted patrolling AI, we can use this in our own game to guard positions or set up groups of AI for our player to defeat.

You have also learned an important technique when using Flow Graph, which is using the output from multiple nodes to trigger a single node in different conditions. The first leg of the patrol route for the AI is triggered through the **Proximity Trigger** entity. However, it wouldn't suit to have the player constantly walking into this trigger to keep the AI walking around, so we loop the output of the last **AI:GoToSpeedStance** back to the start using the **Logic:Any** entity. In this way, it will trigger the first leg of the patrol whenever the last leg is done.

The **AI:GoToSpeedStance** entity is a useful node when scripting AI. It allows you to command the AI entity to execute a specific goal pipe. This is called using atomic goals, which are the simplest instructions we can send the AI entity. If the AI's behavior is not currently busy with other tasks, the AI will proceed to the defined location.

Debugging Flow Graphs using the visual debugger

An extremely valuable tool when using Flow Graphs is the Flow Graph visual debugger tool. Now that we have some basic Flow Graphs already made, we can find out how to debug them to verify when certain events will start to fire.

This will aid any designer to track down any Flow Graph logic errors that might occur.

Time for action - debugging the patrol Flow Graph

1. Open the Flow Graph from the previous example or set up your own Flow Graph to debug.

2. To enable the Flow Graph debugging, click on the icon that resembles a bug, as seen in the following screenshot:

3. Each time that you enter the game mode with the debugger turned on, any of the Flow Graph outputs that are triggered within the level are highlighted in yellow. They will also display the number of times a port has been triggered. Finally, it displays the value triggered at each port, as shown in the following screenshot:

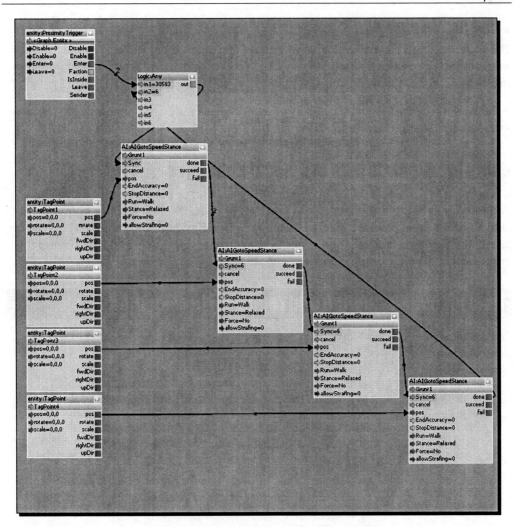

 Press the *F* and *G* keys to highlight the connections going in and out of a selected flow node. On large Flow Graphs, especially with tons of interconnected nodes, this can be very useful.

4. Reset the debugger using the trash icon next to the debug icon.

What just happened?

The visual debugger can be invaluable when the Flow Graph is not reacting as you would expect. It can also be useful to use while actually designing a graph to spot shortcuts or improvements.

It should be recognized that visual debugging will decrease the overall performance. The larger and more complex the Flow Graph becomes, the more performance intensive it will be.

Using breakpoints with the visual debugger

It is possible to add a tool called a breakpoint to any input or output port of a given flow node similar to how breakpoints are set in scripts or code. Once an input or output port with an added breakpoint is triggered by the Flow Graph system, the game will immediately pause; the Flow Graph editor then opens to the current Flow Graph, and it will center the breakpoint in the Flow Graph view.

Time for action - adding and removing breakpoints

The advantage of using the Flow Graph debugger is that you can see the exact values on particular inputs:

1. To add a new breakpoint, press the center mouse button on a specific port or right-click on it to bring up the port context menu, and choose the **Add Breakpoint** option.

2. To remove an existing breakpoint, either press the center mouse button again or choose the **Remove Breakpoint** option. The following screenshot shows the port context menu:

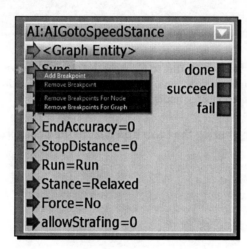

3. Once you have added the breakpoint on a triggered input, switch to game mode.

4. The breakpoint will be hit and it's value displayed in the Treeview in the **Breakpoints** window.

5. To resume the game once a breakpoint has been hit, either press *F5* or click on the **Play** button in the Flow Graph editor toolbar.

6. Remove all the breakpoints for a specific flow node or Flow Graph, by using the context menu options **Remove Breakpoints For Node** or **Remove Breakpoints For Graph**.

Certain context menu options are grayed out if they are not available. For example, if a port already has a breakpoint, the option **Add Breakpoint** will be grayed out; and if no breakpoint exists, it will gray out the **Remove Breakpoint** option.

What just happened?

To give a better overview about all the added breakpoints, the Flow Graph editor now has a Treeview in the **Breakpoints** tab, which is located by default in the bottom right-hand side corner of the Flow Graph window.

If you click on one of the Treeview items, it will open the Flow Graph; if a flow node or port item was clicked, it will also select and center the flow node in the view. With a right-click on one of the Treeview items, it is possible to remove a specific breakpoint, remove all the breakpoints for a flow node, or all the breakpoints for a specific Flow Graph. This is shown in the following screenshot:

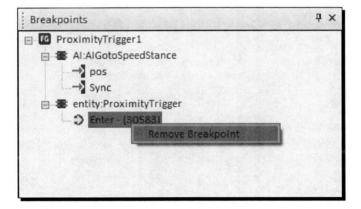

Summary

We learned a good deal about scripting in this chapter, but more specifically we focused on the use of Flow Graph. As we saw, Flow Graph is a very useful visual scripting tool as it gives us the ability to very quickly access functions directly within the CryENGINE SDK. We saw that it was made up of component and entity nodes, and that they are stored on entities within our levels. We created a few examples, and also learned the functions and details of some of the more useful flow nodes. Finally, we saw how to debug our Flow Graphs to know exactly what values are being passed and what ports are being triggered in a visual way.

Using Flow Graph is just one level of scripting available to us in the CryENGINE SDK. In the beginning of the chapter, we introduced the Lua scripting language. In the next chapter, we will learn how to make our very own game code and Lua entities. The techniques learned in this chapter will be helpful in experimenting with the custom entity and game code that you will create in the next chapter.

5
C++ and Compiling Your Own Game Code

When discussing coding versus scripting, you know that scripting gives you the possibility to implement a lot of functionality without changing code. As you already learned in the previous chapter, you can easily add new entities and implement the behaviour in Lua. You can manipulate AI, script your UI, or use the Flow Graph to create game logic. But you are always limited to the functionality that is exposed to Lua/Flow Graph. Also, Lua is always slower in performance than C++.

With C++ there are no limitations, but be aware, if you create a bug in your script you might not get the expected result—a bug in C++ can easily crash the whole game!

In this chapter, you will learn how to use Visual Studio Express Edition to compile and debug CryENGINE 3. Further, you will learn how to expose new functions to Lua by writing code with C++.

In this chapter, we shall:

- ◆ Install Visual C++ Express Edition
- ◆ Compile game code and run CryENGINE 3 with your compiled game code
- ◆ Attach CryENGINE to the Debugger and hit your first breakpoint
- ◆ Create a new Lua entity
- ◆ Expose a new C++ function to Lua
- ◆ Learn a few C++ basics

So let's go and write some code!

Installing Visual C++ 2010 Express Edition

Programmers basically rule the world when it comes to game development. For this reason, having C++ game code released in the Free SDK for CryENGINE is an invaluable tool. I encourage everyone to download the freely available Visual C++ Express to, at the very least, explore the provided game code. This game code is designed to be a template to create your own games and has a huge array of possible functions.

Time for action - downloading and installing Visual C++ 2010 Express

If you are a programmer and do not own the professional version of Visual Studio and wish to complete the later examples that utilize the game code, you will need to download and install Visual Studio Express, which is the free version of Visual Studio available to everyone.

When you installed the CryENGINE Free SDK, a folder is created in your root directory called `Code`. This folder contains the solution files required to edit and recompile the `game.dll` file.

To compile the game code, we need Visual Studio:

1. First, go into **<engine root>** | **Bin32** and rename the original `CryGame.dll` file to `CryGameBACKUP.dll`. Repeat this step in the `Bin64` folder.

2. Download and install Visual C++ 2010 Express Edition. Here's the link—`http://www.microsoft.com/visualstudio/en-us/products/2010-editions/visual-cpp-express`.

3. In the root directory of your build, under **Code** | **Solutions**, open the file `CryEngine_GameCodeOnly_Express.sln`, as seen in the following screenshot:

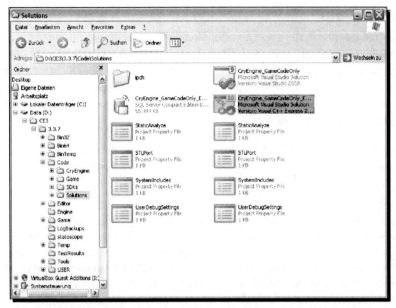

4. Once Visual Studio is opened, press *F7* to compile the **GameDll** file.

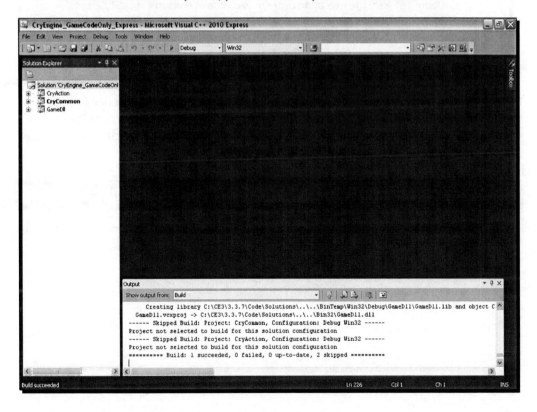

What just happened?

This solution we just opened is the source code, along with the required header files, to create a completely customized `Game.dll`. This gives us access to a huge variety of the CryENGINE functions and allows us to truly tailor the engine for our specific game. Make sure to select **Debug** and **Win32** in the drop-down list next to the green **play** icon in the toolbar. By pressing *F7*, Visual Studio will compile the project. You can achieve the same by selecting **Debug | Build Solution** in the menu.

If you go into the **<engine root>** | **Bin32** folder, you should find a new `CryGame.dll` file besides the `CryGameBACKUP.dll` file. This `.dll` was just made by you!

We just built the Win32 **Debug** version of the code.

If you open the drop-down box, there are three configurations—**Debug**, **Profile**, and **Release**. But for now, we should keep **Debug** selected. The **Debug** configuration is mostly used during development because it will not optimize the code, which makes debugging a lot easier. Since **Debug** is not always optimized, you should use profile configuration if you want to test performance or ship your mod. While it is still possible to debug the profile configuration, most of the time, it is not possible to see the correct current value of a variable in the Debugger. Also, the execution order of each line of code might be different due to compiler optimizations.

Starting CryENGINE 3 with Visual Studio

Because writing new code always requires you to debug your changes, you need to start CryENGINE with the **Debugger** attached. The Debugger is integrated into Visual Studio and enables you with the pause execution option, which lets you stop at a specific point in code (the so-called breakpoints), and step through the code.

Time for action - starting CryENGINE with the debugger attached

1. To be able to start CryENGINE 3 with Visual Studio, we need to do some initial setup.

2. Right-click on the **GameDll** file in the **Solution Explorer** tab found on the left-hand side of the screen, and select the following options as seen in the following screenshot:

   ❑ Select **Set as StartUp Project**

   ❑ Then, click on **Properties**

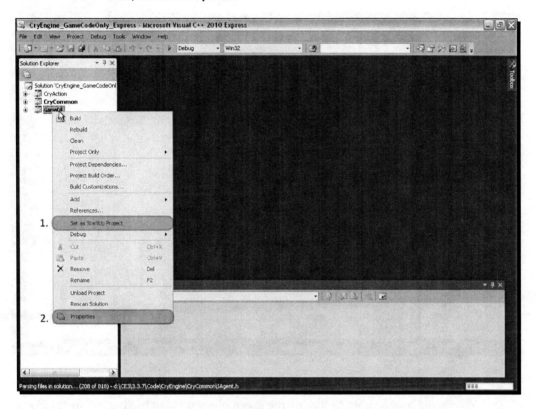

3. Now in the **GameDll Property Pages** window, we have to select **Debugging** present under the **Configuration Properties** tab.

4. In the **Command** property, we have to navigate to the **Editor.exe** file in the `<engine root>` | `Bin32` folder by clicking on the drop-down arrow in the **Command** property and selecting **<Browse...>**, as seen in the following screenshot:

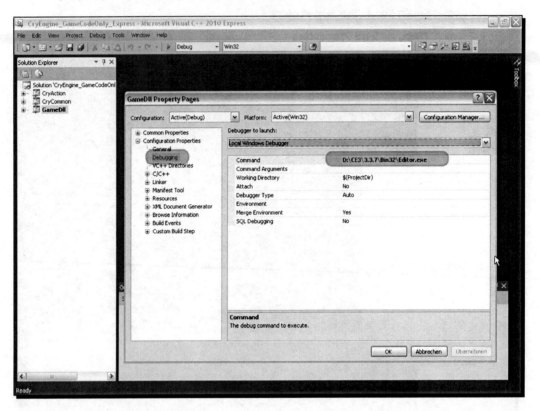

5. Now, click on **OK** to close the property page.

6. You should now be able to click on the green **play** icon in to toolbar (or press *F5*) and see if the CryENGINE Sandbox opens up. If a message box pops up that tells you that **No debug symbols could be found for Editor.exe**, just click on **OK**.

What just happened?

By starting the Sandbox via Visual Studio, we are now able to debug our code. This will help us to modify the code, see what's going on, and track down bugs we might create.

 It is also possible to start the **Launcher.exe** file in the same way as we started the **Editor.exe** file. Just modify the path in the debugging property page as we did with the **Editor.exe** file.

Have a go hero - debugging the launcher

Modify the debugging property to start the **Launcher.exe** application instead of the Sandbox via Visual Studio.

Breakpoints, watches, and code

Running CryENGINE with the Debugger attached will help us to find bugs. If the game crashes somewhere, the Debugger will come to the front and tell you in which function the error occurred.

But it is much more powerful than that!

- ◆ You can add breakpoints everywhere in your game code. Once a breakpoint is hit, the Debugger comes to the front and you are able to step through the code.

- ◆ Once the Debugger hits a breakpoint, you can check the values of the variables.

- ◆ It shows you the **Call Stack** window to see which functions were called before it reached your breakpoint.

- ◆ You can step through the code following each line of code.

- ◆ And much more!

Time for action - setting up your first breakpoint

With the Debugger attached, execution will stop in one of the two ways, either through a crash, which will give you the option to break at the current code location, or by setting your own breakpoints. Let's start with an easy one. Somewhere in code, the camera is set to the player's position. So let's stop execution there, just to see what's happening.

1. If you expand the **GameDll** file in the **Solution Explorer**, on the right-hand side, you will see all source files of the **GameDll** project. Double-click on the **PlayerView.cpp** file, which can be found under **Actor files | player**. In the left-hand side window, you should now see the source code.

2. Now search for **CPlayerView::ViewProcess**. This is the function that sets the position and rotation of the camera. In order to search for a function, open the **Find and Replace** dialog box (*Ctrl + Shift + F*) and type the name of the function into **Find what:**. In the **Look in:** textbox, open the drop-down list and select **Current Document**. Click on **Find All**, as seen in the following screenshot:

3. Once you click on the **Find All** button, the results are displayed in a new window called **Find Results** at the bottom of the page. If you double-click on a line in the **Find Results** window, the source window will directly jump to the correct line of the code (see the following screenshot for reference):

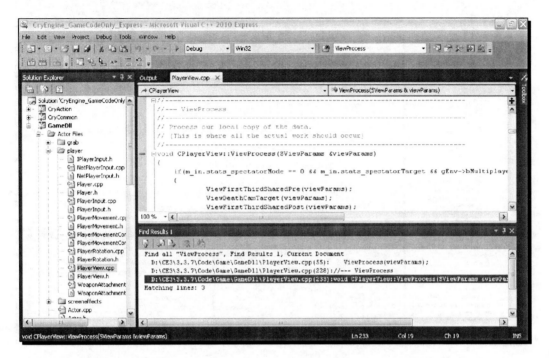

4. In order to add a breakpoint, simply click in the gray area in front of the line where you want to set your breakpoint. A red dot should appear in front of the line if you do so. You can also set a breakpoint in the current line by pressing *F9*.

5. If you now start Sandbox via Visual Studio (press *F5*)and load a level, Visual Studio should pop up in front, as soon as the loading of the level is done. A yellow arrow should now be visible at the top of the breakpoint code line.

Congratulations! You hit your first breakpoint.

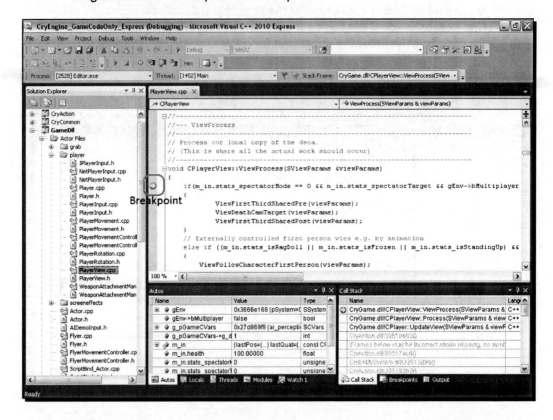

In the bottom right-hand side window, you should see the **Call Stack** window. This is basically a list of functions, which were called before the **breakpoint** was hit. If you double-click on an item in the **Call Stack** window, the Debugger shows the source file of this function and the place where the next function on the **Call Stack** window was called. Since we only have game code, we can only look into the source code of the **CryGame.dll** file. That's why all the other functions below this are grayed out.

The bottom left-hand side window shows the **Autos** tab. This is a list of the variables and their current values. This list is called **Autos** because it displays all the variables that are used in the current function.

You can also just place the mouse cursor over any variable in the code, and a tool tip will appear with the current value.

By pressing *F10*, you will step through the code line by line. If you press *F5*, execution will be resumed. Since we still have the breakpoint set, it will hit the breakpoint again after you press *F5*. So removing the breakpoint (by simply clicking on the breakpoint) and pressing *F5* will allow you to resume with Sandbox.

There are two step-modes:

- Step-over (press *F10*)
- Step-into (press *F11*)

While *step-over* will just execute the current line and stop at the next line, *step-into* will step into the current line (for example, a function) and stop in the first line of this function.

What just happened?

By adding and hitting the breakpoint, we paused execution and so were able to debug the code. With *F10*, we stepped through the code, and with *F5*, we resumed execution. Since debugging your own code is much more interesting, we now have to write some code!

Have a go hero - stepping through the code

Once the breakpoint object is hit, you should start stepping through the code. Use *F10* to step-over the current line and use *F11* to step-into a line.

Create a new Lua entity and call C++ code to interact with it

It's time to write some code of our own. But before we can start writing the C++ code, we will first learn some Lua basics. Let us first begin by creating a simple Lua entity that teleports the player to a different position. Later, we will extend this entity to execute the C++ code.

Let's get started!

Time for action - creating a new entity

In CryENGINE 3, there are various types of Lua entities predefined. Their basic functionality can be easily overwritten and expanded. Additionally, there are interfaces to communicate with C++ and also directly with the flow graph.

A Lua entity has two parts:

◆ The `.ent` definition file defines the name of this entity class and the script file location

◆ The `.lua` code associated with the entity class

In order to create a new entity, we first have to create the `.ent` file. The `.ent` definitions can be found in `<engine root>\Game\Entities` (if this folder does not exist, just create it).

1. Create a new file named `Teleporter.ent` and open it with a text editor such as NotePad++. Each `.ent` file is basically an XML file with a single tag that defines the name of this entity class and the associated Lua script file. Write the following code into the `Teleporter.ent` file:

```
<Entity
Name="Teleporter"
Script="Scripts/Entities/Others/Teleporter.lua"
/ >
```

2. Now, we have to create a new Lua script file for this entity. Create a folder in `<engine root>\Game\Scripts\Entities\Others\` and create a new file, `Teleporter.lua`.

First, we need to create the constructor for this entity. Within this constructor, we can add different properties for the entity:

```
Teleporter = {
  Editor =
  {
    Icon= "AreaTrigger.bmp",
  },
  Properties =
  {
    teleportDirX = 0,
    teleportDirY = 0,
    teleportDirZ = 0,
    object_3DModel = "Editor/Objects/T.cgf",
  },
}
```

A documentation about Lua syntax can be found on the Internet at http://www.lua.org/manual/5.1/manual.html.

3. Within the `Editor` table, we can define an icon for this entity. This is the icon that was displayed in Sandbox once we placed our entity. You can find all icons in `<engine root>\Editor\ObjectIcons\`.

4. The `Properties` table defines the properties that are displayed in Sandbox's **RollupBar**. If you place your entity in Sandbox and select it, you can modify those properties.

5. But before we place our entity, we need to extend the `Teleporter.lua` script with some more basic functions:

```
function Teleporter:OnInit()
  self:OnReset();
end
-----------------------------------------
function Teleporter:OnPropertyChange()
  self:OnReset();
end
-----------------------------------------
function Teleporter:OnReset()
  --this will set the selected 3D Model on the entity
  if (self.Properties.object_MyModel ~= "") then
    self:LoadObject(0, self.Properties.object_3DModel);
  end
end
```

- The `OnInit` function is called every time this entity is spawned.

- The `OnPropertyChange` function is called every time you change a property within Sandbox **RollupBar** for this entity.

- The `OnReset` function is called if the entity gets reset. For example, if you jump into game in Sandbox.

In the `OnReset` function, we simply load the model that is defined in the `object_3DModel` property. First, we check if the `object_3DModel` property is not an empty string. If this is the case, we call the function `self:LoadObject` and pass the name of the object to this function. The first parameter (the `0`) defines the object slot. With this *slot*, we can load multiple objects into different slots.

What just happened?

By creating the `.ent` and `.lua` files, we defined a new entity class for CryENGINE. We are now able to place this entity into our level and change the properties that we defined in the `.lua` file.

Time for action - placing your entity into your level

After we have created both files, we should now be able to place our new entity within Sandbox:

1. Open Sandbox and create a new level (or load your level of choice).

2. In the **RollupBar** tab, select the first tab and choose **Entity** in the **Objects** list. If you scroll in the **Browser** window to **Others** and open this subfolder, you should find your new **Teleporter** entity.

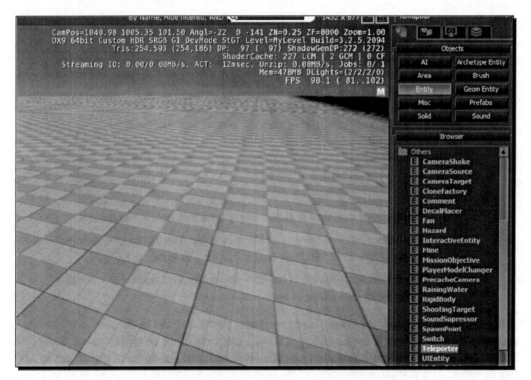

3. You can drag-and-drop the **Teleporter** into your level, as seen in the following screenshot. Once you do this, you can select the entity and just modify the properties in the **RollupBar** tab.

 You can add your entity multiple times and change the properties individually for each **Teleporter** that is placed in your level. The entity that we defined is some sort of template class (a definition about an entity). You can simply drag-and-drop the **Teleporter** entity from the **RollupBar** tab into the level of this entity for which we are creating instances.

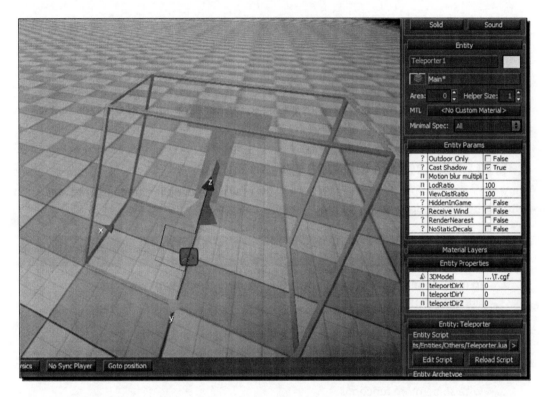

4. If you select your **Teleporter**, you will find the properties, which you just defined in the Lua script, in the **RollupBar** tab under **Entity Properties**.

The property `object_3DModel` is just displayed as **3DModel**, and if you click on it you can open a browser to select a 3D model. This is because we named the property `object_<some name>`. There are a few prefixes that you can use in front of your property name to allow Sandbox to show the correct selection box. Let's see a few prefixes:

- `object_<name>` for the model selection dialog.
- `b<name>` for a checkbox.
- The initial value of a property will also define the type, such as number, string and so on.

What just happened?

With the `.ent` file in place that points to a Lua script, we can easily extend our entity library with our own entities. The basic functions we need are the `constructor`, `OnInit`, `OnPropertyChange`, and `OnReset`. Within the **Properties** table, we can define properties. Those properties can be adjusted separately for each entity of this type that is present in our level.

How to interact with entities via Lua script

Since the entity we just created is a bit boring, we now need to define some interactions with it. This can be done simply by modifying the Lua script we just wrote.

Time for action - making the teleporter usable

1. In order to make any object intractable, we have to add two functions to our lua code:

    - The function `IsUsable`
    - The function `OnUsed`

2. Let's implement these functions. We need to extend the `Teleporter.lua` script with some more functions:

```
--tell the engine that we can interact with this entity
function Teleporter:IsUsable(user)
  return 1;
end
-----------------------------------------
```

```
function Teleporter:OnUsed(user)
  --check „user" being valid
  if (not user) then
    return 0;
  end
  --compute target position from current position + teleport
direction
  local vCurPos = {};
  user:GetWorldPos(vCurPos);
  local vTargetDir = {}; --assign a temp vector as targetDir
„type"
  vTargetDir.x = self.Properties.teleportDirX;
  vTargetDir.y = self.Properties.teleportDirY;
  vTargetDir.z = self.Properties.teleportDirZ;
  local vTargetPos = vecAdd(vCurPos, vTargetDir);
  --set target position on player entity
  user:SetWorldPos(vTargetPos);
end
```

The function `IsUsable` will tell the engine if an entity is usable or not. Returning 1 means that this entity is usable.

The function `OnUsed` is called if the player presses the *F* key while he/she is close enough and looks at this entity.

What just happened?

With the functions `IsUsable` and `OnUsed`, we just made the entity usable.

Now load your level, place the **Teleporter** entity, type in some values for the **teleportDirZ** file (for example, 10), and jump in game and use the **Teleporter** by pressing *F*. (The *F* key is the default *use* key in CryENGINE.) If you did everything well, you should be teleported into the air.

Have a go hero - adding Flownode input/outputs to your Lua entity

It is possible to define flow node inputs and outputs for an entity within the entity Lua script file. The documentation about this can be found here:

```
http://freesdk.crydev.net/display/SDKDOC5/Adding%20Flownode%20
Inputs%20and%20Outputs
```

Now try to add a flow node output for your entity that gets triggered once the teleport action was done.

Time for some real code

Our **Teleporter** entity works fine, but let's write some real C++ code to add functionality. Instead of execution logic in Lua (which can be expensive), we want to write a new C++ function that executes the teleport logic.

Time for action - writing a new scriptbind function in C++

In order to be able to execute C++ code from Lua, we need to write a new, so-called `Scriptbind` function. `Scriptbind` functions are functions that are exposed to Lua, which means that this C++ function can be called from our Lua script code.

1. Open the **ScriptBind_Actor.h** file. You will find all actor-related functions, which are accessible in Lua, as seen in the following screenshot:

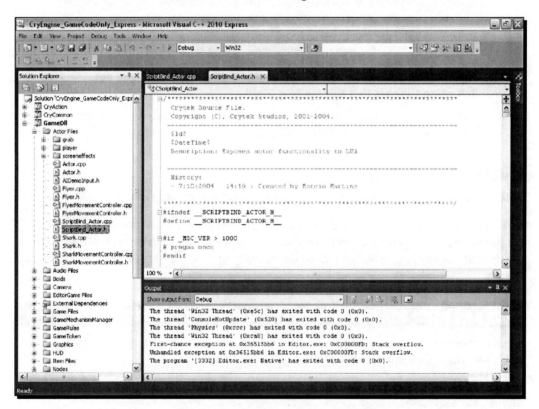

2. If you scroll down, you can simply add a new function there.

3. So, let's add a new function and name it `TeleportTo`. Search for **SetSearchBeam** (which is the last `Scriptbind` function in this file), and add your new function right under it in the `ScriptBind_Actor.h` file:

```
//teleport the actor to targetPos
virtual int TeleportTo(IFunctionHandler* pH, Vec3 targetPos);
```

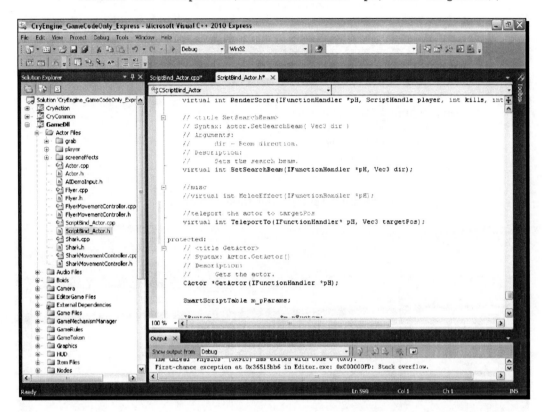

A `Scriptbind` function always returns an `int` (number) and gets an **IFunctionHandler *pH** as the first argument. Each following argument can be user defined. You can add as many arguments as you want, but never forget the first **IFunctionHandler *pH** argument.

4. After we've added the function definition into the header file (`.h`), we now need to implement this function.

5. Open the **ScriptBind_Actor.cpp** file and scroll to the end of this file.

6. Now, we need to implement the function at the end of the **ScriptBind_Actor.cpp** file:

```cpp
int CScriptBind_Actor::TeleportTo(IFunctionHandler *pH, Vec3
targetPos)
{
  //try to get the calling actor
  CActor *pActor = GetActor(pH);
  if (pActor == NULL)
    return pH->EndFunction(0);
  //get world matrix of actor
  Matrix34 tm = pActor->GetEntity()->GetWorldTM();
  //set new position in world matrix
  tm.SetTranslation(targetPos);
  //apply new matrix to actor entity
  pActor->GetEntity()->SetWorldTM(tm);
  //return to LUA (1 means true, 0 means false)
  return pH->EndFunction(1);
}
```

The **ScriptBind_Actor.cpp** file should look similar to this:

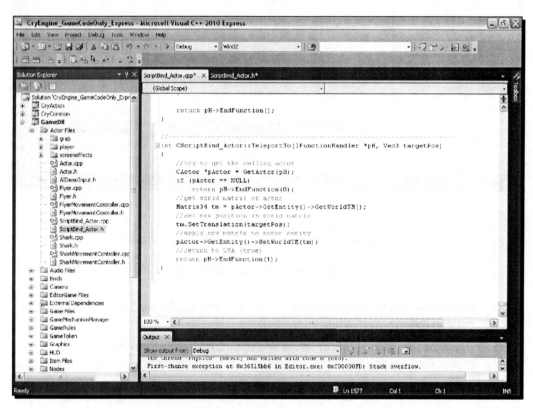

We first get the **CActor*** object from the **IFunctionHandler**. This is the actor on which this function was executed. The little asterisk after **CActor** means that it is a **pointer** to an object and so it can be invalid. If we are working with pointers, we should *always* check this before we access it.

Otherwise, if the pointer is **NULL** and we access it, the game will crash!

So after we check that **pActor** is not **NULL**, we get the world matrix of this player, set the translation (position) of this matrix to **targetPos**, and then set the new matrix to the player.

After we are done, we need to return **pH->EndFunction(1)**. Returning **EndFunction(1)** means that we are returning `true`. With this, it is possible to check in Lua if the function was successfully executed or not.

7. As a final step, we have to expose the new function to Lua. To do so we simple need to go to the function **CScriptBind_Actor::CScriptBind_Actor(...)**, the constructor of the `ScriptBind_Actor` class, and register our new function.

8. Search for **SCRIPT_REG_TEMPLFUNC(StandUp,"")**, and add it under this line. It is the registration of your function in the **ScriptBind_Actor.cpp** file:

```
//register the new TeleportTo function
SCRIPT_REG_TEMPLFUNC(TeleportTo, "pos");
```

Your code should look like the following screenshot:

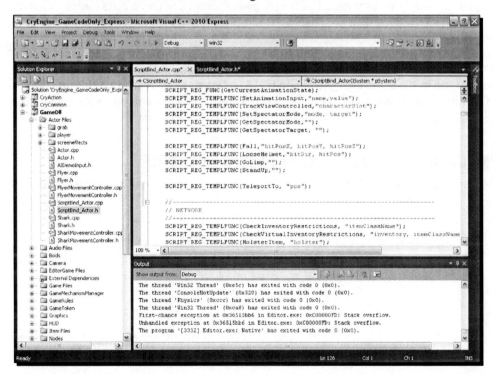

9. Know that you should compile your changes. Select **Debug | Build Solution** (or press *F7*) to trigger the build. If you did everything well, you should get this output as seen in the following screenshot:

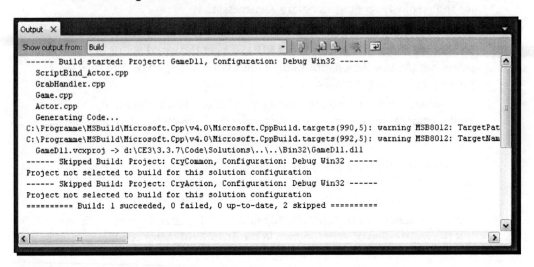

What just happened?

You just compiled the first lines of your very own, custom C++ game code. Before we now hit *F5* and run Sandbox with our changed **GameDll**, we need to change the lua script of the **Teleporter** entity to call our code.

We first defined the function in the **ScriptBind_Actor.h** file. After that, we implemented this function in the **ScriptBind_Actor.cpp** file. As a last step, we registered this function via **SCRIPT_REG_TEMPLFUNC**. With these three steps, we were able to create a new Scriptbind function, which can now be used from any Lua script.

Call the new C++ function from your Lua script

The last step is now to call the C++ code from our previously created **Teleporter** entity.

Time for action - changing the teleporter entity to execute the C++ code

1. First, we need to change the lua script. We want to change the function **Teleporter:OnUsed** to call our C++ function instead of doing the calculation in Lua.

2. This is pretty easy. Change the function as shown below:

```
function Teleporter:OnUsed(user)
  --check „user" being valid
  if (not user) then
    return 0;
  end
  --compute target position from current position + teleport
direction
  local vCurPos = {};
  user:GetWorldPos(vCurPos);
  local vTargetDir = {}; --assign a temp vector as targetDir
„type"
  vTargetDir.x = self.Properties.teleportDirX;
  vTargetDir.y = self.Properties.teleportDirY;
  vTargetDir.z = self.Properties.teleportDirZ;
  local vTargetPos = vecAdd(vCurPos, vTargetDir);
  --call the scriptbind function
  user.actor:TeleportTo(vTargetPos);
end
```

3. Save your changes of **Teleporter.lua**.

4. With the use of **user.actor:<function>**, we can call all the `Scriptbind` functions that are implemented in **ScriptBind_Actor.h**. In this case, we simply call our newly created function.

5. Now it is time to see if everything works as expected. Switch back to Visual Studio and add a breakpoint at the first line of your function.

6. Press *F5* to run Sandbox. Once Sandbox is started, load a level, place your **Teleporter** entity, jump ingame, and use it (Press *F* key). As soon you press *F*, Visual Studio should pop up and your breakpoint is triggered. If you mouse over the **targetPos** argument, you should see the current values.

7. Press *F5* again to see if the teleportation worked.

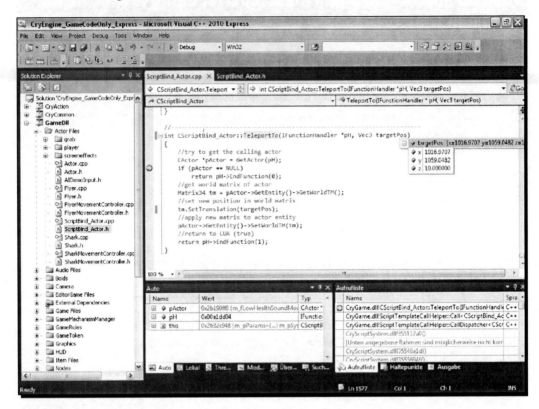

What just happened?

Congratulations! You created a new, interactive entity that calls the C++ code. Good job!

By calling `user.actor:TeleportTo(vTargetPos);`, we executed the C++ `Scriptbind` function. The user object is a reference to the actor that uses the **Teleporter** entity. It was passed to the `Teleporter:OnUsed(user)` function. By using the `user.actor:<fct name>`function, we can access all the `Scriptbind` functions that are defined in the **ScriptBind_Actor.h** file.

So what is this good for? Why don't we use Lua for everything?

♦ Creating complex functionality in C++ can be much cleaner and robust than Lua

♦ Lua can be slow: Run heavy code in C++ (math, physics, and so on)

- It's easier to debug C++ code with Visual Studio
- Not all engine functionality is exposed through Lua, so there are some things you can truly only do through C++

Have a go hero - doing the complete teleporter logic in C++

We still did a lot of logic in the Lua script itself. Try to change the C++ function to do the complete **Teleporter** logic. The Lua script should only call:

```
function Teleporter:OnUsed(user)
  local vTargetDir = {}; --assign a temp vector as targetDir „type"
  vTargetDir.x = self.Properties.teleportDirX;
  vTargetDir.y = self.Properties.teleportDirY;
  vTargetDir.z = self.Properties.teleportDirZ;
  --call the scriptbind function
  user.actor:TeleportTo(vTargetDir);
end
```

To get the current position of an entity in C++ you can call:
```
Vec3 pos = pActor->GetEntity()->GetWorldPos();
```

CryENGINE specific data types

Besides the standard data types, such as `int`, `bool`, `float`, and so on, there are a lot of other data types in CryENGINE 3, which are very helpful if you start writing your own code:

- `Vec3`: It represents a vector of three float values, which is used for positions and 3D-vectors
- `Ang3`: It represents a vector of three floats, which is used to represent Euler rotations
- `Matrix33`: It represents a 3 x 3 float matrix, which is used for the rotation matrix
- `Matrix34`: It represents a 3 x 4 float matrix, which is used to store the rotation matrix with translation
- `Quat`: It represents a **Quaternion**, which is used to efficiently store rotations and interpolate them

While you work with CryENGINE 3, you will use them a lot. All the common operations are supported, such as addition, subtraction, dot product, cross product, and so on.

Let us see an example of a C++ function to determine which of the two points is the closest to a target point:

```
Vec3 GetClosestPositionToTarget(const Vec3 target, const Vec3 posA,
                                const Vec3 posB)
{
    const Vec3 a = target - posA; // vector between target and posA
    const Vec3 b = target - posB; // vector between target and posB

    // squared distance between target to posA
    const float dA = a.GetLengthSquared();
    // squared distance between target to posB
    const float dB = b.GetLengthSquared();

    if(dA < dB)
    {
        return posA; //posA is closer
    }
    return posB; //posB is closer
}
```

 Why use the squared length instead of the normal length? Well, when the normal length of vector dA is smaller than the length of dB, the squared length of dA is smaller than the squared length of dB too.

Pop quiz - Lua entities and scriptbind functions

1. How do you define a new Lua Entity class?
   - ❏ By writing new C++ code
   - ❏ By adding a .ent and .lua file
   - ❏ By using Sandbox **RollupBar**

2. Which Lua function is called to see if an entity can be used?
   - ❏ The IsUsable function
   - ❏ The OnUsed function
   - ❏ The OnInit function

3. How do you make your Scriptbind function accessible from Lua?
   - ❏ Add a new function into the header (.h) file.
   - ❏ Implement the function in the source (.cpp) file.
   - ❏ Do a) and b), but also call **SCRIPT_REG_TEMPLFUNC**.

Summary

In this chapter, you learned how to create your own Lua entity and how to interact with it. Further, you learned how to connect your entity to C++ code. With those basics, it is easy to extend the existing entity library with your own custom entities to create new gameplay elements for your own needs.

In the next chapter, you will learn how to easily create your own user interface with Flash.

Let's go!

6
User Interface and HUD Creation with Flash

Even if the user interface is only a small part of a game, it is very important. There is no game that comes without it. It is the first thing you see once you start a game, and the HUD is visible nearly all the time during gameplay. The style of the UI/HUD has a big impact on the look and feel of a game. While it is needed to show important information (for example, health, current ammo, and so on), it also needs to fit into the rest of the scene. The worst thing will be to have a UI that just feels misplaced over the rest of the scene.

In this chapter, I will show you how to bring your own custom UI and HUD into our engine. Because CryENGINE 3 uses Scaleform GFx as a UI solution, you will need to have Adobe Flash to create your assets.

In this chapter, we shall:

- ◆ Create a new 2D HUD with Adobe Flash
- ◆ Write some simple ActionScript
- ◆ Use the UI Emulator for easy testing and faster development of the UI
- ◆ Load the new HUD and interact with it using UI Action Flow Graphs
- ◆ See basic event handling from Flash to CryENGINE 3
- ◆ See further information on UI Emulator, event handling, and the FreeSDK example menus

Let's start!

Adobe Flash as a very powerful UI design tool

In order to be able to create new UI/HUD assets, we need Adobe Flash. If you don't own Adobe Flash, you can use a 30-day trial of Adobe Flash, which is available at
`http://www.adobe.com/cfusion/tdrc/index.cfm?product=flash&loc=us&prom`
`oid=EBYEO`.

Additionally, I will use Adobe Photoshop, which is also available for a 30-day trial at
`http://www.adobe.com/cfusion/tdrc/index.cfm?product=photoshop&loc=us&`
`promoid=EBYEO`.

Time for action – creating a new Flash asset with Adobe Flash

Once you start Adobe Flash, you need to create a new project. Make sure you choose **ActionScript 2.0**, because CryENGINE 3 only supports AS 2.0.

To make life easier, we will do some initial setup in our new Flash asset:

1. First of all, we will change the resolution to `1280 x 720`. This is a good resolution, because it matches the common aspect ratio of 16:9.

2. The next thing we will do is change the publish settings to **Flash Player 8** and **ActionScript 2.0**.

3. Lastly, we will take an in-game screenshot and place it as a guide in the Flash asset. This helps us to design the HUD that will fit to the rest of the game. To do so, we disable the demo HUD that comes with the FreeSDK and disable the debug information in the upper-right corner.

In order to make a nice screenshot:

1. Start **Sandbox**.

2. Load a level.

3. Jump into the game (press *Ctrl + G*).

4. Open the console (press ^), and disable the demo HUD and profile info via the following console variables:

   ❑ r_DisplayInfo 0

   ❑ g_showHud 0

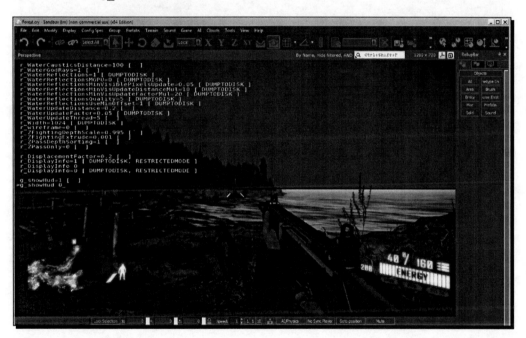

5. Take a screenshot, and crop the render window, for example, in Adobe Photoshop (you should adjust the render window to 1280 x 720). Now, create a new layer in Flash and paste the screenshot of the render window. You should change the layer to be a guide layer and lock the layer.

6. With this setup, we can start designing the new HUD. *Save the file!*

Now, let's start with an easy health and ammo bar:

1. First, create a nice looking health bar. In my example, I simply created a green and blue bar in Photoshop with a bevel filter, and saved both the files as a transparent PNG file (512 x 128).

2. Import both the images into the library by choosing **File |Import | Import to Library...**.

3. If you open the **Library** tab in the right panel, you should find your PNG file along with a new **symbol**.

4. Rename the symbols to something like `greenBar` and `blueBar`. Of course this is not necessary, but it always helps to *name* your Flash assets well, because with time you will get more and more movieclips/symbols, and it will be hard to find the correct one if your naming is weak.

5. I also created a new folder in my library named `picts`. I will put all my images into this folder (which again helps to find the assets later).

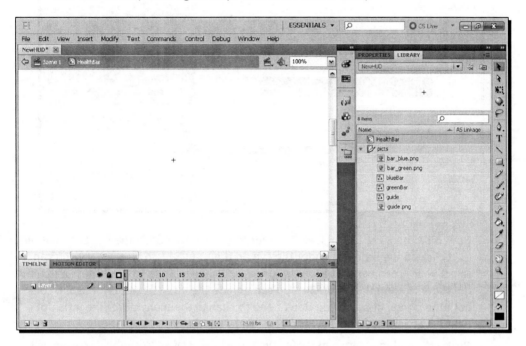

Ok, now let's start with the health bar:

1. Create a new **movieclip** (right-click in **Library** and choose **New Symbol**). I call this one `HealthBar`.

2. Now just drag-and-drop the `greenBar` symbol from the library into the stage of your new `HealthBar` movieclip.

3. Select the layer in the timeline and duplicate it (right-click on layer one and choose **Duplicate Layers**).

4. Rename the layers to something like `BarEmpty` and `BarFilled`.

5. Make sure the `BarFilled` layer is on top of the `BarEmpty` layer.

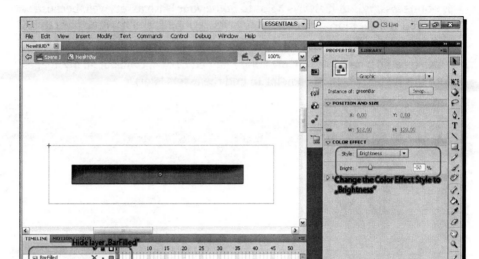

6. Now, hide the `BarFilled` layer in order to be able to modify the `BarEmpty` layer (just click on the little dot under the eye on the `BarFilled` layer). Now you can select your green bar that is on the stage, and change **Style** to **Brightness** and move the slider to something like **-50**. You can unhide the `BarFilled` layer again. Lock both the layers, because you don't need to change them anymore (the little dot right next to the hide dot).

7. Next, we need to create a **mask** for the `BarFilled` layer. With this mask we will be able to hide parts of the filled layer later.

8. Create a new layer (the little icon in the lower-left corner). Make sure this layer is on top of your `BarFilled` layer. Rename the new layer to `MASK`. Now, draw a rectangle over your green bar that covers the green bar completely. Make sure the right border of your rectangle matches the right border of the green bar. You will find the **rectangle tool** in the toolbar on the right side. Right-click on the `MASK` layer, and select **Mask**. The rectangle you just drew now acts as a mask. Everything on the `BarFilled` layer that is under the rectangle is visible, and everything that is not under the rectangle is hidden.

9. Now, we need to animate the `MASK` layer to be able to dynamically *fill* your empty bar.

10. Select the 100th frame of all the three layers in the timeline, right-click on it, and select **Insert Frame**. Then, select the 100th frame of your `MASK` layer and select **Convert to Keyframes**. As a last step, right-click somewhere in the middle of the gray timeline of the `MASK` layer, and select **Create Classic Tween.** An arrow from the first frame to the last frame should appear in the timeline.

11. Select the first frame of the MASK layer, unlock the layer, and move the rectangle to the left so that the right border of the rectangle matches the left border of the green bar.

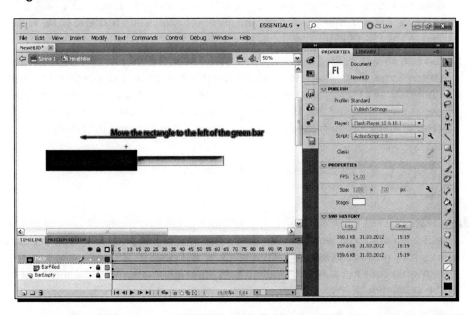

12. Lock the MASK layer again, and move the slider in the timeline to see the result.

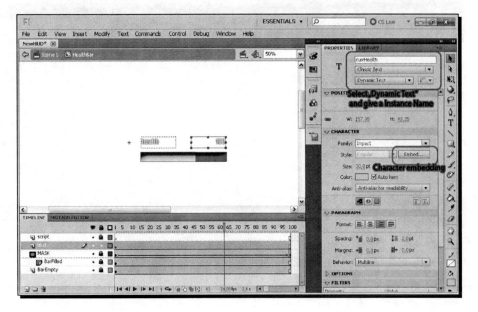

Lastly, we will add some textfields to display the current health:

1. Create a new layer and name it `Text`. Select the **text tool** from the right toolbar, and draw two textboxes. One is for the "health" title, and one is for the current value. Make sure you change the type of the current health value textfield to **Dynamic Text** in the **PROPERTIES** panel and give it the **instance name** `currHealth`.

2. You also have to **embed** the characters. Select your textbox and click on the **Embed...** button. In the dialog that shows up, enable the checkboxes—**Uppercase**, **Lowercase**, **Numerals**, and **Punctuation**—and click **OK**. This will make sure that all the needed glyphs are embedded into the SWF file. If you use dynamic textboxes, you always need to make sure to embed all the characters you will use in this textbox.

> If you use the same font for different dynamic textboxes, you only need to embed them once.

3. Create one last layer, call it `script`, and lock it. Click on the first frame of this layer, and open the **script window** (**Window** | **Actions**, or just press *F9*). Type in a simple `stop();` instruction into the script window and close it. This will make sure that the movieclip does not play the timeline animation automatically. We want to control the animation later via script.

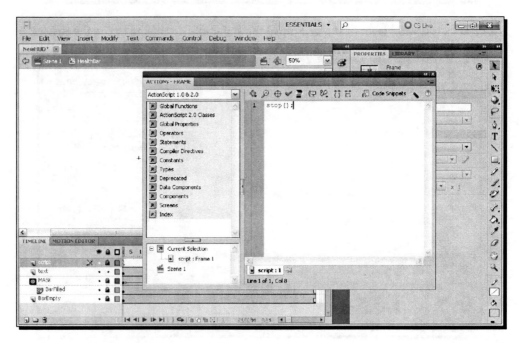

4. Because we also want to have a simple ammo display, we will re-use the `HealthBar` movieclip as an ammo bar. Duplicate the `HealthBar` movieclip, and name it `AmmoBar`. Double-click on it to open this movieclip. Unlock the `BarFilled` layer.

5. Select the green bar and click on the **swap...** button in the **PROPERTIES** panel. Simply choose the blue bar. Repeat this step with the green bar on the `BarEmpty` layer.

6. You should also change the text in the `health` textbox from `health` to `ammo`.

7. Change the instance name of the `currHealth` textfield to `currAmmo` and create two new dynamic textboxes, one for the weapon name, and one for the ammo name. Use the instance names `currWeaponName` and `currAmmoName` on the new textfields.

 Make sure to change the newly created textboxes to **Dynamic Text**.

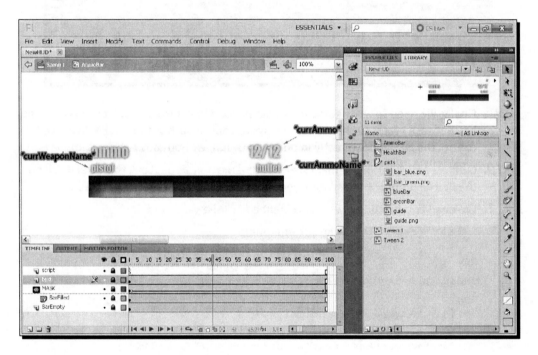

8. That's it! Go to Scene 1 and place your health and ammo bars. Give them the instance names `ammoMC` and `healthMC`.

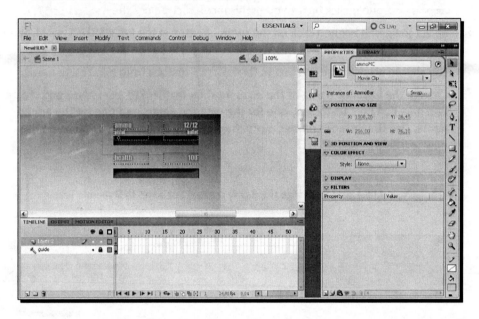

9. Finally, we need to write some ActionScript code to control the values of our ammo bar. Because I want to show several ways to control flash within CryENGINE, we will control the health bar directly in our Flow Graph, without any ActionScript.

10. Create a new layer in the main scene and name it `script`. Lock this layer. Click on the first keyframe of the script layer and press *F9* to open the script editor.

11. We need two functions, which are defined as follows:

    ❑ `setAmmo`: **To set the current ammo**

    ❑ `setCurrentWeapon`: **To set the current weapon**

```
function setAmmo(currAmmo:Number, maxAmmo:Number)
{
  if (maxAmmo > 0) // normal weapon
  {
    ammoMC.currAmmo.text = currAmmo + "/" + maxAmmo;
    ammoMC.gotoAndStop(Math.floor((currAmmo / maxAmmo) * 99) + 1);
  }
  else // melee weapon
  {
    ammoMC.currAmmo.text = "-";
    ammoMC.gotoAndStop(100);
  }
}
```

```
    }
    function setCurrentWeapon(weaponName:String, ammoName:String)
    {
        ammoMC.currAmmoName.text = ammoName;
        ammoMC.currWeaponName.text = weaponName;
    }
```

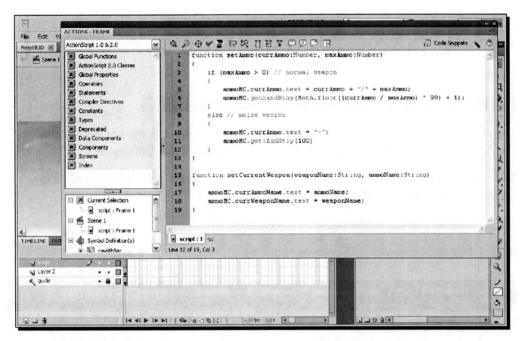

12. Save the NewHUD.fla file, and publish the SWF file. In order to publish the SWF file, you need to choose **File | Publish**, or simply press *Alt + Shift + F12*.

What just happened?

As a first step, we created a new Flash file for our HUD. We added some textfields and an animated bar to display the current health and ammo. We also wrote some ActionScript code to control the ammo bar. Finally, we published the SWF file.

You should now find a NewHUD.swf file in the same folder where you saved your Flash asset. The SWF file we just created can now be used in CryENGINE. In the next part, we will setup everything so that we can display the new HUD in the engine, and use the health and ammo bar to show our actual health and current weapon status.

Have a go hero – adding a crosshair to the HUD

Your HUD should also have a nice crosshair. Try to create a new movieclip for your crosshair and add it to the stage. Optionally, you can design different crosshairs for different weapons. (Remember that the setCurrentWeapon function gets the weapon name as a parameter.)

 In Flash, it is possible to label a keyframe with a name. Create a keyframe for each crosshair and label it with the weapon name. The gotoAndStop ActionScript function can also be used with a label name.

Bringing your Flash asset into CryENGINE 3

After we have created our new Flash asset, we will want to use it in the engine. For this, the first thing we need to do is announce the new Flash asset as a **UIElement**.

To announce a new Flash asset to the engine, we have to create an XML file for it. All the UIElement definition XML files are located in:

```
<engine root>\Game\Libs\UI\UIElements\
```

If this folder does not exist in your Game folder, simply create a new folder.

Time for action – bringing your Flash asset into CryENGINE 3

Let's follow a few simple steps:

1. The first thing we need is an XML file for the newly created Flash asset. Go to the `<engine root>\Game\Libs\UI\UIElements\` folder, and create a new XML file (for example `NewHUD.xml`).

2. The layout of the XML file is pretty easy. Each XML can have multiple Flash assets defined. It starts with a `<UIElements>` tag and ends with a `</UIElements>` tag. Within this tag, you can define your UIElements. Add a new `<UIElement>` definition for your new HUD:

```
<UIElements name="HUD">
 <UIElement name="NewHUD" render_lockless="1">
   <GFx file="NewHUD.swf" layer="1">
    <Constraints>
     <Align mode="dynamic" valign="center" halign="center"
      scale="1" max="0" />
    </Constraints>
   </GFx>
```

```
      </UIElement>
  </UIElements>
```

This is the basic layout for a new UIElement with the name `NewHUD`. Within the `<GFx>` tag you need to define the actual SWF file. Additionally, you can define a layer for this element. If more than one element is visible at the same time, the layer will define in which order those elements are drawn.

Within the `<Constraints>` tag, we can define an alignment for this element. In our case, we want to have dynamic alignment with `halign="center"` and `valign="center"`. With this alignment, the Flash asset will always be centered. With the `scale="1"` flag, the element is automatically scaled to always fit the current resolution without losing its aspect ratio.

What just happened?

By defining the UIElement in the XML file, we announced the new HUD to CryENGINE. It is now possible to display the HUD via Flow Graph. Since we also want to expose the textfields and ActionScript functions, we have to extend the XML file in the next step first, before we can create the Flow Graph to display the new HUD.

Time for action – making functions, variables, and movieclips accessible in CryENGINE 3

Let's follow a few simple steps:

1. In order to call our ActionScript functions and manipulate our movieclips and variables, we have to announce them in the XML file. For this, we need to add some more tags into our `<UIElement>` tag. Let's start with the `<functions>` tag:

    ```
    <functions>
      <function name="SetWeapon" desc=""
       funcname="setCurrentWeapon">
        <param name="WeaponName" desc="" type="string"/>
        <param name="AmmoName" desc="" type="string" />
      </function>
      <function name="SetAmmo" desc="" funcname="setAmmo">
        <param name="CurrAmmo" desc="" type="int"/>
        <param name="MaxAmmo" desc="" type="int" />
      </function>
    </functions>
    ```

2. For each function, you have to define a human-readable name and the corresponding ActionScript function name. Optionally, you can give a description that will be displayed on the Flownode for this function.

3. Within the function tag, you need to define the arguments that are passed to this function. The name must not match the argument name in your ActionScript code. Additionally, you can define a description and a type. As a type, you can use:

   ❑ `bool`: True or false.

   ❑ `int`: Integer number.

   ❑ `float`: Floating point value.

   ❑ `string`: A string.

   ❑ `any`: Default if you don't define the type. It can be any input.

> The types will define the port type of the Flownode. If you use the `any` type, the value will be converted to the best matching type (`bool | int | float | string`).
>
> Defining a type will also increase performance, because no autoconversion is needed. Besides that, it is not possible to type in the value directly into the Flownode if you choose the `any` type.

4. Next, we want to have access to our health bar movieclip. In order to do so, we need to define the movieclip as well.

```
<MovieClips>
  <MovieClip name="HealthBar" desc=""
   instancename="healthMC" />
</MovieClips>
```

5. Each movieclip needs a human-readable name and an instance name. Optionally, you can also give a description.

> Since the movieclip is on the `_root` layer, we will just write the plain instance name. We can also access nested movieclips, for example, `instancename="firstMc.SecondMc.ThirdMc"`.

6. Similar to our movieclip definition, we can announce variables.

```
<Variables>
  <Variable name="HealthValue" desc=""
   varname="healthMC.currHealth.text" />
</Variables>
```

The final XML should look like this:

```xml
<UIElements name="HUD">
 <UIElement name="NewHUD"
  render_lockless="1">render_lockless="1">
   <GFx file="NewHUD.swf" layer="1">
    <Constraints>
     <Align mode="dynamic" valign="center" halign="center"
      scale="1" max="0" />
    </Constraints>
   </GFx>
   <functions>
    <function name="SetWeapon" desc=""
     funcname="setCurrentWeapon">
     <param name="WeaponName" desc="" type="string"/>
     <param name="AmmoName" desc="" type="string" />
    </function>
    <function name="SetAmmo" desc="" funcname="setAmmo">
     <param name="CurrAmmo" desc="" type="int"/>
     <param name="MaxAmmo" desc="" type="int" />
    </function>
   </functions>
   <MovieClips>
    <MovieClip name="HealthBar" desc=""
     instancename="healthMC" />
   </MovieClips>
   <Variables>
   <Variable name="HealthValue" desc=""
    varname="healthMC.currHealth.text" />
   </Variables>
  </UIElement>
</UIElements>
```

7. Save the XML file. Now copy the `NewHUD.swf` file into `<engine root>\Game\Libs\UI\NewHUD.swf`.

8. Because CryENGINE 3 Sandbox supports the reloading of SWF files, it is a good idea to also copy the `NewHUD.fla` file into `<engine root>\Game\Libs\UI\NewHUD.fla`. This allows you to publish your SWF file into the correct folder, and you can reload your changes in Sandbox without coping the SWF file because it was published in the correct folder.

9. Your game folder should look similar to the the following screenshot:

 You can also put your FLA files into a subfolder like `Libs/UI/Assets` and change the Flash publish settings to publish into `../NewHUD.swf`. It is also a good idea to disable publishing the HTML page for the Flash asset because you don't need it.

What just happened?

With your `NewHUD.xml`, the engine now knows your new UIElement. You will now be able to display the new HUD, call functions, and manipulate your movieclips/variables within Sandbox Flow Graph. First, we defined the UIElement and the associated SWF file. Then, we added the movieclips and textfields to the XML file to make them accessible in CryENGINE. Finally, we also added our ActionScript function in the XML file to be able to call this function easily from Flow Graph.

The next part will show you how to use the **UI Emulator** to test your asset. Then we will create a simple **UI Action** in the Flow Graph to feed the data, and call our ActionScript function of the new HUD.

Different alignment modes for UI elements

As you already noticed, we have defined the alignment within the XML file. There are different alignment modes that can be used:

- `dynamic`: A dynamic mode has dynamic horizontal and vertical alignment, without losing aspect ratio
- `fixed`: A fixed position on the screen

◆ `fullscreen`: Always fullscreen; you have to reposition your movieclips by yourself

Each alignment mode has some additional settings that can be used.

Dynamic alignment

In the `dynamic` mode, you need to define a horizontal and vertical alignment and a scale mode:

```
<Constraints>
 <Align mode="dynamic" valign="center" halign="center" scale="1"
  max="0" />
</Constraints>
```

◆ `halign`: Can be `left`, `center`, or `right`.

◆ `valign`: Can be `top`, `center`, or `bottom`.

◆ `scale`: Can be `0` or `1`. If scaling is enabled, the asset is scaled to fit into the screen. The asset is always 100 percent visible. If disabled, it will always stay in its original resolution (if the resolution is smaller than the asset some parts are cut off).

◆ `max`: Can be `0` or `1`. If this is enabled together with `scale="1"`, the asset will be scaled to cover the complete screen. Parts of the asset can be cut off.

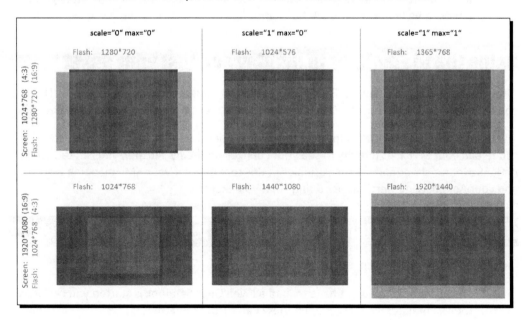

Fixed and fullscreen alignment

While the `fixed` alignment is not very common, you can use it to define the per pixel position of your Flash asset:

```
<Constraints>
  <Align mode="fixed" />
  <Position top="100" left="100" width="800" height="600" />
</Constraints>
```

◆ `top` and `left`: Any number. Defines the position of the asset.

◆ `width` and `height`: Any number. Defines the size of the asset.

With the `fullscreen` mode the asset always has the same viewport as the screen. This is useful if you manage the alignment within your asset (for example, if you are using the **CLIK** constraints ActionScript class).

```
<Constraints>
  <Align mode="fullscreen" scale="0" />
</Constraints>
```

◆ `scale`: Can be `0` or `1`. If set to true, the asset will lose aspect ratio and movieclips are stretched/squished. Otherwise, the aspect ratio stays untouched, but alignment needs to be handled within ActionScript.

Using the UI Emulator to display and test your asset

After you have created a new SWF file and created the UIElement XML file for the HUD, you now want to see the new HUD in Sandbox to make sure everything works as expected.

The UI Emulator is a tool that helps a lot during Flash development for CryENGINE. You can reload your SWF files directly to see your changes on the fly. Further, you can call your ActionScript functions and set the variables in this tool to see if your XML mapping works and your ActionScript functions are doing what you expect.

Time for action – starting Sandbox and testing your UIElement

Let's follow a few simple steps:

1. Start Sandbox. You don't have to load a level. Once Sandbox is started you can start the UI Emulator via **View | Open View Pane | UI Emulator**.

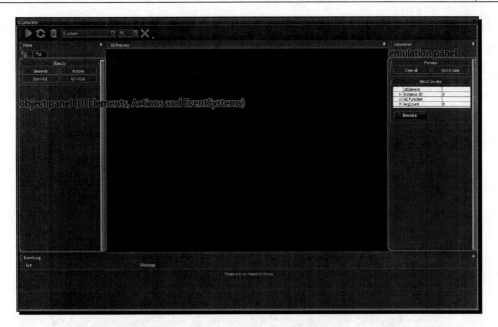

On the left-hand side, you'll find the **Objects** panel. Here you can browse all your **UIElements**, **UIActions**, and **UIEventSystems**. There is also a tab for settings. For example, if you don't want to see the debug info in the upper-left corner of **UI Preview** (frame rate and so on), you can go to the **Settings** tab in the left panel, and click twice on the display info checkbox. On the right-hand side, you will find the **Emulation** panel. With this panel we can call functions on our Flash asset, set variables, and much more. This panel is dynamic, so later we will see how you can attach your functions to this panel to call them.

2. But let's start with the **Objects** panel first. Click on the **Elements** button. A list of all **UIElements** should appear.

3. If you double-click on one of the elements in the list, it will display the Flash asset in **UI Preview**. So, if you double-click on NewHUD, it will be displayed in the preview window.

4. If you scroll down in the left panel a bit, you will find the constraints. You can change them to see the different results.

You can detach the preview window from the main window. If the **UI Preview** window is detached, you can easily change the size of this window to see different resolutions. You can also select different standard resolutions from the drop-down list in the upper-menu bar, which will resize the **UI Preview** window if it is detached.

5. Now, let's start with the emulation of our Flash asset. In the left panel, scroll down until you find the function list. If you click on the **Functions** button, the list will appear.

6. If you double-click on a function, a new item gets attached to the **Emulation** panel on the right-hand side of the screen. Double-click on both the functions of NewHUD. You can do the same for each variable that is in the **Variables** list.

7. Once you have all the functions/variables of interest attached to the **Emulation** panel, you can start typing in some values and call those functions to see if they are working as expected.

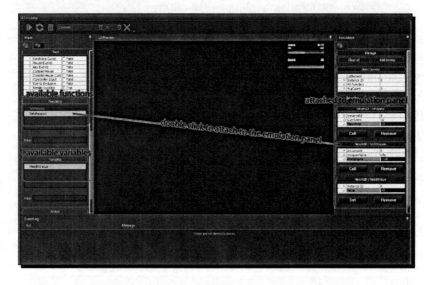

8. If you have copied the `NewHUD.fla` file into the `Game/Libs/UI` folder, you can open it with Adobe Flash and move the bars to some other place. Press *Alt + Shift + F12* to publish your changes. If you switch back to the UI Emulator, you can press the little *trash* icon on the buttons bar at the top of the screen. This will reload all the SWF files. If you double-click on the `NewHUD` element in the **UIElements** list again to display it, you will directly see your changes.

> The *reload* icon next to the *trash* icon will also reload the XML files.
>
> The possibility to reload a changed SWF file directly in Sandbox helps to speed your development process a lot. If something in your ActionScript does not work as expected, just change your code, re-publish, and reload the SWF file to see if your change has fixed the problem.

What just happened?

With the UI Emulator, it is easy to develop and test your Flash assets on the fly. You can also start and test UI Action Flow Graphs and invoke system events to see if your UI logic can handle those events correctly. There will be more details on UI Actions and UIEventSystems later in this chapter.

Have a go Hero – extending the ActionScript function

Extend the `setCurrentWeapon` ActionScript function to receive a third parameter named `bIsZoomed`, and change the function to hide the crosshair movieclip if the parameter is `true`. Add the new parameter in your `NewHUD.xml`. Press the reload button (next to the play button) to reload the SWF and XML files, to test the `setCurrentWeapon` function with the new parameter.

Creating a new UI Action for the new HUD

After we have tested our HUD in the UI Emulator, it is now time to create a new UI Action to get the HUD working. For this purpose, we will create a new UI Action in the Flow Graph, and use the UI Flownodes to call our functions.

Time for action – making the HUD work

Follow the given steps:

1. First of all, we need to load a level. Once this is done, we will disable the old HUD via the `g_showHud 0` CVAR.

2. Because we will use a new UI Action Flow Graph for the HUD, we need to open the Flow Graph. Go to **View | Open View Pane | Flow Graph**. Under **File**, we can select **New UI Action…**. In the file dialog, navigate to `Game\Libs\UI\UIActions`.

3. Name it something like `NewHUD`, and click **Save**. The Flow Graph should be automatically displayed in the Flow Graph Editor. All UI Actions will be found in the `UIActions` folder of the Flow Graph list.

 The final Flow Graph will be shown at the end of this section.

4. We start with a **Start** node. Right-click into the Flow Graph, and select **Add Start Node**. Because we want to display our HUD on level startup, we need to add a **UI:Display:Display** node. In the **Element** port of this node, you can select your `NewHUD` UIElement (select the **Element** port and click on the little browse button to select your UIElement). Connect the **Start** node with the **show** port of the **UI:Display:Display** node.

5. Because we need the weapon info and the local player info (for the current health), we need to add the two nodes **Game:WeaponSensor** and **Game:ActorSensor**. Both nodes need an entity ID as the input (the entity for which it should get the info). So add a **Game:LocalPlayer** node. This node returns the entity ID of the local player. Connect the **Start** node with the **Game:LocalPlayer** node and use the **entityId** port of the **Game:LocalPlayer** node as the input entity on both the sensor nodes. We also use the **entityId** port to **Enable** the sensor nodes, and trigger the **Get** port to get the current info on startup.

6. Now, we use the info of both the sensor nodes to feed our HUD. Let's start with the **Game:WeaponSensor** node for the ActionScript functions `SetWeapon` and `SetAmmo`.

7. You will find all your functions for the `NewHUD` UIElement under **UI:Functions:NewHUD**. Add the two nodes for both the functions (**UI:Functions:NewHUD:SetWeapon** and **UI:Functions:NewHUD:SetAmmo**).

8. Now, connect the **Ammo** port of the **Game:WeaponSensor** node to the **CurrAmmo** port of your **UI:Functions:NewHUD:SetAmmo** node. We will use the same output to trigger the **Call** port, because this port is always triggered when the current ammo changes. We will also use the **MaxAmmo** port of the **Game:WeaponSensor** node to feed the **MaxAmmo** port of the **UI:Functions:NewHUD:SetAmmo** node.

9. The **UI:Functions:NewHUD:SetWeapon** node gets its data also from the **Game:WeaponSensor** node. Because we want to trigger the **UI:Functions:NewHUD:SetWeapon** node every time the weapon changes (**OnWeaponChange**) or the firemode changes (**OnFiremodeChange**), we use a **Logic:Any** node to combine both the triggers of the **Game:WeaponSensor** node to one output. Connect the output of the **Logic:Any** node with the **Call** trigger of the **UI:Functions:NewHUD:SetWeapon** node.

10. Ok, now we also need to connect the health of the local player with our HUD. For this, we only need the **OnHealthChange** port of the **Game:ActorSensor** node. This port will also output the current health. Since the current health could be below zero (to detect the damage the actor received), we will clamp this value between 0 and 100 with the **Math:Clamp** node. Connect the **OnHealthChange** port with the **in** port of the **Math:Clamp** node, and type in the **min** and **max** values (0 and 100).

11. Now, we need to update the variable that we defined in the `NewHUD.xml` file (which points to the textfield of the health bar). We also want to call `GotoAndStop(currHealth)` on the `HealthBar` movieclip (in order to move the timeline to the correct position, which matches the current health).

12. To do so, we need two more nodes—the **UI:Variable:Var** node, and the **UI:MovieClip:GotoAndPlay** node. Place both the nodes on your Flow Graph. The **UI:Variable:Var** node has a **Variable** input . If you select this input, you can open a dialog to select your variable. The **UI:MovieClip:GotoAndPlay** node has a similar **MovieClip** port, where you can select a movieclip. Select the **NewHUD:HealthValue** variable on the **UI:Variable:Var** node and the **NewHUD:HealthBar** movieclip on the **UI:MovieClip:GotoAndPlay** node.

13. Now, connect the output of the **Math:Clamp** node to the **Set** and **Value** ports of the **UI:Variable:Var** node and the **GotoAndStop** and **FrameId** ports of the **UI:MovieClip:GotoAndPlay** node.

14. That's it. Save your UI Action. Your Flow Graph should look like the following screenshot:

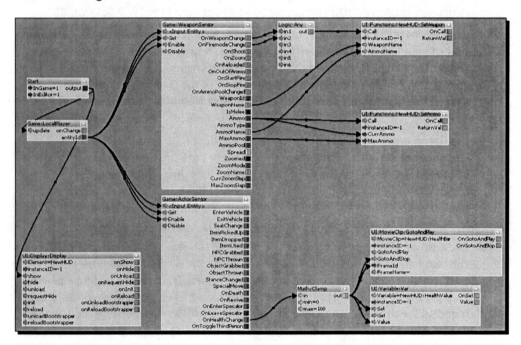

If you jump into the game, your new HUD should appear. If you change the weapon and shoot around a bit, you should see the ammo display working. Try to hit yourself with the rocket launcher (or jump from a high position) to see if the health bar is working.

What just happened?

Hey, you just created a new HUD! Wasn't that easy? Now you can start to add more awesomeness to your HUD.

I also added a simple mini-map and crosshair to the example HUD of this book. Just have a look into the example HUD, and feel free to re-use it and change the design to fit your game!

You will find the Flash asset, UIElement XML, and UI Action Flow Graphs present in the code files of this book. Just copy it into your `Game\Libs\UI` folder and see how it works. Even if I used Adobe Flash CS5.5 in this demo, the example `NewHUD.fla` file of this tutorial is saved in the CS4 format, so you will be able to open the `NewHUD.fla` file even if you are using an older version of Flash.

Have a go Hero – hiding the crosshair if the weapon is zoomed

Extend the Flow Graph to set the `IsZoomed` parameter of the **UI:Functions:NewHUD:SetWeapon** node. Check if the crosshair now hides/shows when you zoom in/out with the weapon.

 You might also need to trigger the **UI:Functions:NewHUD:SetWeapon** node every time the zoom mode of the current weapon changes.

Basic event handling from Flash to CryENGINE 3

The example HUD was just used to output data. But we also want to create interactive menus and handle events, for example, if the user presses a button. In this part, I will create a very basic menu with two buttons to open and close a door in-game.

Time for action – creating a simple interactive menu

Follow the given steps:

1. First of all, we need a simple graphic for the buttons. As you already know my programming art style, I have created three very simple images in Adobe Photoshop.

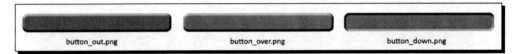

2. Now, start Flash and create a new **ActionScript 2.0** project. Import the three PNGs for the buttons. Create a new movieclip in the library (right-click in **Library**) and call it something like `MyButton`.

3. Open the `MyButton` movieclip and create three keyframes. Place `button_out.png` into the first keyframe, `button_over.png` into the second keyframe, and `button_down.png` into the third keyframe. Now click on each keyframe and type in the label names—out for the first, over for the second, and down for the third keyframe (you can define the label name in the **PROPERTIES** panel if you click on a keyframe).

4. Create a new layer, and add a dynamic textbox to it. Give it the instance name `btnText`. Make sure you embed the font (**Lowercase** and **Uppercase**). It is also important to disable **Selectable** on the textfield.

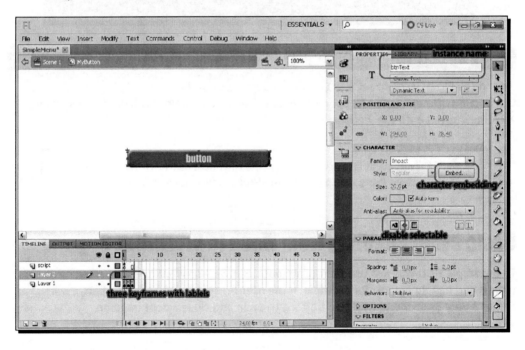

5. Create a third layer for the script, and write a very simple script to handle mouse events:

```
stop();
onRollOver = function()
{
  gotoAndStop("over");
}
onRollOut = function()
{
  gotoAndStop("out");
}
onPress = function()
{
  gotoAndStop("down");
  fscommand("onPressed", btnText.text);
}
onRelease = function()
{
  gotoAndStop("over");
}
```

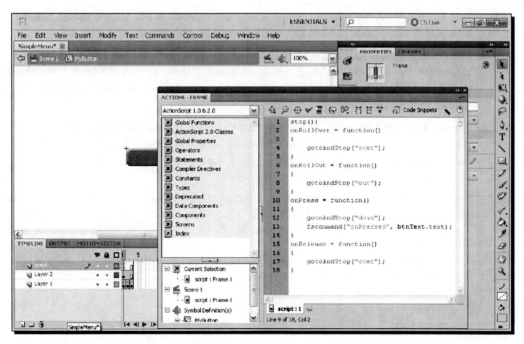

There is `fscommand` in the `onPress()` function. With `fscommand`, we can send events to CryENGINE. The first parameter is a string to identify the event. The second parameter is optional, and can be used as a parameter to pass some additional information to the engine. In this case, we simply use the text that is applied to the textbox as a parameter. This parameter will be used later to identify the button that was pressed.

You can also pass an array as an argument to `fscommand` if you need to pass more than one parameter:

```
var args = new Array();
args.push("arg1");
args.push("arg2");
fscommand("yourEvent", args);
```

6. Now, go to the main scene and place the button movieclip twice. The instance names for the buttons should be `btn1` and `btn2`.

7. Create a new script layer and add the following two lines to set up your buttons:

```
btn1.btnText.text = "open";
btn2.btnText.text = "close";
```

8. Save the `SimpleMenu.fla` file and publish the `SimpleMenu.swf` file.

9. Last but not least, we need to define a new UIElement for our simple menu. Create a new XML file—`Game\Libs\UI\UIElement\SimpleMenu.xml`.

10. The setup is similar to the one from the `NewHUD` UIElement, but we will use a top/left alignment. We will also enable mouse events and a cursor on this element. This means that if the UIElement is visible, the engine cursor is visible, and mouse events are passed to this Flash asset.

11. We will also add a new `<events>` tag to it to define the button events. The event is mapped to `fscommand` and can optionally have arguments. Because we pass the button name as an argument in `fscommand`, we add one `<param>` tag to it.

```
<UIElements name="Menus">
 <UIElement name="SimpleMenu" render_lockless="1"
 mouseevents="1" cursor="1">
  <GFx file="SimpleMenu.swf" layer="1">
   <Constraints>
    <Align mode="dynamic" valign="top" halign="left"
     scale="0" max="0" />
   </Constraints>
  </GFx>
  <events>
   <event name="OnButton" fscommand="onPressed" >
    <param name="Name" type="string" />
```

```
        </event>
      </events>
    </UIElement>
</UIElements>
```

12. Now, save the XML file and start Sandbox. In this example, I will use the `SimpleMenu` UIElement to open and close a door. You will find some doors in the Forest demo level. Just select one door, and create a new Flow Graph for it (right-click on the entity, and select **Create Flow Graph**).

13. Because we defined our events in the XML file, you will find a Flownode for this event under **UI:Events:SimpleMenu**. We will use this event with the **entity:Door** node to open/close it (you can add the **entity:Door** node by right-clicking on the Flow Graph and choosing **Add Graph Default Entity**).

14. We will also use an **Input:Key** node to display the `SimpleMenu` UIElement on press, and hide it again on release. We will also use the **Input:ActionFilter** node to enable the **only_ui** filter so long as the *Tab* key is pressed. This filter will lock all the input in the game and only pass the input to the UI.

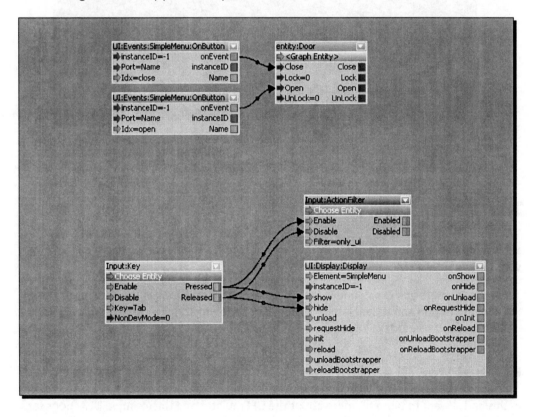

All event nodes have a **Port** input. If this is set to `<TriggerAlways>`, it will always trigger if the event is fired. In our case, we select the **Name** port. This means that this node is only triggered if the **Name** output of this node is equal to the string that is defined in the **Idx** input. With this setup, we can use this node to trigger only if an event is fired that has a specific value (**Idx**) on the chosen output (**Port**). In our case, we check the button text to see if the **open** or **close** button was pressed.

15. If you now jump into the game, you can press *Tab*, and the menu should appear. Click on the buttons to see if they work as expected.

What just happened?

With `fscommand` and the `<event>` tag, it is really easy to handle Flash events in CryENGINE. You should now be able to write your own menus. Mouse events can be easily enabled for your UIElement via XML.

There is a lot more you can define in the XML files. Just have a look at `CryDev.net`. The full documentation about the Flash UI system can be found at `http://freesdk.crydev.net/display/SDKDOC4/Flash+UI+System`.

UI Emulator, UI Actions, and FreeSDK example menus

In this part, I want to talk a bit more about the UI Emulator and the example UI Actions for the FreeSDK example menus.

We already used the UI Emulator to test the simple functions of our HUD. But this is not the only thing you can do with the UI Emulator. You can also trigger UI Actions and emulate system events, such as `OnSystemStarted`, to see if your UI Action flow behaves as expected. For this purpose, you can enable Flow Graph updates on all UI Actions via the UI Emulator.

But first let's have a look at UI Actions.

UI Actions – Flow Graphs to control the UI

If you create a new UI Action, it is basically just a normal Flow Graph that behaves like any other Flow Graph. But there are some differences, which are listed as follows:

- Although a normal Flow Graph belongs to an entity, this Flow Graph only exists if the belonging entity is loaded. A UI Action is a standalone Flow Graph.
- Normal Flow Graphs only exist if a level is loaded, because entities are only spawned within a level. UI Actions are level independent, and so are always existent.
- So each UI Action gets updates every time, even if no level is loaded (for example, in the main menu or during loading).
- UI Actions can have start and end nodes. And they can be controlled via control nodes.
- UI Actions can be in a disabled state as long as the UI Action is not started.
- UI Actions support multitriggering. Normal Flow Graphs do not have this feature.

So what does this mean?

UI Action is a standalone, level-independent Flow Graph

This means that a UI Action always exists. It gets loaded once during system initialization and exists as long as the game runs. As a result, you can control menu logic for the main menu, in-game menus, level loading, matchmaking, and so on.

UI Action can have start and end nodes

While a normal Flow Graph uses various nodes to trigger different things, a UI Action can have **UI:Action:Start** and **UI:Action:End** nodes. If you add these nodes to a UI Action, you can control this UI Action from any other Flow Graph via a **UI:Action:Control** node.

For example, consider that you have a movieclip with a textbox in your HUD, which should display a message for a few seconds. You can set up this UI Action (call it **DisplayHudMessage** for example) as shown in the following screenshot:

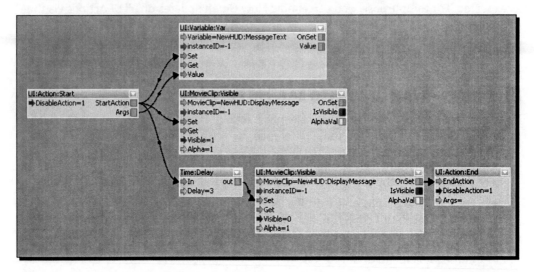

Now, you can add a **ProximityTrigger** entity with an explosion somewhere in your level and create a Flow Graph that uses the **DisplayHudMessage** UI Action to inform the player that he/she has to run away.

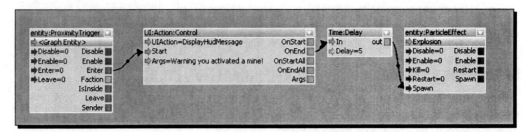

Now if the player walks into the trigger, he/she will get the warning in the HUD that is displayed for three seconds. After the three seconds, we have another five seconds to run away before the explosion happens.

You can also start UI Actions from C++ code or via Lua.

UI Action can be in a disabled state

Once you use a **Start** and **End** node in your UI Action, you can set the `DisableAction` port on those nodes to `true`. If you do so, this UI Action is completely disabled as long as it is not started. Once you start a UI Action via any **Control** node, the UI Action gets enabled and will be disabled again once the **End** node is triggered.

This is useful to help performance, because the UI Action Flow Graph does not need to be updated as long as it is not started.

But there is another big advantage with this. Consider that you have a node in your UI Action that is used as a trigger to do something. For example, an **Input:Key** node to call an ActionScript function that highlights the next button. You don't want to call this ActionScript function if the menu is not visible. If your UI Action would be enabled always, the **Input:Key** node would call the ActionScript function always, even if the menu is not visible at the time. But if you use a **Start** and **End** node with `DisableAction=true` and only start this UI Action if the menu is visible, the ActionScript function is only called as long as the menu is visible.

 You can display the state of all UI Actions via the `gfx_debugdraw 2` CVAR. This will show a list of all UI Actions and if they are enabled or not.

UI Actions support multitriggering

This is a feature that allows one node to trigger the same port multiple times during one update call. As an example, let's have a look at the part of the UI Action that creates the button list for the single player-level selection. Open the **mm_singleplayer** UI Action (which can be found under **UIActions | MM_PagesMain**) in the Flow Graph and enable Flow Graph debugging (the button with the *bug icon*).

Now, open the UI Emulator, enable the Flow Graph updates (the *play button* at the top), and display the main menu (just double-click on **MainMenu** in the **UIElements** list).

Now, click on **Actions** in the **Objects** panel, and double-click on the **mm_singleplayer** UI Action. The UI Action should now be attached to the **Emulation** panel. Click on the **Start** button and look at the UI Action Flow Graph.

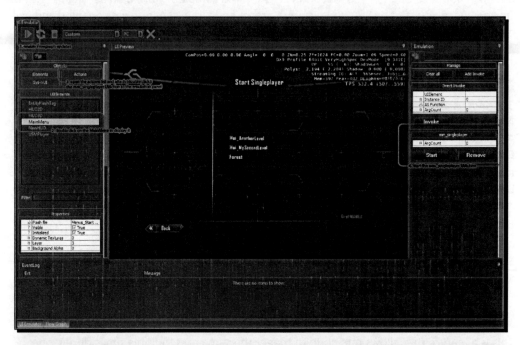

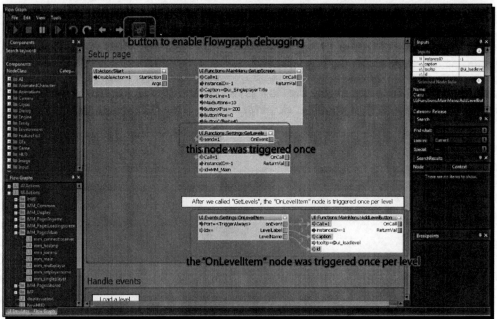

As you clicked on the **Start** button for the UI Action in the **Emulation** panel, the **UI:Action:Start** node was triggered. Later in the flow, the **UI:Functions:Settings:GetLevels** node was triggered. This node is a UIEventSystem node. Internally, the UIEventSystem executed code to get all the levels, and then called the **UI:Events:Settings:OnLevelItem** node once for each level that is in the Game\Levels folder. Everything happened in one frame.

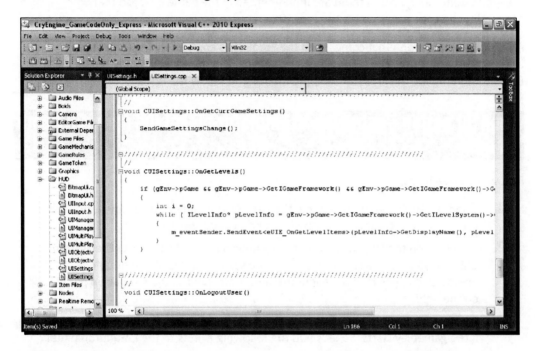

The code for the UIEventSystem (in this case UISettings.h / .cpp in the CryGame project under the HUD filter) can be found in the CryGame project under HUD. A short look at the callback function for the **UI:Functions:Settings:GetLevels** node shows us that it sends a UIEvent for each level. This will trigger the **UI:Events:Settings:OnLevelItem** node once per level.

 The CUISettings class is a good and easy example of how to create C++ UIEventSystems, which can be used in your UI Action Flow Graphs. So, if you are interested in writing your own UIEventSystem, this is a very good starting point.

UIEventSystems and UI Emulator to test your UI

The cool thing about UIEventSystems is that you can emulate all events within the UI Emulator. This helps a lot, to create your UI Actions to handle those events correctly. Most of the communication between Flash and CryENGINE 3 is realized through UIEventSystems, and most of them are implemented in the game code, so that you can modify the code easily within the FreeSDK.

Also, the example menu that comes with the FreeSDK is completely implemented as UI Actions and it uses the UIEventSystems heavily. This allows you to use the UI Emulator to emulate the FreeSDK example menus and follow the flow.

Time for action – using the UI Emulator to test the FreeSDK demo menus

Follow the given steps:

1. Open the UI Emulator and enable the Flow Graph updates (the *play button* in the top menu bar). Clear the state by pressing the little *trash icon*.

2. Now click on the **Sys->UI** button in the **Objects** panel. If you select the **System** UIEventSytem, you will find a list of all the system events. If you double-click on one of the events in the event list, it gets attached to the **Emulation** panel on the right.

3. For now, we want to see what happens if the game starts, if a level loads, and if the gameplay starts. So let's add the following events to the **Emulation** panel:

    - ❑ OnSystemStart
    - ❑ OnLoadingStart
    - ❑ OnGameplayStated

4. If you call OnSystemStart, the main menu should appear. You can also look into the Flow Graph and enable Flow Graph debugging to see which nodes are triggered to fill the main menu. The flow starts in the sys_statecontrol UI Action (there should be the **UI:Events:System:OnSystemStart** node that then starts another UI Action).

5. You can always reset the state by pressing the *trash icon*. If you enable UI Action logging (in the **Settings** tab on the left-hand side of the UI Emulator, or with the gfx_uiaction_log 1 CVAR), you will see what happens in the **EventLog** window.

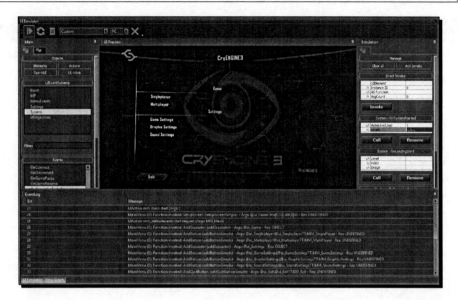

 With the big **X** button in the top button bar, you can clear the log.

6. Repeat the steps with the `OnLoadingStart` and `OnGameplayStarted` events.

What just happened?

By using the UI Emulator, you can easily see how the UI Action flow handles the different system events. This is a great tool that helps a lot in setting up your menus without the need of starting the launcher and restarting it every time you changed something. You can also change your UI Actions and see the result directly, without the need of using Sandbox to create/change your UI Actions and then starting the launcher to see the results.

Have a go Hero – creating a new menu page

Try to create a new menu page for the main menu. Look into the **MM_Main** UI Action Flow Graph and add a new button for your new menu page. Look into **MM_SoundSettings**, on how this page is set up and how the button in the **MM_Main** UI Action is set up to go to the **Sound Settings** menu.

 Look in the **UI:Functions:MainMenu:AddButton** node of the **mm_main** UI Action that creates the button with the **@ui_SoundSettings** caption. Look for it's **id**. Isn't it the same name as the **MM_SoundSettings** UI Action?

Pop quiz – UI Actions

1. Where are the Flash element XML definition files located?

    a. `Libs\UI`

    b. `Libs\UI\UIElements`

    c. `Libs\UI\UIActions`

2. When using a textfield to display some info, such as the current health, what type of textfield do you have to use?

    a. Input Text

    b. Static Text

    c. Dynamic Text

3. If you want to raise an event from Flash, what ActionScript function do you need to call?

    a. `sendEvent`

    b. `fsCommand`

    c. `onEnterFrame`

Summary

This chapter showed us how to connect Flash to CryENGINE 3 using the Flow Graph. We learned a few Flash basics, and how to use ActionScript and Flow Graph to interact between the engine and our UI.

You should now be able to create your own custom HUD and menus, and hook them up with CryENGINE 3!

In the next chapter, you will learn how to create new 3D assets for CryENGINE using 3ds Max.

7
Creating Assets for the CryENGINE 3

CryENGINE doesn't make bad art look good, it makes good art look even better. Art and assets are truly what defines the visual style and appeal of your game. Thus being able to leverage the material, shader and lighting technologies available in the CryENGINE will allows us to bring our art and assets to AAA quality. All you need to do is follow some simple guidelines for asset creation.

In this chapter, we will explore the fundamentals as well as some advanced techniques used for creating real-time game assets for the CryENGINE 3.

In this chapter, we shall explore:

- ◆ Establishing what assets we need for our game
- ◆ Creating a texture for use within the CryENGINE
- ◆ Creating a basic model
- ◆ Creating a material and exporting the model to the CryENGINE
- ◆ Creating a destructible asset
- ◆ Creating a skinned character for CryENGINE 3
- ◆ Creating animation for the skinned character
- ◆ Applying **physics** and **ragdoll** properties to the character
- ◆ Animating rigid body data

So let's get on with it!

What are assets?

In game development, we typically refer to any artwork related to our games as assets. This distinction differentiates asset creation from programming and scripting, and even level design. Any 3D model, texture, or animation can be referred to as an asset.

Understanding the CryENGINE 3 asset pipeline

The following diagram displays the workflow or pipeline of creating assets with various pieces of software. In the following examples, we will use **Autodesk 3ds Max**, which uses the **CryExport Plugin** to send the asset to the resource compiler. Once processed by the resource compiler, the asset is ready for use within the CryENGINE Sandbox.

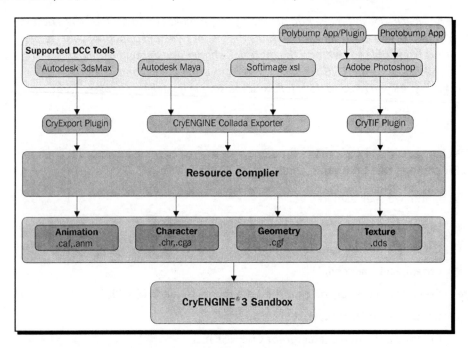

Exploring the CryENGINE 3 asset file types

Before we start making any new assets of our own, we must first understand the different files and formats that the CryENGINE uses.

In the above screenshot, we see a mix of different assets; some of them are animated, such as the tank, helicopter, and character, and some of them are static, such as the tree, rock, and plant. These assets can be broken down into three distinct file types.

For **static art assets**, the **Crytek Geometry Format** (`.cfg`) is used.

The `.cfg` file is created and exported from a 3D application, such as Maya or 3ds Max. It contains the geometry data of grouped triangles, vertex colors, and optional physics data for the 3D models. In the previous screenshot, the rock, plants, and tree are all `.cfg` files.

For non-deforming animated geometry, the **Crytek Geometry Animation** (`.cga`) format is used.

`.cga` assets are created in a fashion similar to `.cfg` files. However, the main difference is that `.cga` files can contain animation data that animates different main objects or subobjects in the model. In the previous screenshot, the tank and helicopter are both `.cga` assets, as they have animated parts.

For assets that are skinned to a skeleton for animation, the **character** (`.chr`) format is used.

The `.chr` file is exported from the 3D application and it contains character data. A character can be any asset that is animated with bone-weighted vertices, such as humans, aliens, ropes, lamps, heads, and parachutes. The `.chr` file includes the mesh, the skeleton in the default position, vertex weights, vertex colors, and morph targets. In the previous screenshot, the human male is a `.chr` asset.

Following a workflow for artists

Throughout this chapter, we will try to maintain a workflow similar to that of any professional 3D artist working with the CryENGINE 3. A typical workflow begins in Sandbox with a white box version of the model we need to create. As discussed in *Chapter 3, Playable Levels in No Time*, the white box is a basic visual representation of a volume or object that a designer wants created. We then export it directly to the desired DCC tool, for example, 3ds Max. Once the white box object is in 3ds, it can then be modified or even recreated, and the size and shape will be easy for the artist to follow or to remain within when creating geometry.

After the artist has sufficiently polished the asset, it is then exported from the DCC tool to the CryENGINE, where textures and materials are adjusted for the best look.

The first step we need to take to be able to follow this workflow is to set up our units within the DCC tool, which is the topic of our next example.

Working with units and scale in CryENGINE 3

The CryENGINE 3 uses the metric scale to represent objects, distance, and size. It is important to keep this in mind when making your game assets. To ensure your asset matches the scale you intended, it is highly recommended that the unit setup in your DCC package be set up to match the scale in the CryENGINE. Let's do just that.

Time for action - setting up 3ds Max units to match CryENGINE scale

Different game engines use a different scale to represent objects; in our case, let's set up our 3ds Max application to work with the CryENGINE 3.

1. Open 3ds Max.
2. On the top menu bar of 3ds, locate the **Customize** tab. Click on it and select **Units Setup** from the list.

   You will now see a dialog box as seen in the following screenshot:

3. In the **Units Setup** dialog box, change the **Display Unit Scale** option to **Metric**, and in the drop-down box, select **Meters**.

4. Next, click on the **System Unit Setup** button.

5. In this new dialog box, change the **System Unit Scale** to **1 Unit = 100.0 Centimeters**. This effectively matches 3ds Max to the same scale as the CryENGINE SDK.

6. Click on **OK** to save the settings and go back to your 3ds scene.

   There is a very useful function available in Sandbox for us, to test our unit setup within 3ds Max.

7. Open the Sandbox application to any level.

8. Create a 1 x 1 x 1 meter **Solid** entity.

 Review *Chapter 3, Playable Levels in No Time* if you do not know how to create CSG or white box solids within the editor application.

9. Make sure to have the **Solid** selected, and then go to **Menu | File | Export Selected Geometry to .OBJ**, as seen in the following screenshot:

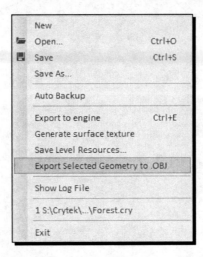

10. Create a directory in your CryENGINE build under **Game | Objects | Reference**, and save the cube as 1m_cube.obj.

 .obj is a fairly standard format that is compatible with almost all 3D DCC tools.

11. Next, use **File | Import** from within 3ds and import the 1m_cube.obj to your 3ds Max's scene.

12. You see that you can now use this as a reference for future creations or simply follow the grid, which is now identical to the CryENGINE's grid, as seen in the following screenshot:

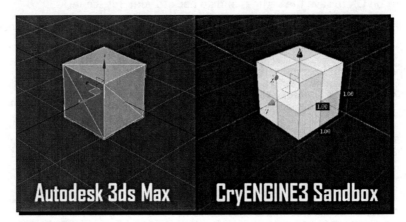

What just happened?

Now that the scale and unit size have been properly set up, we can accurately represent our models in 3ds Max the way they are meant to be rendered in CryENGINE. It is common for some artists to load a scale human model when making some assets to maintain believability. One of the major advantages of using metric with 3ds is that it makes all unit inputs and calculations; for example, when creating primitives, match the metric values.

Matching grid and snap settings between 3ds Max and Sandbox

Depending on the type of asset you may be creating, it is recommended to adjust the viewport grid to a suitable setting in both 3ds Max and the editor application. Click on the **Tools | Grids and Snaps | Grids and Snaps Settings**. In these settings, you can change the **Grid Spacing** option to other values. For large objects, using a grid spacing of 1 meter is recommended. For smaller objects use 1 cm. In the editor, locate the grid icon in the edit mode toolbar and activate it by clicking on it, or set the grid size using the pull-down menu beside the grid icon, as seen in the following screenshot:

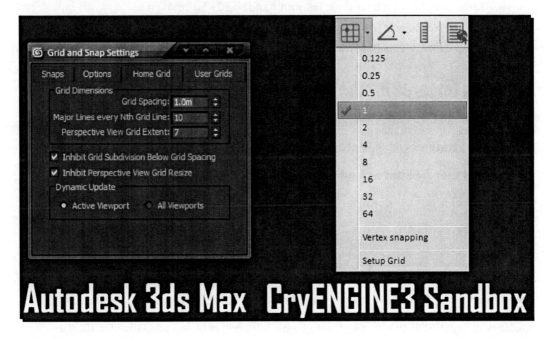

Using real-world measurement reference

The following reference measurements were originally created for **Crysis**, but are useful can be used as a guide for creating new assets:

- Table height (top of the table) = 75 cm
- Seat height (top of the chair, seat) = 46 cm
- Stairs height = power of 75 cm (150 cm, 225 cm, 300 cm, 375 cm, 450 cm)
- Stair steps = 18.75 cm (4 steps will sum up to 75 cm)
- Boxes = 60 cm x 40 cm x 40 cm
- Hide Objects (which AI are prone to hide behind) = objects that are smaller than 120 cm
- Hide Objects (which AI crouch to hide behind) = objects that are bigger than 120 cm
- Hide Objects (which AI stand to hide behind and strafe left/right to leave cover) = objects that are bigger than 180 cm
- Jump over Objects (standing, without hand) = 30 - 50 cm high
- Jump over Objects (running jumps) = 50 - 100 cm high
- Jump over Objects (sideways, using hand) = 120 - 150 cm high

Creating textures for the CryENGINE

Before we get to exporting our own objects, let's take some time to learn how to make our own textures. There are many different avenues available online for acquiring or learning how to make textures within Photoshop online.

Some useful sites are listed as follows:

http://www.3dtotal.com/

http://www.cgtextures.com/

http://www.turbosquid.com/

This example is designed to take you through the process of getting the texture ready for use within the CryENGINE, rather than the process of actually painting the texture.

Textures in CryENGINE are usually created with Adobe Photoshop and stored in the TIF image format by using the **CryTIF Plugin**. However, the TIF images are not used directly in the game but converted to a more optimized format, usually .dds, by the resource compiler. Not all textures use the same settings; normal maps, for example, require a different compression type than diffuse maps. For this reason, the resource compiler does the conversion based on presets, which can be selected by the user when saving the .tif file from Photoshop.

Time for action - creating your own texture

Let's create a .tif file within Photoshop and then save it within CryTIF using an appropriate compression method.

1. Start Photoshop.

    As all we want to do is simply create our first .tif file, a complex texture is not required here. You can import the example texture from the example assets.

2. Create a new image with the dimensions of 1024 X 1024.

3. Create a simple pattern or open the sample texture provided, which is stored under objects/wooden_props/textures/wood_prop_dif.tif.

4. Save this file as a CryTIF (.tif) file type. This format is made available upon the installation of the CryTIF plugin.

5. Save this texture under the game/textures/ folder and name it test_pattern.TIF.

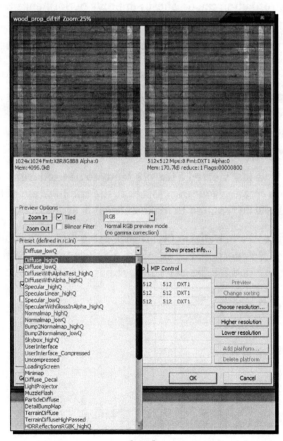

Once you select save, you will be presented with the CryTIF texture dialog box.

The primary function of this dialog box is to add metadata to the texture, which can later be used by the resource compiler to compress the texture appropriately, for whatever platform it is being created for, or even the type of texture it will be used as.

In the upper area of the CryTIF dialog box, you can see two images, the original image on the left-hand side, and a preview of the processed image using the preset on the right-hand side.

Directly below the two images are different image properties, such as the resolution, number of mip maps, texture format, and memory.

6. In this example, select the **Diffuse_hiqhQ** preset.

7. Click on one of the image previews and use your mouse wheel to preview the appearance of texture, should it be tiled or repeated.

8. Finally, notice the effects of reducing the resolution in this image by clicking on the **Higher resolution** and **Lower resolution** buttons. Understand, however, that reducing resolution can drastically improve performance but can degrade the visual appearance.

The preview image window updates to show the compression results.

9. Click on **Generate Output** to manually perform the `.tif` to `.dds` conversion.

10. Finally, click on **OK** to write the metadata containing the **Preset** and **Resolution** settings.

What just happened?

Congratulations! You have just created a texture ready to be used with the CryENGINE. This is a major step into creating your own assets as the combination of the geometry, material, and textures will be required to make believable assets.

When applying a texture to a material in CryENGINE using the `.tif` extension, it will automatically load the `.dds` version. For example, a diffuse texture path of `textures/test_pattern.tif` will load the file `textures/test_pattern.dds` at runtime.

Working with the CryTIF (.TIF) format

The CryTIF format is used in the asset creation pipeline for almost all artists. The reason why the CryENGINE uses `.tif` files and not `.jpeg` or other popular image formats is that the `.tif` extension stores uncompressed texture information, as well as, has the ability to store different settings for the resource compiler as meta information. It is not recommended to create `.dds` files manually or without the resource compiler, as the results may not be accurate or even compatible. Should an error occur, and the system path to the root directory is lost by the plugin, you can restore the path in Photoshop under the menu **Help | About Plug-In | CryTIFPlugin**.

If the RC stored under **Bin32/RC** is executable and cannot be found, the configuration dialog box will be opened automatically and the path to your root directory can be entered.

Creating and exporting custom assets

Now, it's time to get our own creations into the engine.

As discussed earlier, `.cgf` geometry is used for most static geometry. It is also the most simple of all the model formats used by the CryENGINE. **Static geometry** is commonly used for various objects in the environment that do not require special properties assigned to them. Some obvious examples of this could be walls, structural components of buildings, and other environmental features such as rocks.

In this example, we will make a typical wooden prop. This example is meant to show the process of exporting a basic mesh, so I would encourage you to try your own custom models and consider this example as a guideline to creating static `.cgf` models. It is important to note that the process for exporting an animated or **skinned mesh** will be discussed later in this book. For now, we will keep our objects simple.

All directories containing objects must be placed under the root game folder in the `Game\Objects` folder. Objects placed outside of the `Game` folder will not be read by the CryENGINE SDK, and so you will not have access to them when using the **Editor.exe**.

Time for action - creating and exporting your first model

In this example, we begin with a simple, cylinder-type mesh that will become a wooden barrel. First, let's create some geometry for your first object:

1. Create your own custom mesh; or for this example, open the example file **wooden_barrel_simple.max** as seen in the following screenshot:

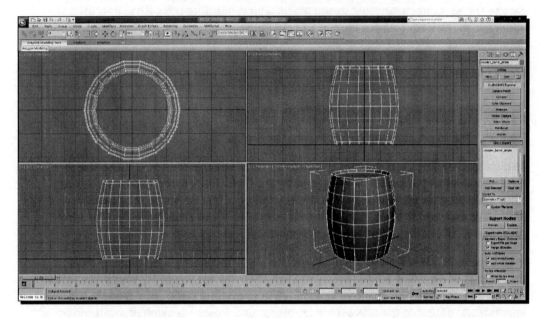

The pivot of the object in 3ds Max will become the pivot of the object when used in the engine. This is important to know, because moving the pivot point of the object to different locations will make placing it easier later on in the engine.

2. Align the pivot of the object to 0, 0, 0. This will make aligning the object to terrain or even other objects easier later on, when using from the editor.

Let's create a material for our object now, which we can use to texture and modify some physical parameters.

3. Open the **Material Editor** window in 3ds Max by pressing the keyboard shortcut *M*.

4. Create a new **Multi/Sub-Object material** in the first material slot by clicking on the **Standard** button, as seen in the following screenshot:

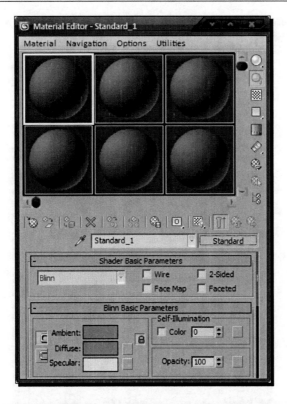

5. Select **Multi/Sub-Object** from the dialog box that opens.

6. Next, set the number of submaterials to two by clicking on the **Set Number** button in the newly created material.

> CryENGINE 3 supports up to 32 submaterials; however, every submaterial that is rendered will add to the overall draw call count of the asset. We will discuss the performance implications of too many draw calls later, but for now, understand that they should be kept as low as possible. For the best performance, keep the number of submaterials low to manage this.

We should give the material and all the submaterials appropriate names; as and when we create the .mtl file, these names will be exported and used by the engine.

The name of the material that you assign to an object in 3ds Max must be the same as the name of the .mtl file created.

7. Name the parent material **wooden_prop** and the subsequent **Sub-Material** as **texture** and **proxy**, as seen in the following screenshot:

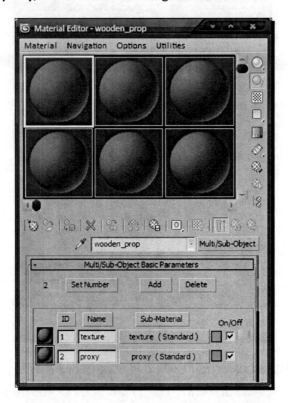

8. This step is very important as you must open each submaterial and set the **Shader Basic Parameters** to the **Crytek Shader** type, as seen in the following screenshot:

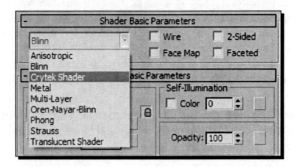

 Only use the **Crytek Shader** option for materials on objects when the ultimate goal is to export that material to the CryENGINE.

Having selected the **Crytek Shader** option for both the submaterials, you will see a new parameter for these materials under the heading of **Physicalization**.

This setting controls the way the material acts in the engine, particularly with physics properties.

The **default** setting can be used for most materials because it has no additional physics capabilities.

9. Select the **Proxy** submaterial and change its **Physicalization** type to **Physical Proxy (NoDraw)**. This will cause any geometry assigned to this submaterial to be ignored by the renderer, making it invisible to the user.

10. Next, to actually physicalize the material in the engine, select the **Physicalize** checkbox as seen in the following screenshot:

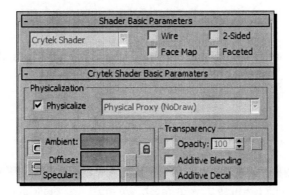

If **Physicalize** is disabled, the object will not physically interact with anything in the game world.

Now that our material is set up, we can create the .mtl file.

The .mtl file must be created in the directory in which you plan to save your assets.

11. Open the **CryENGINE Exporter** and locate the **Material** rollout, as seen in the following screenshot:

Ensure that the topmost material is active; you should see all the submaterial in their list. If a submaterial is active while creating the `.mtl` file, the file will contain only that submaterial.

12. Create the `.mtl` file by clicking on **Create Material**.

The Sandbox **Material Editor** window will open.

13. Click on **Create Material** in 3ds Max a second time. You will then, finally, be asked to enter a filename for the new MTL file.

Again, ensure that this name is same as the material in 3ds Max.

14. For this example, save this material as `wooden_prop.mtl` to a directory named `objects/wooden_props/`.

Let's assign the **wooden_prop** material to the **wooden_barrel_simple** object in 3ds Max now.

15. Click on the **Assign Material to Selection** icon in the 3ds Max's **Material Editor**, ensuring you have the object selected.

Now that we have our material applied, we can assign a texture to it.

Before assigning textures to your mesh, we must first make sure we have **UV** mapped our object. **UV** mapping is a technique where the 3D object is laid out flat onto a 2D texture map. **UV** mapping of an object also determines how the faces of a particular mesh will display texture.

For this object, a simple automatic cylindrical unwrap makes the most sense, as shown in the following screenshot:

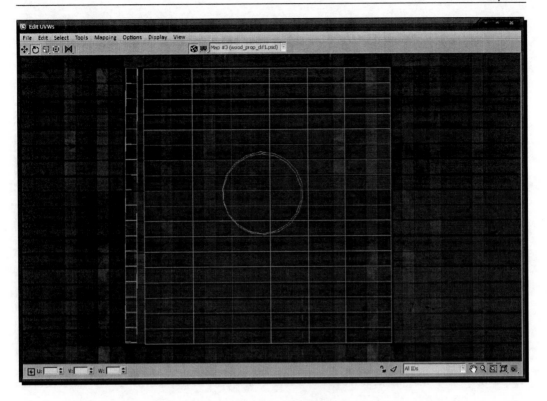

We can now assign a texture to the first submaterial.

Ensure that all the polygons in your object are set to `material ID 1`.

16. Assign an appropriate, wooden-type texture to the texture submaterial.

17. When exporting, it is important that your mesh be an editable poly or editable mesh, and the modifier stack be collapsed to avoid any unsupported modifiers on export.

18. Save your `.max` scene in the same location as where you want to store the asset. In this case, save the `.max` scene to `Game\objects\wooden_props\wooden_barrel_simple.max`.

19. To export the object, open the 3ds exporter and locate the **Object Export** section at the top of the interface, then select your prop, and click on the **Add Selected** button. You will notice that its name is added to the export list, as seen in the following screenshot:

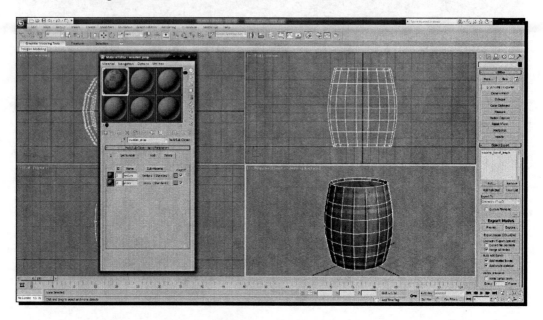

20. Next, select the type of file you'd like to create from the **Export To** pull-down menu; in this case it is a **Geometry (*.CGF)** file.

21. Next, click the **Export Nodes** button. This will export the object to the same folder as the 3ds Max file. By default, the exported object will be given the same name as the 3ds Max filename, which in our case is `wooden_barrel_simple.cgf`.

One thing should be noted about smoothing groups. Smoothing groups should be assigned during export. If they are not found on the mesh, the exporter will generate and apply a single unified group automatically, which can cause rendering errors on the mesh. Smoothing defines the way the faces of a 3D model interact with light and shading to give the illusion of a rounder or smoother mesh.

The final step of this example is to preview the asset in the engine!

22. Open up the CryENGINE **Sandbox Editor** and load any level.

23. On the **RollupBar**, select **Brush** and browse to **wooden_props/wooden_barrel_simple.cgf**. Click-and-drag it into the perspective viewport in the level.

You will notice that the geometry is there, but the texture is red and reads **Replace me**.

This is simply telling us that our `.mtl` file does not have a valid texture in the **Diffuse** slot.

24. To rectify this, select the prop and open the Sandbox **Material Editor** by using the keyboard shortcut *M*.

25. Click on the **Get material from selection** tool.

26. Go to the **Diffuse** slot of the first submaterial of your object, using the browse button. Locate the texture you want to use for the object. For this example, use the texture **objects/wooden_props/textures/wood_prop_dif.tif** (see the following screenshot for reference).

Congratulations! You have created your own custom object with material and texture.

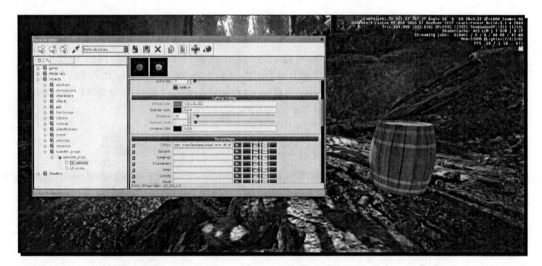

What just happened?

We've just broken the biggest barrier to the entry when working with our own custom assets and a game engine; we've successfully created and exported our own creation to the CryENGINE. We created a basic mesh and material within 3ds Max, and then exported it in a CryENGINE compatible format. Finally, we placed the object within a level and adjusted basic material parameters. As all material parameters can be changed and previewed in real time, it is easy and fun to experiment with different colors, textures, shader settings, and other parameters. Happily, this is only the beginning; there are many more things to consider when working with static objects. Physical dynamics is one such consideration.

Using a physics proxy instead of the render geometry for collision

The **physics proxy** is the geometry that is used for collision detection by the physics system. It can be part of the visible geometry as seen in the preceding example, or linked to it as a separate node completely and made invisible. Usually, the physics proxy geometry is a simplified version of the render geometry, but it is also possible to use the render geometry directly for physics. For performance reasons, the collision geometry should be kept as simple as possible, because checking for intersections on complex geometry is very expensive, especially if it happens often. A physics proxy is set up in the DCC tool exclusively. The only setup needed in Sandbox is assigning the surface type.

> Adjusting the physical properties of collision will likely require a re-export of your mesh.

Adjusting physical dynamics with user-defined properties

It may be required that some objects have specific physics or dynamic properties applied. These properties can be added using the **User Defined Properties** option within 3ds Max. Select an object and, on the **Edit** menu, click **Object Properties** to access the **User Defined Properties** list of that object, as seen in the following screenshot:

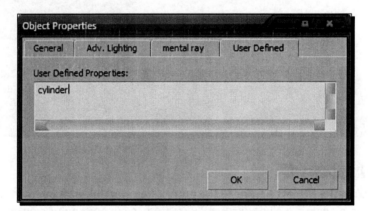

Some common parameters that can be used are:

- **box**: Force this proxy to be a box primitive in the engine.
- **cylinder**: Force this proxy to be a cylinder primitive in the engine.
- **capsule**: Force this proxy to be a capsule primitive in the engine.
- **sphere**: Force this proxy to be a sphere primitive in the engine.

◆ **Mass**: This value defines the weight of an object. If the value is set to zero, it sets the object to unmovable mode, which is perfect for static meshes.

◆ **no_explosion_occlusion**: It will allow the physical forces and the damage from explosions to penetrate through the geometry. A good example of this could be a chain-link fence, where explosions should not be blocked.

Creating destructible objects

There are several methods of setting up breakable assets, which the player can destroy in CryENGINE. In this example, we will be going through the process of creating a destroyable object entity.

Destroyable objects are assets that contain the original object and some precreated pieces, which spawn when this original object is destroyed. It destroys into the precreated pieces when taking more damage than the specified health property of the entity.

Good candidates for destroyable objects are glass bottles, explosive barrels, computer monitors, and, consequently, wooden barrels. Larger objects can also be destroyable, but it will depend mostly on what the gameplay requires, such as a destroyable vehicle or wall.

All of these assets normally consist of precreated pieces, which emit when the object is destroyed.

Time for action - making your object destructible

In this example, we will use the `wooden_barrel_simple` asset created earlier in the chapter. Alternatively, you can open the example file **objects\wooden_props\ wooden_barrell_destructible.max**.

To create a `.cgf` containing the object's broken pieces, we must create them as submodels for our main mesh. Each submodel must also have a physics proxy geometry. The submodel's name and **User Defined Properties** will determine its behavior.

1. Create the original model to be used as the non-destroyed mesh. In this example, it is the unbroken barrel.

2. Name the non-destroyed mesh **main**. It will act as the alive geometry for the entity within CryENGINE.

3. At this point, you can use various methods within 3ds Max to break up an object. For this example, you can simply cut out the shape using the cut tool within 3ds Max.

4. First, create the destroyed geometry that will replace the original geometry when the object is destroyed and name this object **remain**.

    The **remain** model will be used as the permanent, post-destruction submodel, which replaces **main** when the destroyable object's entity state changes from alive to dead. You could also add a new, destroyed submaterial and assign it to this mesh as a destroyed texture may appear drastically different.

    If no node is named **remain**, then all the pieces other than main will be destruction pieces, which are physically dynamic.

5. Create different and relatively realistically broken pieces, which will be spawned as the destroyable object is destroyed within the CryENIGNE. Name them **broken_piece_1** and **broken_piece_2**, as seen in the following screenshot. If you want to create more pieces, you can simply increment the numbers to **broken_piece_3** and so on, depending on how many unique pieces you want created.

6. Create a physics proxy for each one of these pieces.

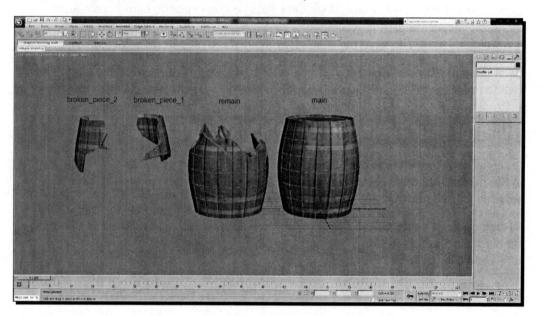

7. Before exporting the **main** object, move all the objects to the origin so that they are intersecting each other.

8. Set the **Pivot** orientation, if not already set, in world coordinates, to 0,0,0 for all the pieces.

9. Link all the objects to a 3ds Max **Helper** named **wooden_barrel_breakable**, as seen in the following screenshot:

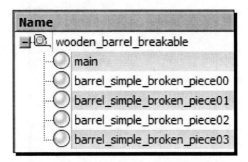

10. Uncheck the **Merge All Nodes** option and click on **Export Nodes**, as seen in the following screenshot:

 The CGF must be exported, with the **Merge All Nodes** checkbox deselected, to produce multipiece geometry.

11. Now, we can place the object as a destroyable entity found under the **Physics** subfolder of the **Entity** browser in the **RollupBar** tab, as seen in the following screenshot:

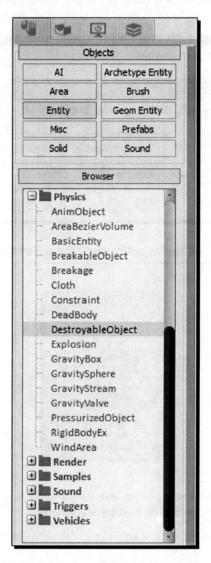

12. Set the parameters for the **DestroyableObject** as follows:

- ❏ Set **MaxHealth** to a relatively low value of **200**
- ❏ Set the **Mass** to **50**
- ❏ Finally, set **Invulnerable** to **False** by deselecting the checkbox, as seen in the following screenshot:

⊞	Breakage		
⊞	DamageMultipliers		
⊞	Explosion		
⊟	Health		
?	Invulnerable	☐ False	
n	MaxHealth	200	
?	OnlyEnemyFire	☑ True	
⊞	Interest		
⊟	Physics		
?	ActivateOnDamage	☐ False	
?	CanBreakOthers	☐ False	
n	Density	-1	
n	Mass	50	
?	PushableByPlayers	☑ True	
?	RigidBody	☑ True	
?	RigidBodyActive	☑ True	
?	RigidBodyAfterDeal	☑ True	
☐	MP		
☐	Simulation		
⊞	Sounds		
⊞	Vulnerability		

13. Switch to game mode, and shoot or otherwise damage the object.

Note that, when the object is destroyed, the pieces spawn in the position in which they were placed in the CGF, relative to the original model, and can be physically simulated as seen in the following screenshot:

What just happened?

You can use this destructible object for many different functions now as it has two different physical states, an **alive state** or a **dead state**. In the alive state, the object acts precisely like you'd expect a normal physical entity to react. It can be set up to be a rigid body or static physical entity. Some fun examples are cliffs, platforms that the character might walk on, bridges, buildings, and so on.

After taking more damage than the specified **Maxhealth**, the entity will go into the dead state. When going into the dead state, a destroyable object entity can optionally generate a physical explosion and apply area damage to the surrounding entities. It can spawn a particle effect, and finally replace the original geometry of the entity with either the destroyed geometry and/or prebroken pieces of the original geometry. When the object breaks due to a hit from a projectile, this hit impulse is applied to the pieces, in addition to any explosion impulse that occurs on the entity.

Have a go hero - use some of the other breakability types

There are a few different types of destructibility available in the CryENGINE. Try using some of the other types of destructible objects available.

Specifying physics and render dynamics with user defined properties

Similar to static and simple objects, some parameters can be added to the individual objects in a destroyable object asset. Try adding some of the following **User Defined Properties** to the pieces from the preceding example:

1. **generic** = **count**: This causes the piece to be spawned multiple times in random locations, throughout the original model. The count specifies how many times it has been spawned. There can be multiple, generic pieces.

2. **sizevar** = **var**: For generic pieces, this randomizes the size of each piece from a scale of `1-var` to `1+var`.

3. **entity**: If this is set, the piece is spawned as a persistent entity. Otherwise, it is spawned as a particle.

4. **density** (density or =mass) = **mass**: This overrides either the density or the mass of the piece. Otherwise, it uses the same density as the whole object.

Breaking two-dimensional assets

Using 2D, breakable objects is a useful technique for level objects, such as glass, ice, wood, or walls, which typically don't have a lot of volume or thickness. The technique works very well with thin and mostly flat mesh objects.

Two-dimensional breakables are controlled through the surface type of an object set in its `.mtl` file.

Some surface types have been specifically set up for two-dimensional breakage already within the CryENGINE Free SDK. Some of these are **mat_glass, mat_glass_ breakable_safetyglass_large,**and **mat_glass_breakable_thin_large**. Some rules for objects using these surface types are as follows:

- ◆ The object must be seven times thinner, in the direction of breaking, than the length of the other two axes.
- ◆ Each triangle on the object cannot exceed a 15 degrees deflection between them, so keeping these meshes flat is the best practice.

  For example, this type of breakability within the CryENGINE can be seen in the following screenshot:

Designing breakables with constraints

Breakable objects are also sometimes referred to as **jointed breakables**. These are structures that are built of separate meshes being held together by virtual joints; rather than having submodels spawn on destruction, all the pieces are already rendered.

You can create these within 3ds Max or, alternatively, use a very useful CryENGINE entity called a **constraint**.

A constraint can be used to hold two physical objects together. The parts can then be individually disjointed by applying physical force greater than the joint limits, by using objects such as a gun, or by player interactions such as explosions and so on.

Some good examples of breakable objects are road signs, wooden fences, or a wooden shack. All these assets are made of parts that are assembled as they appear in the real world, as seen in the following screenshot:

 For furniture or anything that doesn't require a base attached to the ground that remains after it's broken, it is better to use a **rigidbodyEx** or **basicentity**. If you need the remaining part to stay static, then it is better to use a breakable object and specify the mass of the part as 0. If this isn't done, the engine will determine at random which part remains as the static object.

Pop quiz - creating assets for your games

1. What file format is mostly used for static assets?

   - ❑ `.chr`
   - ❑ `.cga`
   - ❑ `.cgf`
   - ❑ `.cpp`

2. For creating textures for the CryENGINE game engine, what plugin and tool must be installed when using Adobe Photoshop?

   - ❑ CryTIF plugin and extension
   - ❑ Max scripts
   - ❑ Polybump tool
   - ❑ `.mel` scripts

3. What entity is best used when creating a destructible asset within the editor?

   ❑ **BasicEntity**
   ❑ **RigidBoxyEx**
   ❑ Destroyable object
   ❑ Breakable object

Using character assets

A character is a combination of geometry data that is attached to a predefined skeletal hierarchy. Examples include human bodies, aquatic animals, aliens, horses, and ropes. In the following examples, we will be dealing with humans, but keep in mind that most of these concepts can be applied to other types of animated assets as well.

Animated characters are integral to any game. Whenever you want to have realistic-looking movement, you need to be able to skin the asset's mesh to a skeleton. Once the mesh has been skinned, it can be exported to engine as a `.chr`. There is also a second format used mostly in vehicles or rigid body assets called `.cga`.

Following the character creation pipeline

There are four important steps involved in preparing and animating your character from CryENGINE 3:

1. Create a character and export a `.chr` file.
2. Enter the character's information into the `.cba` file.
3. Animate the character and export a `.caf` file.
4. Add the exported `.caf` file to the character `.chrparams` file.

We will follow this workflow over the next few examples.

Creating your own characters

When creating **character assets** for CryENGINE, they are typically saved to two or even three separate scene or `.max` files:

1. The first file contains the main character.
2. The second file contains the first **LOD** or **level of detail**, explained further below, of the character as well as the ragdoll physics mesh.
3. The third file is optional because it usually contains just the head of the character. The head is separated as it makes it easier to edit and animate independently from the rest of the character.

Before we begin, some important things to note about the geometry used for the characters for CryENGINE are:

- The characters must be facing forward on the Y+ axis in 3ds Max
- The skinned geometry must have no transformations applied, and its pivot should be set to origin or 0, 0, 0

As there are many tutorials available online and elsewhere for character modeling and texturing, we will not go into depth on the actual process of modeling the character. Rather, we will learn to manipulate the example SDK character and explore how we can use this to create our own characters and animations.

Time for action - creating your own skinned character

In this example, we will create our own skinned character asset that we will rig to the default skeleton. We will then export and test this within the Sandbox **Character Editor**.

1. Locate the `.max` file named **SDK_Agent.max** stored under `objects\Characters\ agent\` in the downloaded example files.

2. Open the scene.

The assembly on the left-hand side of the following screenshot is the **Live Deforming Skeleton**. It is, at its core, a 3ds Max **Biped system** with some extensions added. The deforming skeleton is the typical starting point for all characters as it is responsible for many tasks. Let's see some of its tasks:

- ❏ It deforms the render meshes of the character based on the skinning information.
- ❏ The actual geometry of the bones in this skeleton will be used for the hit detection and physics for an active or alive character.
- ❏ Materials applied to the deforming skeleton are also used for hit detection, and can be used to apply physical impulses or to read where the character has been hit.

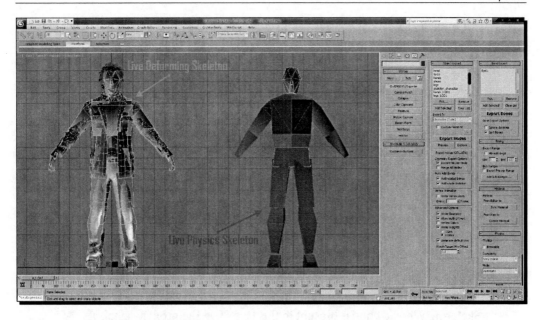

3. Open the **Select By Name** list in 3ds Max by pressing the shortcut *H* or clicking on the **Select By Name** icon.

All the bones, otherwise known as nodes, that are parented/linked to the object **Bip01**, together comprise the **Live Deforming Skeleton**.

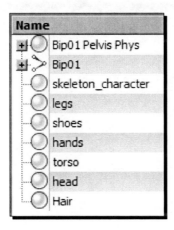

For human characters, it is easiest if you retain the same hierarchy as shown in the example scene. New bones can be added, but they should not interfere with the 3ds Max Biped's default hierarchy, as there are specific nodes used for automatic foot plant and ground alignment.

4. At this point, if you are working on a custom character, you will want to import your custom geometry into the **SDK_Agent.max** scene.

To achieve high-fidelity animations, current generation games sometimes include several hundreds of individual animations, so to get a character in the game quickly, it is best to use the pre-built example skeleton and structure.

The second skeleton within the **SDK_Agent.max** scene is the **Live Physics Skeleton**, which is also called the **Live Phys Skeleton**.

The best way to understand the **Live Phys Skeleton** is to think about it in terms of a set of constraints or movement restrictions to each bone in the **Live Deforming Skeleton**. When a bone is present in this **Live Phys Skeleton**, it signals its counterpart in the **Live Deforming Skeleton** that it should be physical in the world when the character is alive. The **Live Phys Skeleton** for your character also stores physical properties for its counterpart, which is stored in the **Live Phys Skeleton** bones' **IK** properties, as seen in the following screenshot:

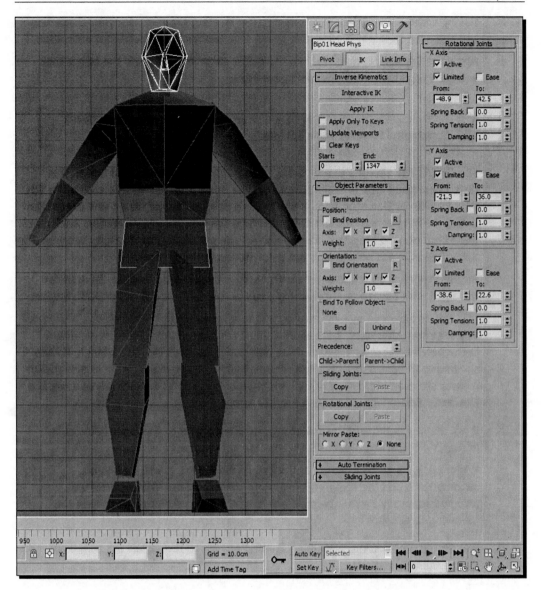

Now that we understand the function of both the skeletons in the **SDK_Agent.max** max file, we will discuss the setup of different portions of the character.

Whenever you are modeling humans for animation, the model should match the joints in the skeleton. For example, the knee geometry lines up with the joint between the calf and thigh bones of the skeleton.

5. Having created, imported, or decided to use existing geometry for your character, you will have to skin this geometry to the **Live Deforming Skeleton** for animation.

6. Apply the **CrySkin** Modifier to your character mesh and then add the bones that you wish will affect the character's geometry.

 The **CrySkin** Modifier will give you an accurate preview of the CryENGINE's **Spherical Skinning** within 3ds Max.

The CryENGINE allows a single vertex to be deformed by a max of 4 bones. It is thus a very good idea to make sure to set the **Bone Affect Limit** to 4 within the 3ds Max **CrySkin** or Skin Modifiers. If you set this amount higher than 4 and export the .chr, the Resource compiler tries to average the weights of this vertices back to a bone limit of 4, so keep this in mind should you get inconsistent results between the deformation in 3ds Max versus the deformation in the CryENGINE.

Before exporting your character mesh, there is a technique that can be used for making it very easy to modify certain parts of the character directly within engine.

This can be achieved by exporting a character containing only a skeleton, also know as a **skeleton_character**. It is simply a single triangle usually placed somewhere in the pelvis and set to use a no draw material to be invisible. This triangle is then skinned to the entire live skeleton. This will allow you to export what is essentially a blank skeleton to the CryENGINE, onto which you can add attachments using the **Character Editor** within Sandbox's editor application.

7. If not already done, add the **skeleton_character** object to the **Export Nodes** list in the CryENGINE exporter.

When adding a skinned object to the **Export Nodes** list, it will, by default, automatically add the required skeleton to the export list. The exporter will also automatically add all the child bones of the listed skeleton, as seen in the following screenshot.

8. You should now add the remaining skinned objects to the export list, and finally export them to engine!

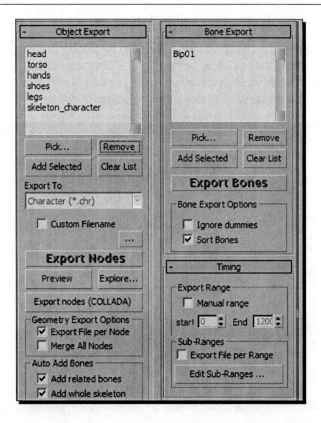

9. For this example, make sure to add the **shirt** mesh to the export list.

10. Click on the **Export Nodes** button.

   As we want to assemble our character into a single, manageable file, we can now create a `.cdf` or **Character Definition File** using the **Character Editor**.

11. Open Sandbox and then open the **Character Editor** by clicking on **View | Open View Pane | Character Editor**.

12. Using **File | Open** in the **Character Editor**, you can now open the exported `.chr` files.

13. First, open the **skeleton_character.chr** exported earlier.

You can preview the **Live Deforming Skeleton** by setting the **ShowSkeleton** property to **True**, in the **Debug Options** of the **Character Editor**. You can also preview the **Live Phys Skeleton** by enabling the **Display Physics** property in the debug options, as seen in the following screenshot:

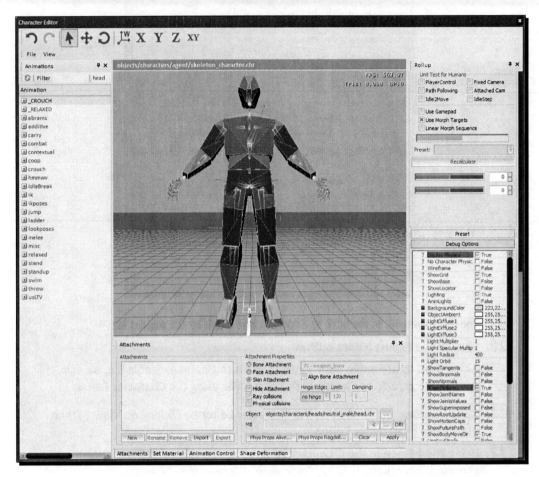

14. In the **Attachment Properties** section, select **Skin Attachment** as seen in the previous screenshot.

15. Under the **Attachments** window, click on **New**. Name the new attachment **shirt**.

16. Select the browse (**...**) button beside the **Object** string, and browse to the **shirt.chr** file we exported earlier.

17. Leave the material field (**Mtl**) blank for now, because it takes the default material applied to the **Attachments** model. To apply attachments on the character, click on **Apply**.

You will see that the shirt is now attached to the skeleton, and if an animation is played by selecting an animation in the **Animation** list, the **shirt** reacts to the parent skeleton appropriately.

18. Add the remaining pieces of the character we exported earlier.

Having now assembled this character, we need to save it for later use in our levels or games.

19. To do this, navigate to **File | Save as** and save the file as a **.cdf**. You can name it as you see fit. For this example, I am saving it as **mycustom_character.cdf**.

This character can now be used later as many different animated assets within your games. It can be used as the player model, as AI's friendly and enemy characters, and also for animated cinematics!

What just happened?

Characters allow for animation and locomotion on characters, and so being able to create working and realistic characters is imperative when creating a game. It can be used as the player's representative model, in the game, in cut scenes, and finally as artificial intelligence.

The **Attachment** system is one of the principle reasons behind the **Character Editor**. Current generation games can have more than 20 to 30 different character models, and so using attachments is one way to avoid repeatedly displaying the same character to the player over and over again. The **Attachment** system also allows designers and artists to give the character a unique look in a very intuitive and easy way.

Creating a character LOD (Level of Detail)

Character LODs (Level of Detail) are meshes with lower polygonal resolution, which will automatically be faded in between based on the character's distance from the camera in the game engine.

To create LODs, you must copy the original character mesh and then reduce its triangle count, which can done manually or for the sake of speed; you can use automated modifiers in 3ds Max, such as **Multires**.

Once the polygon count has been lowered, the fastest way to skin the LOD similarly to the main character is to use the **Skin Wrap** Modifier in 3ds Max and use the original skinned mesh as the target. You can then convert this **Skin Wrap** Modifier to a regular **Skin** Modifier and then export the newly created LOD.

LOD object names must follow the _LODn naming convention, where n is the number of the LOD. A number of LOD objects have already been created for this example's character, as seen in the following screenshot:

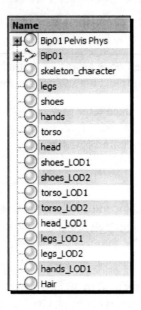

Bone attachments

When using the **Character Editor** in Sandbox, you can add other types of attachments to the characters other than skin attachments, as seen in the following screenshot:

One of these is called a **Bone Attachment**. Adding a **Bone Attachment** is a way to have any asset (.cgf, .cga, and .chr) constrained to a single bone within your character. This can be useful for rigid body attachments such as weapons and even props such as sunglasses or helmets. When applying a **Bone Attachment**, you may sometimes have to use the **Align Bone Attachment** checkbox. When set, it aligns the pivot of the asset with the bone. In other words, the rotation of the joint and the rotation of the attachment will remain identical throughout all animations played on the skeleton.

Creating animations for your character

Characters wouldn't be very interesting without animations! In this example, we will cover the task of making a relatively basic animation for a skeleton and exporting that animation for playback later in Sandbox.

Time for action - creating animation for a skinned character

Having learned in the previous example how to create, export, and skeleton a character, we will now learn the basics of animating it. For this example, you can use your own custom character created in the previous example or open the example character provided.

1. Open the file named `Objects\Characters\agent\SDK_Agent.max`.

2. Now, open the `animations.cba` file with any text editor, for example Notepad. You will find this file under the `game/animations` folder.

    In the `animations.cba` file, each entry is a character animated within the Free SDK. You will notice that developer comments already exist to explain each of the parameters.

    When creating a custom character, it is common practice to copy the definition for a similar character and set the `Model File path`, `Animation Path` and `Database path` to that of your own skeleton.

3. Make an entry in the `animations.cba` file (as seen in the example), paying special attention to the `Model`, `Animation Path` and `Database Path` values:

    ```
    <AnimationDefinition>
      <!--the reference model-->
      <Model File="/../Objects/Characters/agent/skeleton_character.
    chr"/>
      <!--the path with ALL animation we can use on this model-->
      <Animation Path="human_male"/>
      <!--for all animations use compression level 1-->
      <COMPRESSION value="2"/>
      <RotEpsilon value="0.0000001" />
      <PosEpsilon value="0.0000001" />
      <Database Path="human_male/human_male.dba"/>
      <!--for all animations need to detect footplants-->
      <FOOTPLANTS value="NO"/>
      <!--we apply the Locomotion_Locator modification just on BIP-
    files. Aliens, vehicles and weapons don't need it. -->
      <LOCOMOTION_LOCATOR value="YES"/>
      <!--we apply different modifications to the weapons . Human
    and Aliens don't need it. -->
      <!--a list of animation that need special handling-->
    ```

```
      <SpecialAnimsList>

        <!-- AIMPOSES COMMON -->
        <Animation APath="Aim" footplants="NO" compression="0"
autocompression="0" SkipSaveToDatabase="1" />
        <Animation APath="vehicle" footplants="NO"/>

      </SpecialAnimsList>
    </AnimationDefinition>
```

In the previous code snippet, I have left the developer comments intact; however, I have made the adjustments to use the character created in the previous example.

Having now added this character to the .cba, we can begin animating.

Let's now create a simple, arm-waving animation that will take us through the basics of exporting skeletal animation.

 Make sure the biped is not in figure mode as you will not be able to keyframe any bones otherwise.

As this is a 3ds Max Biped, you could now apply motion capture data to the **Live Deforming Skeleton**. You can find such data online or in the example files provided on http://crydev.net. For now, we will assume that such data is not available for the animation we require.

4. Set the animation mode in 3ds Max to **Auto Key** and move the **Bip01 R Hand** bone into a wave position, as seen in the following screenshot. You will notice, once you move the bone, that a **keyframe** is automatically created.

5. You may have to rotate the upper and lower arm to get a more realistic pose.

6. Once you are happy with the position, move the time slider to the tenth frame and set the arm to a different pose.

   As we want this animation to loop, we must set the last keyframe of our animation to the same position as the first keyframe.

7. This can be done by selecting all the bones that have been keyframed, shift-clicking on the first keyframe in the time line, and then dragging the newly copied keyframe to the final frame.

   For this example, copy the first keyframe to the twentieth frame.

8. Since we will only be exporting a single animation, we can set the time configuration in 3ds Max to only show frames from 0 to 20.

[The exporter will automatically export the currently displayed frames in the animation time line, if not set otherwise.]

9. To export the animation, open the CryENGINE exporter in the **Tools** tab and ensure that the **skeleton_character** has been added to the export nodes list, as seen in the following screenshot.

As discussed earlier, this will automatically add the parent node of the skeleton to the export bones list.

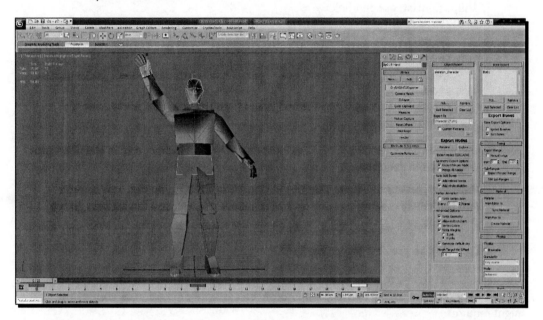

10. Clicking on the **Export Bones** button will open the save dialog, which will allow you to save the animation as a `.caf` file.

11. Save our waving animation under the defined path in the **animations.cba** for your particular character. In this case, save it as `custom_wave.caf` under the `Animations/human_male` folder.

There is one final step that we must complete before being able to view our character animation in Sandbox's character editor.

We must add this new animation to the characters parameter file or `.chrparams`.

12. For this example, using a text editor, open the skeleton_character's `.chrparams` file found under `Game\objects\Characters\Agent\skeleton_character.chrparams`.

13. Locate the **AnimationList** entry:

```
<AnimationList>
    <Animation name="$AnimEventDatabase" path="animations\human_male\events.animevents"/>
    <Animation name="$Include" path="animations\human_male\male.chrparams"/>
</AnimationList>
```

14. Insert a new entry for our animation and a comment preceding it in the **AnimationList**, as seen below:

```
<AnimationList>
    <Animation name="$AnimEventDatabase" path="animations\human_male\events.animevents"/>
    <Animation name="$Include" path="animations\human_male\male.chrparams"/>
    <Animation name="mycustom_wave" path="custom_wave.caf"/>
</AnimationList>
```

15. Open the character `Objects/Characters/Agent/Agent.cdf` in the **Character Editor** within Sandbox.

Note that, on the left-hand side of the **Character Editor**, you can now browse into the newly created `mycustom` folder, where you will see the **custom_wave** animation.

16. Click on it to preview the animation.

Congratulations! You have created and exported your own animation to the CryENGINE. You can now start animating more complex or more extreme animation as your game might require.

What just happened?

When a character is loaded by the engine, it checks for a `.chrparams` file that defines a list of valid animations and other properties, such as **IK** limits, for the particular character. These animations then become accessible through code, cut scenes, and the character editor to be played back.

In this example, we dealt with the `.caf` animation data that is created by exporting the animation range from 3ds Max. Upon export, the resource compiler is invoked and a certain amount of compression and optimization is applied to the animation to make it ready for real-time playback.

.chrparams wildcard mapping

Assigning each animation definition in the `.chrparams` file, line by line, can take an unacceptable amount of time and lead to very big `.chrparams` files.

It is only necessary if the in-game name that is supposed to be assigned to the animation is substantially different than the filename of the `.caf`.

Wildcard Mapping uses the asterisk (*) to represent the filename. Using the asterisk in the ingame name will replace it with the part of the actual filename that is wildcarded.

For example:

```
<Animation name="Custom_*" path="custom_wave_*.caf"/>
```

This code line will load all the animations from the folder `Custom` that start with the words `custom_wave` and have the extension `.caf`.

Wildcard Mapping can even be used on an entire folder. It requires, however, that these folders are kept clean of old and unused assets to not waste memory.

One important advantage of using wildcards is that, once a folder is mapped, new animations can be quickly added to that folder without the need to add an animation definition in the `.chrparams` file each time.

Have a go hero - using the animobject entity for animation playback

A useful entity for testing animations is the **animobject** entity found under **Entities | Physics | animobject** of the entity section in the **RollupBar** tab.

Once placed in a level, you can assign a model, and then enter the string of the in game animation name, as seen in the following screenshot:

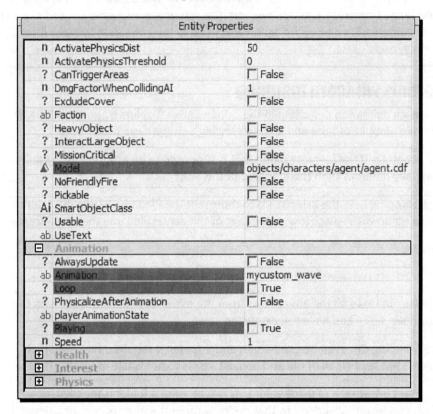

A good technique is to add this **animobject** to a Flow Graph and assign the animation to it using the **Animation:PlayAnimation** flow graph node.

Creating animation for rigid body assets

Sometimes it is not required to skin the geometry to bones for deformation, but rather animating the nodes' movement and rotation directly within 3ds Max might be preferred. Animated hard body geometry data only supports directly linked objects and does not support skeletal-based animation. Some good examples of Rigid Body animation could be a rotating radar dish, the precomputed destruction of a building, or other such assets.

It is composed of two file types:

- ◆ `.cga` (Crytek Geometry Animation)
- ◆ `.anm` (**Additonal Animation**)

Time for action - creating animation using rigid body data

Let's create some of our own `.anm` files that will animate a series of nodes we will create in 3ds max:

1. In 3ds Max, create two simple sphere primitives in the scene.

2. Convert the primitives to an editable poly by right-clicking on the object and selecting the function **Convert To Editable Poly**.

3. As we will be exporting a `.anm` file for a `.cga` geometry, we must convert all the objects that will be animated to the **Tension Continuity and Bias controller** or **TCB**.

4. Change the controller types for **Position** and **Rotation** to **TCB** under the **3ds Motion Tab**.

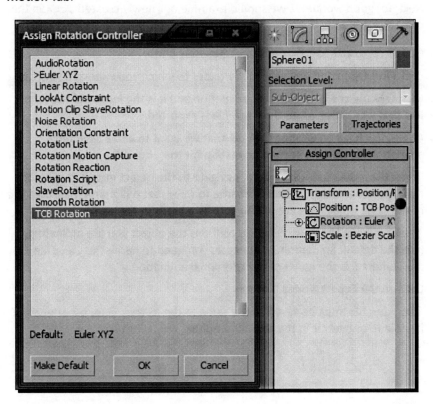

5. Now, create a very simple animation for the objects in the scene (bouncing the spheres is a simple animation to make).

6. Next, we must export the geometry before exporting the animation for it.

7. Select all the objects and add them to the **Object Export** list by clicking on **Add Selected**.

8. For this example, make sure **Export File Per Node** is set to false, because we would like to have both the geometric objects in a single `.cga` file.

9. Next, make sure that the CGA file type is selected in the **Export To** drop-down box.

10. Save the max file as `mycustom_bouncing_spheres.max` under the `game/objects/bouncingspheres` folder.

11. Click the **Export Nodes** button.

   This will export the objects to the same folder in which the source file is located.

   The file will assume the source file's name unless you check **Custom Filename**. This will allow you to type in a unique name.

   Next, for good workflow, we should examine our newly created `.cga` in the character editor.

12. Open CryENGINE Sandbox and the **Character Editor**.

13. Click **File| Open** and navigate to the folder to which you exported your `.cga` file.

14. Each CGA file contains a default animation and it is the length of the time line that was active when the `.cga` file is exported.

15. As we now have an existing CGA file that we want to add a selectable animation to, create a second animation for the `.cga` file.

16. When the animation is complete, navigate to the object export section of the exporter and set **Custom Filename** to `true`; set a filename that uses the name of the `.cga` object you are adding it to as a prefix in the name.

17. As an example, the `test.cga` file contains the object you are animating, plus the default animation. In our case, you need to name the `.anm` file `test_[n].anm`, where n is the name of the additional animation.

18. Click on the **Export Nodes** button.

19. The `.anm` file must be saved to the same folder as the `.cga`, otherwise you will not be able to preview it in the character editor.

What just happened?

.anm files are the simplest animation that you can export to the CryENGINE. They do not require as much processing power as a skinned mesh and can be animated fairly easily. These types of animations can be used on a variety of environmental objects, which require some moving parts. The .anm file format is also the principal animation format for any vehicle animation.

Have a go hero - using pre-baked physics with .cga objects

To pre-bake physical destruction, you can use .cga objects with baked .anm animations.

This can be very useful for the complex destruction of large objects.

The same rules apply when creating pre-baked physics for .cga objects, because all the position and rotation controllers of the objects in CGA need to be set to TCB.

When exporting pre-baked physics animations, select **merge all nodes** in the export options.

Turn off all bone export options, but tell the exporter to **export every '1' frames**.

Select one object that is not moving and parent all the other pieces to it. This object can be the one you set to **unyielding**. In buildings, use the foundation.

The current animation will show up as **Default** in the CGA you export; no .chrparams file is needed to play it.

Open your CGA in the **Character Editor** and play the animation labeled **Default**; you should see your animation play here.

 When using the pre-baked .cga in the game environment, it must be placed as an **animobject**.

There are two important properties available when using pre-baked .cga; the first is that **ActivatePhysicsThreshold** is a fraction of levels gravity, so a heavier piece will be harder to activate, since the gravity force that acts on it is stronger. The second is the **mass**. Mass is set as the overall value for the entire CGA; for instance, a **Mass** of 100 on a CGA with 100 pieces would yield 1kg per piece.

Summary

In this chapter, we learned a lot about creating assets for the CryENGINE 3. This opens up a world of possibilities allowing you to create any object you can imagine and importing that into your levels. These examples are just scratching the surface of how you can use these features. Experimentation is highly encouraged!

We can now experiment with materials and textures, and apply them to our own models. We also know how to adjust the physical dynamics of our static, physical, and destructible object. The ability to create simple and some complex assets will be more than enough to create any prototype project. The skills learned within this chapter should give you the ability to create and move any mesh from 3ds Max to the CryENGINE.

Now that we've learned about asset creation, we're ready to explore characters, animation, and cut scenes, which are the topics of the next chapter.

8
Creating Real-time Cutscenes and Cinematic Events

Cinematics and cutscenes are historically non-interactive sequences used by many games to provide a back story. With the advent of stronger hardware and more sophisticated technology in recent years, cinematics and cutscenes have become far more interactive and don't necessarily need to take control away from the player, though they are still useful to frame specific and important events.

In this chapter, we will use the cinematic and cutscene system known as **Track View** within CryENGINE, to create real-time scripted sequences and later on to render these sequences to video.

In this chapter, we will be:

- Creating a new Track View sequence
- Learning how to animate cameras in Track View
- Triggering a sequence using Flow Graph scripting
- Animating entities in Track View
- Playing animations on entities in Track View
- Using Console Variables in Track View
- Using Track Events to send triggers to Flow Graph
- Capturing video from CryENGINE 3

Let's get started.

Discovering the Track View editor

The **Track View editor**, shown in the next screenshot, is the embedded Sandbox cutscene creation tool for making interactive, film-like sequences with time line dependent key-frame control over objects and events in CryENGINE 3. For those already familiar with the CryENGINE 2 Track View system, you will see that it is quite similar; although, improvements have been made as tools such as a Curve Editor and director tracks can now be used for fine-tuning control on, what used to be, hard-to-manage, complex sequences.

Using Track View, creating cinematic cutscenes and scripted events are both possible, which allow you to sequence objects, animations, and sounds in a scene that can be triggered during a game and played either as a detached cutscene from the third-person perspective, or from the first-person perspective of the player as he plays the game.

Sequences created with Track View can be triggered in a game with a specific Flow Graph node, which will be covered in a later example in this chapter. We will also see that we can set a variety of different properties to enable our Track View sequences to range from passive, in-game scenarios to fully uncoupled cutscenes.

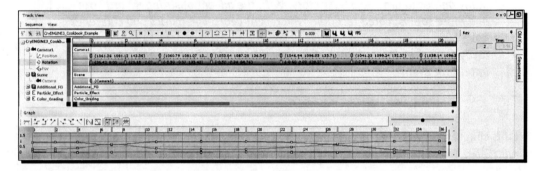

This system and its application will be familiar to anyone who has used animation software such as 3ds Max, but this guide will also help those unfamiliar with cutscene editors to start creating simple scenes for your levels.

Creating a new Track View sequence

Creating Track View sequences is very similar to creating animation within other key frame animation DCC tools, such as 3ds Max and Maya. However, you do not have to have any previous animation experience to complete this chapter.

This example with thus familiarize you with the Track View editor as well as take you through some of the important interface controls.

Time for action – creating a new sequence

Whenever you are adding cutscenes or Track View sequences to a level, you should always make a new layer to add your objects onto. This will allow you to control all these objects independently of the level and hide or show them when needed.

1. Open Sandbox and then open the Forest sample level.

[When a new track sequence is added, an object is placed onto whatever layer is active when the new Track View sequence is created.]

2. Add a layer named **Cinematic**.

3. Once the layer is added, ensure that it is the active layer by checking that it is highlighted.

4. To create a Track View sequence, open the Track View panel by selecting the menu option **View | Open View Pane | Track View**.

5. Click on the **Add Sequence** icon in the Track View editor to create a new sequence, as shown in the following screenshot:

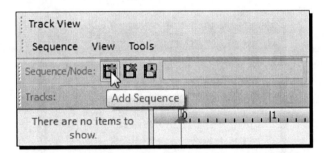

Clicking on the **Add Sequence** icon will present you with the opportunity to name the sequence.

6. Name this sequence `my_first_cutscene`.

When the sequence is added, a new object is placed on the active layer. This object is named a **sequence object** and will store all the information for our Track View sequence.

Now that we have created a new sequence, it's time to adjust some of the fundamental settings for it.

7. Click on the **Edit Sequence** icon.

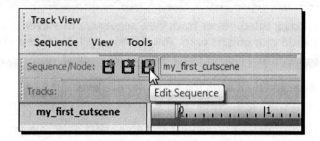

Upon clicking **Edit Sequence**, you will be presented with the properties window, as shown in the next screenshot.

Many of the properties shown in the properties window are self-explanatory.

8. In our case, let's simply adjust the length of the sequence by changing the **EndTime** parameter to 30.

[By default, the Track View editor's time line will display the time in seconds.]

Now that we have the basics set up for this sequence, let's add some additional tracks.

The first track that we will add is a director node.

The **director node** allows us to activate different cameras throughout the course of the Track View sequence, allowing a simple form of camera cutting. In our example, we will only use a single camera, but it is good practice to always add a director node to your sequences.

9. To add the director node, right-click in the empty whitespace within the **Tracks** window on the left-hand side of the **Track View** editor. You will see a large dialog with many different track additions that you can make.

10. Select **Add Director(Scene) Node**, as shown in the following screenshot:

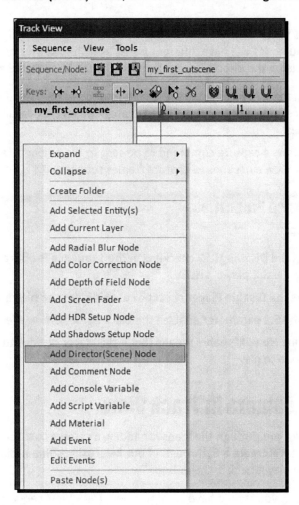

We will use this director node to activate a different camera in the next example.

What just happened?

The sequence we just added is the cutscene itself. For each sequence, you can add a number of nodes for each object that you use, including the top-level node of the scene itself. To this is what we added the director node. For each node that you have, you can have a number of tracks, depending on what kind of node it is. Each track is measured in seconds and has points marked on it to indicate where a key frame or event starts.

Have a go hero – using Sequence Properties and director node tracks

Adding a track to any node can be done by right-clicking on the node and selecting an available track.

Adding tracks to the director node

Different entities and nodes will have different tracks available, but for now we will try some of the tracks available on the director node. Some of the tracks available are as follows:

- **Console**: Allows a key frame to contain information to be passed to the engine's console. An example of this could be to change the level of detail settings to high, for cutscenes.

- **Capture**: Allows a capture command to be sent to the engine to allow for the output of the Track View cutscenes to capture frames sequentially.

Adjusting Sequence Properties

Follow the given steps:

1. Try enabling the **Disable HUD** checkbox in the **Sequence Properties** window, which disables the default player's HUD.

2. Try selecting the **Disable Player** checkbox as this hides the player during the scene.

3. Enabling the **16:9** parameter enables the black bar letterbox effect.

4. Finally, setting **Non-Skippable** means that if the player decides to skip the scene, it will continue to play.

Animating a camera in Track View

This example will take you through the steps for adding a camera to a Track View sequence and animating it. We will create a flythrough of our level using some basic animation techniques and then play it back in the editor.

To follow this example, you should have created a new Track View sequence with a director track already added, as shown in the previous example.

Time for action – animating a camera

Having added a new Track View sequence and director node, we need some objects to be added to this sequence for us to direct. In this example, we will animate a camera.

1. First, navigate to the **Misc** section in the Rollup Bar, and click-and-drag a **Camera** entity into the level. This will create a wireframe preview of the camera showing its direction and **Field Of View** (**FOV**). You can move the camera object in your game world, as you would any other entity, using the **Move** and **Rotate** tools.

2. Rename the newly created camera to cinematic_camera1. At this point, you should adjust your view to be able to quickly preview the view from the actual camera.

For this example, we will only animate the camera movement from the camera's viewpoint and not from the perspective view.

3. To change your active view to cinematic_camera1, right-click on the top bar in the viewport.

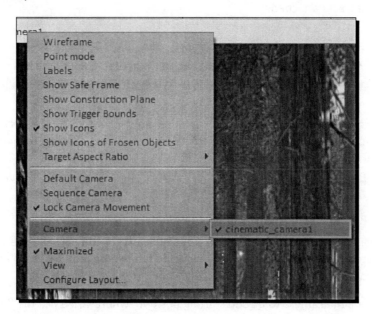

4. Reopen the dialog and also deactivate **Lock Camera Movement**. This will allow us to control the movement of the camera from its own perspective.

5. Back in the Track View editor, let's now add this camera to the sequence.

6. To add any entity to a Track View sequence, simply select the entity in the editor, in our case the `cinematic_camera1` entity, and then add it to the Track View sequence using the **Add Selected Node** icon.

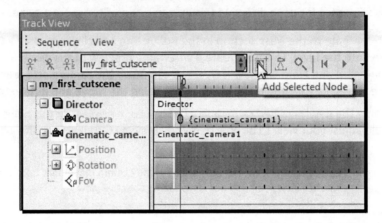

You will notice that when the camera is added to the sequence, it already has some default tracks attached.

 A camera node can have only the default tracks of FOV, Position, and Rotation, plus an events track, but animated objects and characters can have many more.

7. Having unlocked the camera movement, we must now click on the **Record** icon in Track View to automatically key frame any movement changes to an object in the editor.

8. Select the camera in the editor; you can do this quickly by double-clicking on the entity in Track View.

9. Click **Record** and move the camera to its initial starting position.

   You can move the camera in the exact same way that you navigate the viewport in Sandbox. It does, however, allow us to do interesting motions, such as banking and rotating the camera.

10. Navigate the camera to a good starting position, where you'd like the flythrough of the environment to begin.

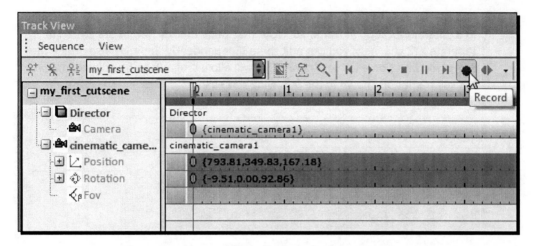

Note that the key frames are added for **Position** and **Rotation** automatically, while the **Record** icon is active.

 You can also animate FOV, which is helpful for zooming in on an object quickly.

11. Next, move the active time slider to **10** seconds.

12. Keeping in mind that the animation will be interpolated between two key frames, make another key frame at **10** seconds by moving the camera to a different position.

At this new position, let's add some roll to the camera.

13. With the camera selected, click on the rotate tool, and then in the type-in dialogs at the bottom of the viewport, type in a value in the **Y** parameter.

14. The higher the value, the more the camera will roll. Use negative values to roll in the opposite direction, as shown in the following screenshot:

15. Another effective way of adding variations to the movement is by using the Curve Editor. The Curve Editor can be accessed through the **View** section of the Track View editor.

16. Change the view to the Curve Editor, and select-and-drag one of the axis key frames to a different location at frame **10**. Note that since the key frames are stored in seperate XYZ channels, you can edit them independently. You may also notice the Bezier modifiers on each key frame. This will allow tangents to be adjusted between the key frames, as shown in the following screenshot:

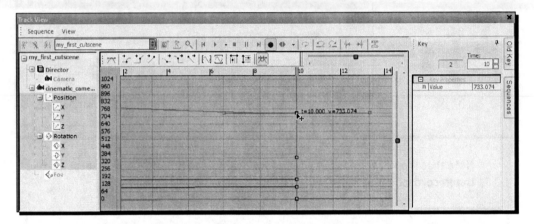

17. Change the view back to the Dope Sheet and scrub the time slider from frame **10** to frame **0** and back. Notice that you are instantly able to preview the animation!

18. Drag the time slider to **20** seconds, and create a new position for the camera in a forward direction from the last key frame. For this example, this will be the final key frame for the camera.

Because we are animating a flythrough, you can of course create as many key frames as you like by dragging the time slider forward and moving the camera to a new position for as long as you want your sequence to last.

For this example, our sequence is only three key frames long.

19. You can now preview the entire sequence by clicking on the **Play** icon.

Having created key frames at **0**, **10**, and **20** seconds, you may find that the camera movement is either too fast or too slow. There are two ways to adjust this. The first way is the most accurate, which is to select all the key frames at a particular time and bring the time between key frames down by dragging them closer. Alternatively, drag them further apart for longer sequences.

20. To return to the default camera view, in the same dialog used earlier to unlock the camera's movement, click on the **Default Camera** entry.

Make sure to save this sequence as we will re-use it later on in this chapter.

21. Save the `.cry` file as `Forest_sequences.cry`.

What just happened?

The sequence that we have just created can be triggered via different means during game mode for a variety of purposes. A simple flythrough can be used to introduce areas, give the player a unique view of events, and to further the story and narrative. Commonly, it is also used to create gameplay-specific events to occur, such as the movement of certain entities within the game world and so forth.

Have a go hero – doing more with the tools available

We explored some tools in the previous example, which are used to create cutscenes. We did not, however, explore all of them. Let's try to use a few of the different settings available to us.

FOV

The FOV on a camera can be set and animated by changing the value on the **Camera** entity, which will be key-framed while the record is active. Alternatively, you can type in the values to a manually created key frame by double-clicking anywhere on the FOV track. Some good FOV values for cutscenes are usually between 35 and 45, depending on the required shot.

Playback speed

You can adjust the play speed of the Track View editor by clicking on the *pull down icon* beside the **Play** button.

Options available will not translate to in-game triggering of this sequence, and will only be used for previewing in the editor.

Curve Editor

Animators will likely be familiar with a Curve Editor approach to key framing objects within Track View. You can adjust your view to contain both the Curve Editor and the Dope Sheet by selecting both of them from the **View** menu.

There are many Curve Editor tools, most of which are pertaining to the editing of the tangents between key frames.

Triggering a sequence using Flow Graph

Depending on the game or scenario you may be creating, you will likely need different requirements for when and how cutscenes should be triggered. This is catered to nicely for designers because of the cross communication within certain tools and systems of CryENGINE 3.

Time for action – triggering a sequence

In this example, we will use a simple Flow Graph to trigger a cutscene when a player walks into a certain trigger.

You must have a level open that has a previously saved Track View sequence in it.

If you have already completed the *Animating a camera in Track View* and *Creating a new Track View sequence* sections covered earlier in the chapter, then you can use the `my_first_cutscene` sequence to build onto.

1. Click-and-drag a proximity trigger into the level. This can be found under the entities/triggers section in the Rollup Bar.

2. Once you have added the trigger to the level, set the trigger bounds to be big enough to trigger when the player enters it. Good values are as follows:

   ```
   DimX Value="5"
   DimY Value="5"
   DimZ Value="5"
   ```

3. Next, right-click on the proximity trigger and create a Flow Graph on it, as shown in the following screenshot:

4. Name the Flow Graph `cutscene_trigger`. Next, let's create a Flow Graph to handle the triggering logic.

5. Add the proximity trigger itself by right-clicking and selecting **Add Selected Entity** in the Flow Graph.

6. Also add the **Animations:PlaySequence** FlowNode.

7. Connect the **Enter** output of the proximity trigger to the start trigger of the **Animations:PlaySequence** node. Your resulting Flow Graph will look like the following screenshot:

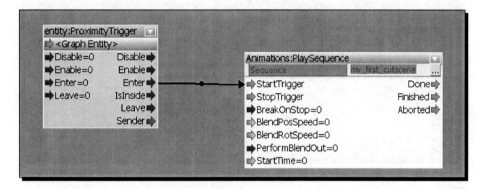

You can now enter the game mode, and whenever you enter the proximity trigger, the sequence defined in the sequence parameters of the **Animations:PlaySequence** FlowNode will be played.

What just happened?

As you have seen now, one of the fastest ways to trigger a sequence is to attach it to a trigger object, such as the proximity trigger, which can be positioned in the level.

By building a Flow Graph that connects the trigger output of the proximity trigger to the start trigger of the **Animations:PlaySequence** Flow Graph node, one can easily activate a sequence by having a player enter the proximity trigger in the game.

Have a go hero – triggering sequences even faster and adjusting the PlaySequence FlowNode

There are other techniques that can be used to trigger sequences quickly. Additionally, there are some useful parameters on the **Animations:PlaySequence** node, which we will touch on now.

Using the Input:Key node to trigger a sequence

Sometimes, for cutscenes, it can be easier to not be forced to enter a trigger every time you wish to run the cutscene. Another useful trigger is the **Input:Key** FlowNode that allows you to press a defined key that will trigger the cutscene. Try to use it in a Flow Graph, as shown in the following screenshot:

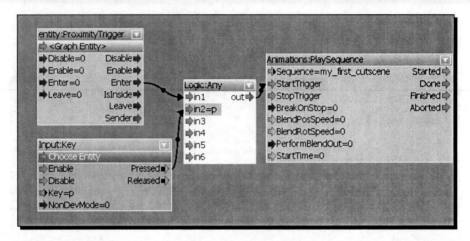

StartTime property

When a sequence is triggered from the **Animations:PlaySequence** node, you can force it to jump to a particular start time. This can be useful if you wish to have multiple, different events stored within a single sequence.

BreakOnStop property

When the sequence is stopped, by default, the time slider will go to the very last frame and trigger the logic that may be stored there. This is typically used because when a scene is skipped, you can still trigger all the logic and positional info on that last frame. Setting **BreakOnStop** to true will overwrite these defaults and cause the logic on the last frame to not trigger.

Animating entities in Track View

The animation of objects and entities in Track View can be as complex or as simple as the animator or designer requires. In this example, we will animate a dead tree falling into water. This will involve animating the tree itself, as well as triggering some particle effects at specific times. The interesting part about this particular example is that this cutscene could be used as a scripted event, one that does not take the control away from the player, or as a cinematic cutscene.

Time for action – animating an entity in Track View

We will focus on setting this example up as a scripted event, as the cinematic process of animating a camera has been touched on already in previous examples.

You should have the `forest.cry` example level open for this example.

You should also have created a new blank sequence with no entities named `my_second_cutscene`.

1. The first step is that we must add some geometry to animate. It is important to remember the difference between brushes and entities.

 Brushes cannot be added to Track View.

2. To allow us to animate the geometry, drag-and-drop **BasicEntity** into the level found under the entities/physics section of the Rollup Bar.

3. Once placed, name **BasicEntity** to `falling_tree_01` and set its model string to `objects/natural/vegetation/rocky_ravine/d_spruce_dead_a.cgf`.

4. Drag **BasicEntity** somewhere near the waterfront, where it might look like it could fall in and allow the player to walk up.

5. Create an initial key frame to set it's original position and then drag the active time slider over to **1** second.

6. Reposition the tree to a fallen pose with the record active, and note the different values being set in the key frame at **1** second for **Position** and **Rotation**.

For the ease of this example, we will only create the two poses, but you can of course add more key frames for better-looking animation.

With this kind of animation, you can rely on the preview timing for collision-type events such as particle effects. The alternative would be to simulate this in the physics engine physically, which could be good but not deterministic enough to be used for reliable in-game play.

Next, let's add two particle effects to this sequence. The first will be the breaking of the tree at the base with a wood splintering effect.

7. Add a particle effect from **DataBase View** under the `particles/breakable_objects/tree_break/small` library to the scene and align it to the base of the tree.

8. Add this particle effect to **Track View** and create a key frame on the **Event** time line for the particle effect. The property on this key frame must be set to **Spawn**. Create this key frame at the beginning of the scene to coincide with the destruction of the tree, as shown in the following screenshot:

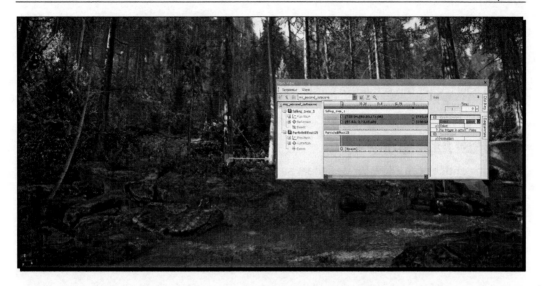

9. Scrub the time line until you find the point where the tree impacts the water.

10. Once you find the first frame that has contact between the water and the tree, place a second particle effect from **Database View** under `particles/water/body_splash/corpse`.

11. Add the **Spawn** key frame for this particle effect just at the contact time between the water and the tree.

12. Play the sequence back to preview the results!

You can now trigger this sequence through the Flow Graph depending on many different events!

What just happened?

Animating entities can allow for designers and animators to control scripted events. This allows a fairly advanced manipulation of a wide variety of entities for these events. One important use of this kind of rudimentary animation is to white box certain cinematic events, which may be polished further later on.

Have a go hero – using other tracks on entities

Try using some of the other tracks available on the entities within Track View.

Entity Visibility track

A track available to most entities is the **Visibility** track. Add this by right-clicking on the entity in the sequence and selecting the **Visibility** track.

When a key frame is created on this track it will change the state of the object to hidden or vice versa. The easiest way to visualize it is to see that when the track is *blue*, the object is seen, when it is not, the object is *hidden*.

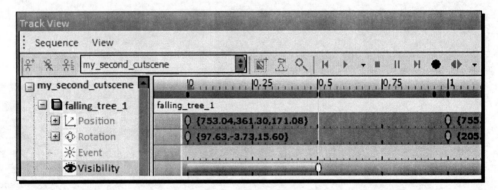

Animating scale

Scale is also accessible to most entities via Track View. A Scale track can be added by right-clicking the added node and selecting scale.

Entities and their tracks

Some entities have unique tracks. For example, characters can play animations and explosion entities can have explode events. Experiment with the different entities in your cutscene to see what is exposed.

Playing animations on entities in Track View

There are situations where you might not want to animate an entity directly in Track View, as we did in the previous example. A good example of when not to animate in the mentioned fashion is when dealing with skinned characters. Track View does not give you a bone-level control when dealing with characters, and thus the next example will cover how to import a previously authored animation for characters or entities into Track View for playback.

Time for action – playing an animation on an entity in Track View

Let's discover how to play an animation on entities in Track View:

1. To begin with, you must have created a new cutscene in a level and added a camera to it, all of which has been covered in previous examples.

2. Add an object of interest to the scene for the camera to focus on. In this example, we will add a human character with a simple animation.

 For characters in cinematics, an AnimObject entity is used as opposed to an AI entity, for performance reasons. Also, because an AnimObject entity doesn't have AI, the AI system won't conflict/fight with the Track View system.

3. Select the **AnimObject** entity in **RollupBar** and drag it into the level.

4. With **AnimObject** selected, click on **Entity Properties** in **RollupBar** and set the string of the model to that of a human character. For example, setting it as `objects/characters/Agent/Agent.cdf` is a good choice.

5. In the Track View, click on the **Add Selected Node** icon.

    With the AnimObject entity added, you can now add an Animation track to animate the character.

6. Right-click on the entity, and on the **Add Track** menu, click on **Animation**.

7. Double-click at frame **0** to add a key in the Event track, and then select the key to bring up the **Key Properties** section.

8. Then, from the drop-down list, select the **standup_tocombat_nw_back_01**
    animation, as shown in the following screenshot:

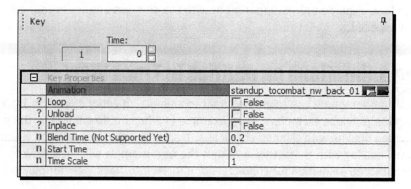

What just happened?

AnimObject entities can have the Animation track available to them, which allows us to
add preauthored animations to the entity in the game. This is preferable for many cutscenes
where AI would be inefficient, or it would be difficult to perform the exact same movements
at the right times.

 It is typical to hide an AI entity and then to unhide the AnimObject version
of the AI for cutscenes.

Have a go hero – using more properties for animations on entities

There are some additional properties that could be used when playing animations on the
entities in Track View. Some of these are useful in different situations. Try adjusting the
following parameters for yourself:

- **Loop animation**: When you want the animation asset to loop on the character, you
  can simply set the **Loop** Boolean to **True**. This will loop the asset until told to stop.

- **Start Time**: You can manually set a time in the **Start Time** dialog to go to a certain
  frame of the animation. This can be useful for different facial sequences as well as
  for climbing animations.

- **Time Scale**: Using Time Scale, you can adjust the speed of animation to faster or
  slower than originally intended. When adjusting the Time Scale dialog, you will
  notice that the Animation track will extend the length of the selected animation
  when **Loop** is not selected, as shown in the following screenshot:

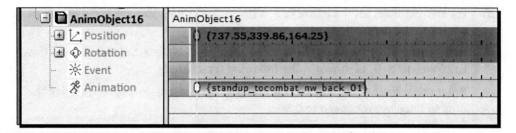

Using Console Variables in Track View

Now that we have learned to create a variety of different sequences, we will explore some of the bridges to connect to the different systems of CryENGINE with which Track View has been designed.

Time for action – adding a Console Variable to a sequence

For this example, we will add some console commands to the Track View sequence created in the *Creating a new Track View sequence* and *Animating a camera in Track View* sections of this chapter. These two sections must be completed before going forward with the following example:

1. You should have the `my_first_cutscene` cutscene open in Track View and your view set to that of the camera.

2. Right-click on the parent node of `my_first_cutscene` and select **Add Console Variable** as shown in the following screenshot:

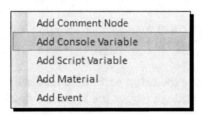

You will then be asked to name this **Console Variable (CVAR)**.

 It is very important that you name the CVAR the *exact* name of the variable you would type into the console.

3. For this example, set the name to `e_TimeofDaySpeed`. You will see it added as a track to the parent node of the sequence.

4. Next, create a key frame on the `e_TimeofDaySpeed` track. Set the value of this key frame to `0.5`, as shown in the following screenshot:

What this will now do is force a command to the console, in this case setting the time of the playback speed to **0.50**.

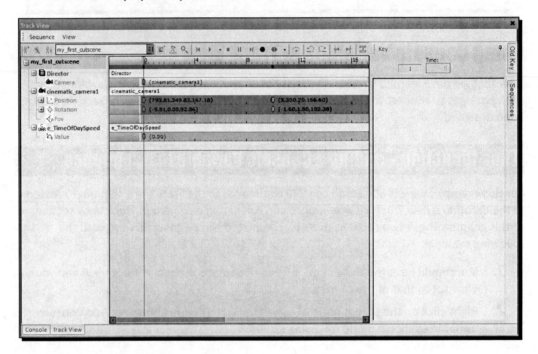

 It should be noted that you cannot preview the CVAR events if the sequence is not triggered from within the game.

5. In this case you can use the setup performed earlier by creating a Flow Graph and adding an **Input:Key** node to trigger the sequence quickly.

6. Trigger the flythrough sequence and notice that the time of day in the level now plays according to the value set in Track View.

What just happened?

Setting CVARs can sometimes be an easy way of achieving some quick effects and changes. Some examples of this are disabling all LODs for marketing videos, or changing rendering effects. In any case, it's valuable to leverage the connection between events happening within a track sequence and the engines console.

Have a go hero – animating CVAR values

CVARs that are added to the sequence can have many different key frames, which allow for the animation of these values. For example, you may want to change the play speed of the time of day within the level to change gradually from fast to slow or vice versa.

The t_scale CVAR in Track View

Sometimes to slow down an entire sequence at once, the t_scale CVAR is used. This can be used quite safely as long as it's understood that the default value is **1**. A good setting for a slow motion, bullet-time feel is about **0.2**.

Using Track Events

A Track Event is a one-way signal that will allow you to further leverage the interconnectivity of Track View with other systems. In the case of Track Events, that system is Flow Graph, as you can send this signal to branch Flow graph logic from a Track View sequence.

Each sequence may have any arbitrary number of Track Events defined. These events can be called at any time from a Track Event Node. Each event may also carry with it a string value assigned to the key frame in the Track View editor. When a Track Event is triggered from the sequence, its corresponding output port in a special Flow graph node is activated, allowing you to branch Flow graph logic very easily.

Time for action – creating some Track Events for a sequence

For this example, we will add some Track Events to the Track View sequence created in the *Creating a new Track View sequence* and *Animating a camera in Track View* sections of this chapter.

1. You should have the my_first_cutscene cutscene open in Track View and your view set to that of the camera.

2. First we must define some Track Events. Open the my_first_cutscene sequence.

 Track Events are defined per the Track View sequence.

3. Once opened, right-click on the sequence in the tree view on the left-hand side of the **Track View** window, and select the **Edit Events** option, as shown in the following screenshot:

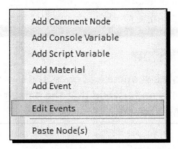

A dialog box labeled **Track View Events** will open.

4. To create a Track Event, select the **Add** button and give the event a name. The event will then be added to the list.

5. To remove this event, select it from the list and select the **Remove** button. When you are done, select the **OK** button to save your changes.

6. Create a new event named `sequence_started`, as shown in the following screenshot:

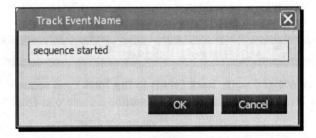

The Track Event Node will allow you to call a Track Event from the sequence.

7. To add the node to your sequence, right-click on the sequence in the tree view on the left-hand side of the **Track View** window, and select the **Add Event** option towards the bottom.

8. Give the node a name and it will then be added to your sequence.

From here, you will be able to add keys to toggle the Track Events just like any other node.

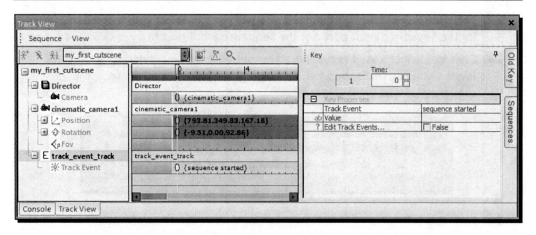

9. If you select any of the keys you created on the Event track, you can assign one of your predefined event names to it by choosing them on the right-hand side menu, called **Key Properties**. You can also edit the list of Track Events for the sequence quickly by double-clicking on **Edit Track Events**.

    The next step will be to add this event to a Flow Graph.

10. To add your Flow graph logic, you will first need to either create a new graph or open an existing one.

11. Place a Track Event Node, which can be done by right-clicking anywhere in the graph and selecting it from the context menu, as shown in the following screenshot:

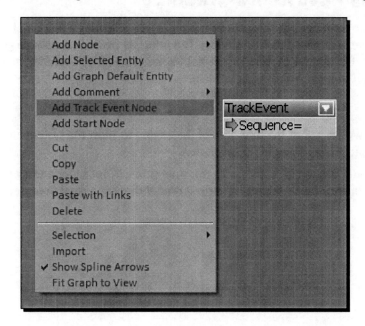

12. The node will initially be empty and you will need to select your animation sequence for the **Sequence** input port. Set the **Sequence** input port to `my_first_cutscene`.

13. Once you select a valid sequence, an output port will be created for each Track Event owned by that sequence. As shown in the following screenshot, the **sequence started** event was created:

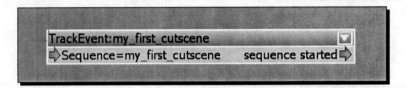

14. From this point, create your Flow graph logic using the created output ports.

When these events are triggered from the animation sequence as it plays through, the output ports will trigger, allowing your Flow graph logic to execute.

What just happened?

Track Events allow for direct triggering at particular times within a sequence to the Flow Graph. This allows for an extremely complex combination of animation and Flow Graphed physics or effects to be triggered directly from a sequence.

Capturing video from CryENGINE 3

Capturing video from CryENGINE 3 can be quite easy. By following a few simple guidelines, you can achieve near photorealistic renders. The principle behind capturing a good video from CryENGINE is that we capture sequential frames rather than capturing real-time video or direct-to-video.

There are a few reasons for this:

◆ First, we can adjust the time step of the engine to allow the system enough time to capture the frames in full resolution.

◆ Secondly, sequential frames with this time step will not suffer any lag due to performance-heavy scenes, as we will render them at a fixed time step.

Time for action – capturing frames from CryENGINE

For this example, we will capture video from the Track View sequence created in the *Creating a new Track View sequence* and *Animating a camera in Track View* sections of this chapter.

There are two ways to capture frames from the engine. The first is by using a Capture track, which is unique to the director node. The second is by using typed console commands which are discussed at the end of this example.

1. To add the Capture track open the `my_first_sequence` sequence and right-click on the director node.

2. On the director node there should be a track titled **Capture**. Set the key frame at the start of the sequence in the Capture track and adjust **Duration** that you'd like to capture in seconds, as shown in the next screenshot.

3. The next value to set is the **Time Step** value, which allows for a fixed frame rate capture. This will adjust the engine timing so that it gives the renderer enough time to capture the frames during the capture process.

    Time step = 1 second / amount of frames

    Example: 1 second / 30 frames = 0.033333333

    0.0166666667 would be 60 frames per second and so on

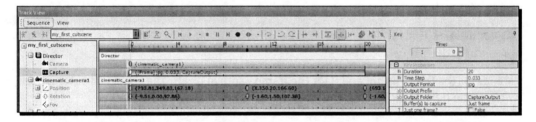

4. We now define the **Output Format** settings. Supported formats for export will appear when clicking in the space beside the parameter. Some of these include TGA, TIF, and PNG.

5. You can also define the **Output Folder** settings, which will create a folder that is named what you define here in the root directory of your build. This will store all the sequential images that will be captured.

6. Leave **Buffer(s) to capture** at its default settings; you can explore the settings which allow for stereo capture as well as `.hdr` images.

7. Once you are ready to capture, switch to game mode and trigger the sequence.

You will notice that playback is significantly slower when capturing. This is to be expected! Results will vary depending on the power of the machine used.

What just happened?

At its core, the Capture track parameters are all CVARs that could be set as well. You can find these commands under the `capture_` prefix in the CVARs. We successfully output all our frames and can now use freely available tools, such as VirtualDub, to composite our frames together into a video. One important consideration is to render the video as the time-stepped frame rate meaning 30 frames per second at a 0.033 time step.

A huge variety of video editing software will be able to accept the input of sequential frames quickly and easily. One such program would be Sony Vegas, where you can simply select a numbered sequence when importing the first image in the sequence.

Have a go hero – increasing frame size and setting useful CVARs for video recording

The height and width of the captured frames in the editor is exactly the size as that of your perspective window. You can easily resize the view size by rescaling the docked windows (such as Rollup Bar or the console). The size of the frame is displayed in the upper-right corner of the perspective window.

In game mode, you can change the resolution of the captured frames by changing the resolution in the **Options** menu or using the commands `r_height` and `r_width`.

Set the following two variables:

```
r_height N
r_width M
```

N stands for the frame height and M for the frame width in pixels. The game will automatically switch to the next possible size if the size entered is not available.

Useful CVARs for high resolution capturing

Try adding some of the following CVARs to your sequences for various situations:

- `e_lods = 0`: This will force the highest LOD on all objects.
- `e_ViewDistRatio = 255`: This will force all the objects in the level to be rendered at all times. The maximum value is `255`.
- `e_ViewDistRatioVegetation = 150`: This will increase the range to which the vegetation is rendered.
- `e_TerrainTextureLodRatio = 0`: This will force the maximum resolution of terrain low detail textures.

- `e_TerrainLodRatio = 0`: This will turn off any dynamic LOD on the terrain, making it render at full resolution, all the time. Warning—this will severely impact performance, as a full map with no terrain LOD will cost around 5 to 6 million triangles.
- `e_ShadowsMaxTexRes = 2048`: This value will allow more texture memory and a higher resolution to be used for shadows maps in the engine. The default is `1024` for a high system spec.

Pop quiz – creating cinematics and cutscenes

1. Which is the main tool used when animating entities and cameras within Sandbox?
    a. Flow Graph
    b. Animation Graph
    c. DataBase View
    d. Track View

2. When playing back animations on characters in Track View, what entity is placed within the level and added to TrackView?
    a. AnimObject
    b. Geom
    c. Basic
    d. RigidBody

3. Which track does the director node contain that allows for the easy capturing of video?
    a. Animation
    b. Event
    c. Visibility
    d. Capture

4. Which system can be used to send signals directly to Flow Graph from a key frame within Track View?
    a. Sequence objects
    b. Track Events
    c. Field Of View
    d. Connected feature enabler

Summary

We've discussed and explored some practical uses of using Track View for creating cinematic cutscenes and scripted events. We've seen how to sequence objects, animations, and entities in a scene, and how they can be triggered by our player or by debug inputs. We saw that the sequences can be played either as a detached cutscene or from a completely different perspective of another camera.

We also saw that sequences created with Track View can be triggered in the game with a specific Flow Graph node named **Animations:PlaySequence**. Now that we are able to make our own prescripted events and cutscenes, we can add a good deal of experience and variety to our levels and games.

Now that we've learned about animating and sequences, let's learn how to make these as immersive as possible by adding sound and music to our game, which is the topic of the next chapter.

9

Immersion through Audio Design

Music and audio design in video games had an unglamorous start. Arcade machines, computers, and even some of the early consoles were far more known for their flashing lights and images on screen rather than their attention seeking and arguably irritating beep, pop, and ringing noises. Fortunately, for all gamers, these days have long since past. Modern games now use sophisticated sound hardware, software, and logic, allowing the imagination of the audio engineers and composers to run free.

As the technical capabilities of sound hardware increase, so does the professionalism and technical expertise of the people creating music and sound effects for games. Once, making sounds for a game might have been the domain of bedroom coders, however, most music and sound for modern games are produced in expensive studios using the same kind of equipment as a blockbuster film might use.

In this chapter, we shall:

- Get a sound into engine as an **ambient sound**
- Use some advanced features of ambient sounds
- Use **area shapes** and boxes for sound obstruction
- Learn how to set up random sounds
- Learn how to set up reverb volumes
- Learn how to add sounds to particle effects
- Learn how to add sound to a weapon

So, let's get started!

Introducing sound design

The sound system within the CryENGINE is a hierarchical class system that supports many different sound libraries and different target platforms. The sound system offers interfaces and is used by sound entities in a level, or can even be called from code to play sounds systematically. The principal focus was set to support the **FMOD-EX** library by FireLight Technologies (`http://www.fmod.org/`), but there is also support for the Xaudio port for Xbox360 and a dummy/null system.

A typical production workflow for integrating a new project contains the following steps:

1. Create a new project using the **FMOD Design tool**. Projects are stored as `.fdp` files.
2. Add groups, events, and sound definitions.
3. Organize sound assets into **wavebanks**.
4. Build the project that converts source `.wav` files to the target more compressed and optimized format for real-time playback formats such as `.fev` and `.fsb`. These formats are discussed later in the chapter.
5. Reference a sound event name in code or in the Editor to load the project and play the event `Sounds/mycustomproject:duck:quack`.

Understanding the CryENGINE sound event system

The CryENGINE sound event system introduces some new terms, which we will explain here. The sound event system can be seen from two different perspectives:

1. From the view of the sound designer, who works mostly with a sound specification tool called **FMOD Designer** to create sound events and to organize them.
2. From the programmer's perspective, who sees the event system as a data structure where information and sound data gets loaded and from which sound events get spawned.

The examples given in this chapter will focus principally on the first perspective; however, in some of the later examples, simple code blocks will be used to add sound events to weapons and other entities in the game.

Setting up a project structure

The sound system is composed of several projects. Each project is a well-defined set of sound events. These events can be structured into event groups and independently added to a category. A project must first be exported for it to be loaded into the event system, and only then can one of its events be played. The build project step generates an event datafile and several wavebanks.

CryENGINE does not allow for nested project folders (for example, `folder1/folder2/fmodproject.fdp`), so you must always use one folder per project to avoid project files not being recognized in the CryENGINE.

Event grouping

An **event group** holds several sound events. The workflow for a designer is straightforward as he/she organizes similar events into a group. The programmer can then preload all sound data of a specific group or free the data of a group if its events are no longer needed for saving valuable memory.

Using categories

A **category** is part of a hierarchical structure, which gives some additional semantic meaning to an event. An event can only be sorted in one category.

Adding events

A **sound event** combines sound assets with varied properties to create full sound. Among many properties, sound designers can specify basic characteristics. For example, whether a sound is looping, if it is being played in 2D or 3D, what its radius is, and how the sound attenuates over distance. All these properties are stored within the event. An event can be composed of one or several sound definitions, which hold the real sound data. A sound event is played by specifying it with its event name, using the following format:

```
Path/projectname:groupname:eventname
```

For example:

```
sounds/weapons:scar:reload
```

It is preferable that all project, group, and event names within the event system be written in lowercase.

Reviewing sound event system file formats

The event system uses three different file types:

- Project file: It contains the data of a project to be used by the FMOD Designer tool.
- FEV - Event datafile: It contains the data of a project to be loaded at runtime.
- FSB - Wavebank: It contains sound data.

Using wavebanks

In each project, the sound data of a sound definition can be organized into different wavebanks. These wavebanks have various options for compression (PCM/ADPCM/MP3/MPEG2) and to check whether the data gets streamed or fully loaded out of it at runtime.

Getting your first sound into the CryENGINE

Now that we've sufficiently beat the theory behind the sound system to death, let's get to the more exciting process of getting our first sound assets into the engine! Background environment sound often consists of both ambient sound loops and random one-shots. A good example of this is inside a cave, where there is an ambient wind, and some random one-shots of drips of water falling. Typically, the random one-shots are used to sweeten the environmental sound, whereas the main environment loop is there to set the atmosphere.

Time for action - creating an ambient sound event

Using the entities **AmbientVolume** and **RandomSoundVolume** attached to area shapes, one can create convincing sounding environments. This example will take you through the process of setting up a sound event and getting your own sound in the engine. It will also include some important interface steps, which will be used throughout the chapter. The following screenshot is an example of an ambience setup in the forest example level from the Free SDK:

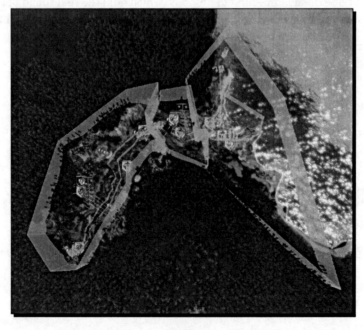

To get your first sound into engine, we must first open **FMOD Designer**, which is the tool we will use to create our sound events for the CryENGINE.

1. Open **FMOD Designer**, which can be found in your build directory under `Tools\FmodDesigner\fmod_designer.exe`.

2. Once opened, create a new project.

3. Name the project `mygame_environment.fdp` and save this project under the game directory in `game/sound/mygame_environment/`.

    You will notice that a default event group and event will be created in your project.

4. Rename the event group to **Cave** by typing it into the name property.

5. Rename the event from **event00** to **cave_ambience** by typing it into **Property | Name**.

    Now that we have our event, we need to give the event a sound to play.

6. Right-click on the first layer of the event, and select the **Add sound** function, as seen in the following screenshot:

7. From the **New Sound** dialog box, click on the **Add sound file...** button, and browse to the file `sounds/mygame_environment/cave_ambience.wav` ensuring **Loop mode** is set to **Looping**, as seen in the following screenshot:

8. Set the sound to be a three-dimensional sound by changing the **Mode** property of the sound from 2D to 3D.

The next step is to now add some parameters to the sound. These parameters will be adjusted by the engine and will trigger different effects, which we will add onto the sound.

9. Add a parameter by right-clicking just above the layer of the event that says **(Right-click here to add an event paramater)** and select the **Add parameter** function, as seen in the following screenshot:

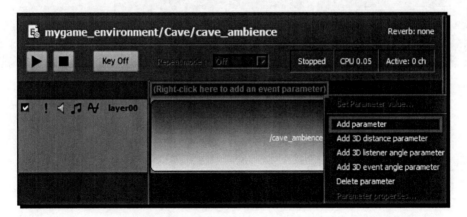

10. Right-click on the newly created **param00** parameter and select **Parameter properties** from the context window.

11. Rename the parameter from **param00** to spread.

Having assigned a parameter to this sound for the engine to modify, we must now add some effects that will change the way the sound is played, depending on the values of the spread parameter coming from the sound system.

12. To add effect, right-click under **layer00**, as seen in the following screenshot, and select the **Add effect...** option:

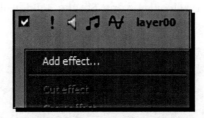

The **New Effect** window will appear and a large list of effects will be available to assign to the layer.

13. Add two Effects—**3D Speaker Spread** and **3D Pan Level**.

14. Next, adjust the angle of the **3D Speaker Spread** and the level of the **3D Pan** by adding some points along the parameter values.

15. In this example, I set relatively low **3D Pan Level** and high **3D Speaker Spread Angle** when the spread parameter is zero. Then, I increased the **3D Pan Level** quickly as the spread parameter hit around **0.1**. I then adjusted the **3D Speaker Spread** to have a very small angle once the spread parameter was high, as seen in the following screenshot:

These effects, in combination with the spread parameter, adjust how the sound behaves as you approach or leave the area shape.

We must now build our project so that the sound is compressed and the event is created for use within the editor application or launcher.

16. Click on the **Project** menu at the top of the FMOD interface and then select **Build**.

17. In the **Build Project** dialog box, select the **Select which wave banks to build:** option; in this example, there will only be one. Set the **Build project for:** setting to **PC**, as seen in the following screenshot:

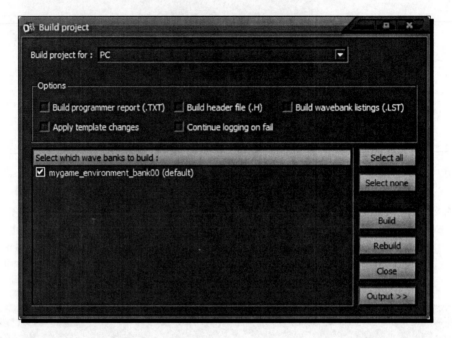

18. Click on the **Build** button when ready.

19. FMOD will then compress the `.wav` audio into a `.fsb` format and the sound event into a `.fev` file and will output a message when completed successfully.

Now that we have the formats, we require to play back the sound within the CryENGINE. Let's place this sound into a level so that we can iterate and try different settings for effects!

20. Open the level into which you'd like to add sound. For this example, the forest level will suffice.

21. Under **Entities | Sound** in the **RollupBar** tab, select the **AmbientVolume** entity and drag this entity into the level.

22. Next, draw a simple area shape by clicking on **Area** in the **RollupBar** tab and then selecting **Shape**. For this example, create a simple four-sided box that's big enough for the player to enter.

23. Under the **Entity Links** of the area shape, click the **PickTarget** icon, and then select the **AmbientVolume** entity, which will link it to the area shape. You will now see that this worked, when you can see a gray line connecting the area shape to the **AmbientVolume**.

24. In the **AmbientVolume** entity properties, click on the name string and then click on the browse icon, which will open the **Sound Browser** window.

25. Browse to the directory `Sounds/mygame_environment/Cave/` and select the **cave_ambience** event.

Note that you can preview the sound as well as the way it reacts to different parameters within the **Sound Browser** using the sliders and **Play** button, as seen in the following screenshot:

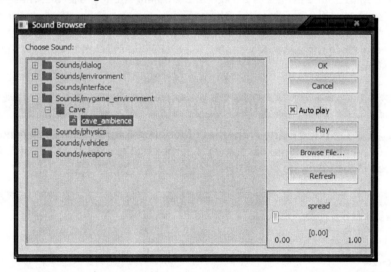

Double-click on the **cave_ambience** sound file, and it will then be assigned to the **AmbientVolume** entity. Now we are ready!

26. Type the console command `s_SoundInfo=1` that will display the all playing sounds and some debugging and profiling tools.

27. Switch to game mode and walk into the area shape.

If everything is working correctly, you will hear the sound as well as see, using `s_soundinfo`, that the entry **3d sounds/mygame_environment:cave:cave_ambience** is playing.

You'll now notice that whenever you approach or enter that area shape, the ambient sound will play.

28. As a final example, set the **Height** value of the area shape created earlier to 20.

The area shape will now limit the vertical dimensions of the **AmbientVolume** entity.

 If you leave the **Height** value undefined, the **AmbientVolume** entity will have an unlimited vertical dimension.

What just happened?

Congratulations! You have learned many different skills in this example. We successfully created a new FMOD project, created an event group, added an event, assigned sound to that event, and finally added some effects and parameters for this event. We even went so far as to build our project and get our sound working in the engine!

We can use looping sound events as background ambient sounds in levels. These are typically 3D sounds, which reside within the confines of an area shape. When the player enters the area shape, the ambient sound travels with the player becoming, in effect, a surround sound. Once the player leaves the shape, the sound is left behind on the perimeter of the area shape.

Have a go hero - using more ambient volume properties

Try using some of the other **Entity Properties** of **AmbientVolume**. As with any entity within the CryENGINE, **AmbientVolume** has some properties that can easily be adjusted in the editor, as seen in the following screenshot:

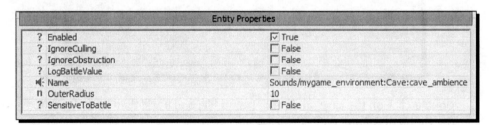

Some of these properties are:

◆ **IgnoreCulling**: This is set to true, by default, and means that ambient volumes will be culled by distance, and if separated by **VisArea**.

- ◆ **OuterRadius**: This setting will cause a falloff or ramp up in the sound as you leave or approach the area.

- ◆ **IgnoreObstruction**: This setting is used to enable or disable obstructions to the sound used, often in interiors, where the player might not always have a line of sight to the **AmbientVolume** entity.

Leveraging advanced parameters of ambient sounds

An obvious problem that can occur when using ambient volumes and shapes is that most ambient volumes will bleed through into your inner ambient shapes, which are being used for interior ambience.

Scenarios for this are pretty common, in which you have your player in an exterior, natural environment with birds chirping, wind gust sounds, and leaves rustling. Once the player enters a building, the exterior natural sounds should be cancelled. In the next example, we learn how to adjust for this scenario.

Time for action - nesting ambient sounds and using other parameters for sound events

As we saw previously, each **AmbientVolume** has a radius. As you get closer to an area, the ambience will begin to fade at a certain distance away from the perimeter of the area shape. That distance is controlled by setting the radius in the **AmbientVolume** properties. However, in this scenario where the player goes from natural exterior into a man-made building, we need to nest a smaller shape inside the large one.

1. Create a large area shape.

2. Inside the large area shape, create a smaller second shape.

3. Following the previous example, link two separate and unique **AmbientVolume** entities to each area shape.

4. Select the area shapes and assign a **GroupID** of 1 or higher to each; the **GroupID** parameter can be found in the entity parameters rollout of the **Areashape** entity.

   Assigning the same **GroupID** to both areas causes them to interact with respect to their ambient sounds.

An example of this setup is seen in the following screenshot:

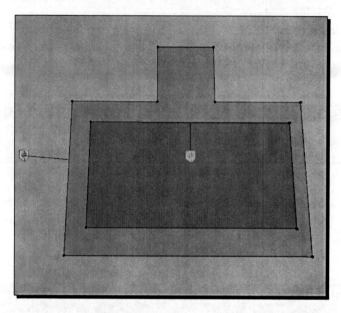

5. Next, we must assign a **Priority** parameter to both areas. You can also find this setting in the shape parameters for the area shapes.

   The higher priority shape will cause the ambient sound of the lower priority shape to cancel out when the players enter the higher priority shape.

6. For our example, we will set the smaller nested ambient shape to a **Priority** of 2 and set the larger one to a **Priority** of 1.

   The radius of the higher priority shape will be used when cross fading between nested **AmbientVolumes**. For example, if the large shape has a **Radius** set to 20 and the small shape has a **Radius** of 1, when the player enters the small shape, the large shape's sound will fade out over one meter. If the player walks out from the large shape, the sound will fade out over 20 meters.

   Ambiences can also be set to change according to the dynamic day/night cycle. A good example would be that during the day, bird calls would be frequent and at night, insect and night animal sounds would probably be heard.

7. Add a parameter to the sound called **daylight**. It should be noted that **daylight** is not the same as the day/night cycle in **Time Of Day**. It simply checks whether the sun is up or down, so the transition is fast.

8. Create a second layer for the night ambience. To do this, copy-paste the first layer, and then choose new ambiences for the night layer, as seen in the following screenshot:

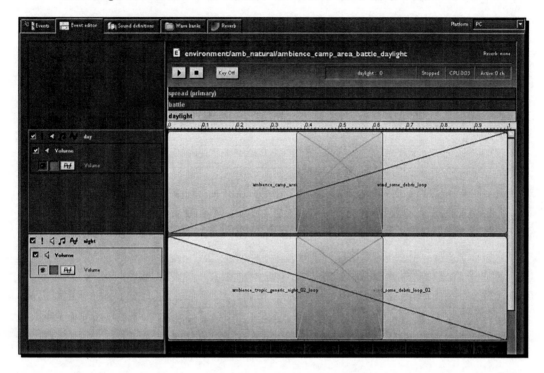

9. As you can see in the previous screenshot, the **daylight** parameter is highlighted. Now you will be able to add a **Volume** effect to each layer, and also a specific fade curve. During the day, the parameter is close to 1.0, thus playing the day ambience at full volume. As the sunlight reduces, it gradually slides to 0.0, and the night ambience fades in while the day ambience fades out.

What just happened?

Congratulations! You are fast becoming an expert sound designer. In this example, we saw how to apply some additional, slightly more advanced parameters to our ambient sound events. We explored how to use the radius of the **AmbientVolume** entity, as well as how to use the **GroupID** entity and priority parameters of area shapes. Furthermore, we saw that you can create composite sound in layers with multiple parameters and events to suit specific situations.

Have a go hero - sound obstruction using area shapes and boxes

Try using area shapes and boxes for **Sound Obstruction**.

The edges of area shapes and area boxes can be flagged for obstruction by the sound system, by enabling the **DisplaySoundInfo** parameter in the area shape. Enabling **DisplaySoundInfo** will display obstructed sides in a different color from that of the unobstructed ones. You can simply enable or disable obstruction in the **Sound Obstruction** rollout, as seen in the screenshot:

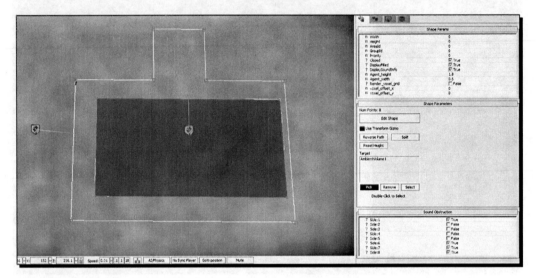

Obstructed sides (red) will not calculate the ambience updates for that segment. **Non obstructed sides** (green) will calculate ambience updates for that segment. They can be used to define doorways and windows, as well as for offering greater flexibility in a complex shape in shape setups.

Randomizing sounds

To add more variety and authenticity to the ambiences, you can combine the **AmbientVolume** entity, used in the first example of this chapter, with an entity called **RandomSoundVolume**. Using this entity, a one-shot sound event can be randomly fired off at a particular 3D position or within a given area.

Time for action - creating random sounds

In FMOD, we have the ability to add multiple tracks to individual sound definitions. This can be used to good measure when creating random sound volumes. This example will demonstrate how to create a sound definition with multiple sound files and how to randomly play these within your level.

1. Open the FMOD project created in the previous example `mygame_environment.fdp`.

2. Create a new sound event and name it `random_bats_oneshot`.

3. Switch to the **Sound Defs** view in FMOD.

4. Right-click in the **Sound Defs** list and select the **Add sound def...** option.

5. Name the new **Sound Def** file as **bat_flying_cave**.

6. Select the **bat_flying_cave** sound def, and in the **Sounds** window, right-click and select the **Add sound file...** option.

7. Add the three provided `.wav` files named **bat_flying_cave_01.wav** , **bat_flying_cave_02.wav**, and **bat_flying_cave_03.wav**.

8. Keep the **Play Percentage** set to **33.33%**, as it gives all sound files an equal chance to play.

9. The final results of the project and it's settings are seen in the following screenshot:

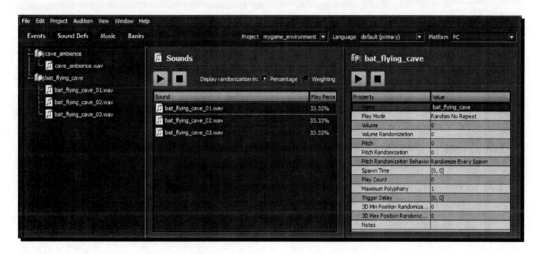

10. Switch back to the **Events** view.

11. Right-click on **Layer00** and select the **Add Sound...** option.

12. You will now see the sound def—**bat_flying_cave**—created earlier in the list. Select it and click on **OK**.

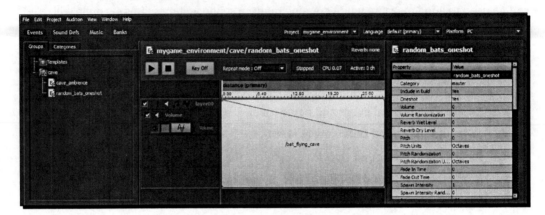

In the preceding screenshot, you can see that I have set a distance parameter with a **Volume** effect over **30** units. Depending on the distance into which the random sound event is placed, the sound will not only play one of the three different events but will also adjust their volumes based on the distance to the sound. It is all up to the creativity of the designer to combine and balance the available parameters and values to create a believable and living atmosphere.

13. Rebuild the FMOD project and save it.

Now that we have our random sound definition setup, let's play it in the game.

14. Open any level to which you wish to add random sound, and place an **Entity** from **RandomSoundVolume** into the level.

15. Assign this new sound event, created earlier, named **bat_flying_cave** to the **RandomSoundVolume** entity.

16. Create an area shape, and under the shape, target pick the **RandomSoundVolume** entity as you did earlier with an **AmbientVolume** entity.

17. Assign parameters as seen in the screenshot that follows:

∏	DiscRadius	10
?	Enabled	☑ True
?	IgnoreCulling	☐ False
?	IgnoreObstruction	☐ False
?	LogBattleValue	☐ False
∏	MaxWaitTime	15
∏	MinWaitTime	5
◀:	Name	Sounds/mygame_environment:cave:random_bats_oneshot
?	RandomPosition	☑ True
?	SensitiveToBattle	☐ False

18. Setting the **DiscRadius** to **10** will control the distance surrounding the player at which the sound will be played.

19. Setting the **MinWaitTime** and **MaxWaitTime** parameters controls the time frame within which a sound will start. This value is measured from when the last sound started.

What just happened?

You have now used random sounds to sweeten up your ambient environmental sounds! As you have now seen, nearly the same FMOD parameters used for the ambience loops can be assigned to the random one-shots, such as battle, daylight, distance, and others. However, spread is not needed because the **RandomSoundVolume** does not roll off outside the area shape. Instead, we assigned a distance parameter as we would to any other sound event.

Reverb volumes

Levels can have different reverb settings in different areas. A simple example of this is underwater versus outside of the water. Rather than having to create many different variations to a .wav file, reverb volumes can be designed directly in the Editor and can drastically change the way sound events are played back. Like **AmbientVolumes**, **ReverbVolumes** are attached to area shapes or boxes. They can be attached to the same area shape/box as an **AmbientVolume** already is, and will affect that **AmbientVolume** entity's sound events.

Time for action - create your own reverb preset

In this example, we will create and place our own **ReverbVolume** as well as explore the parameters and settings within **Reverb Presets**.

1. Open the editor application and then open the **Forest** level.

2. Open the **DataBase View** and select the **Reverb Presets** tab.

3. Click on **P+** to create a new reverb preset.

4. Adjust the values in the **Parameters** window, and click on the icon resembling a bar graph or a play icon, to preview the effects.

    Any sound played once the **play/audition** button is clicked will have the specific **Reverb Preset** added onto it. Thus you can quickly preview parameter changes by adjusting the parameters and clicking on play, and then triggering sounds in the game.

5. Save the preset as seen in the following screenshot:

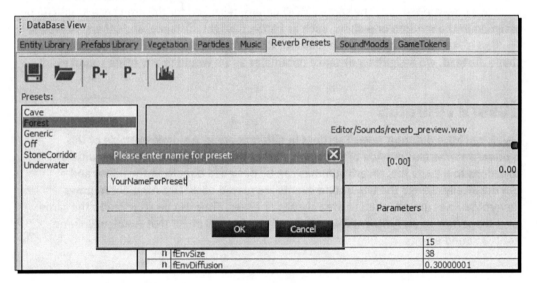

6. To test your preset right away in the database viewport, make sure to select a sound by clicking on the folder icon and then picking the desired sound.

You will notice the sound loaded and its wet settings automatically present in the slider.

7. In the **RollupBar** tab, select **Entity | Sound | ReverbVolume**.

8. Drag this entity to the level. You will notice that the properties of the **ReverbVolume** entity are adjustable when it is selected.

9. Link the area shape to a **ReverbVolume**. Like **AmbientVolumes**, when the player approaches the area shape, the **ReverbVolume** fades in, reaching full effect when the player enters the shape.

10. Set the parameter **FullEffectWhenInside** to **True**, which controls the overlapping of reverb volumes. This is similar to setting priorities in **AmbientVolume**.

11. Set the parameter **OuterRadius** to **2**, which controls the falloff distance.

?	Enabled	☑ True
n	Environment	1
?	FullEffectWhenInside	☑ True
n	OuterRadius	2
☞	ReverbPreset	Hall

What just happened?

You have created your first reverb preset, and can now set up multiple **Presets** to easily adapt the way it sounds in certain areas of the environment. Having learned how to set up your own preset, let's review some of the parameters that are available to use in the **Reverb Presets** tool.

Have a go hero - setting parameters in the reverb preset editor

In the **Reverb Presets** window, you create and save **Presets** as we've just done in the previous example. You can also access the parameters for a **Reverb Presets** tab by simply highlighting it as in the screenshot. Try adjusting some of these **Parameters** to see how they affect your sound events.

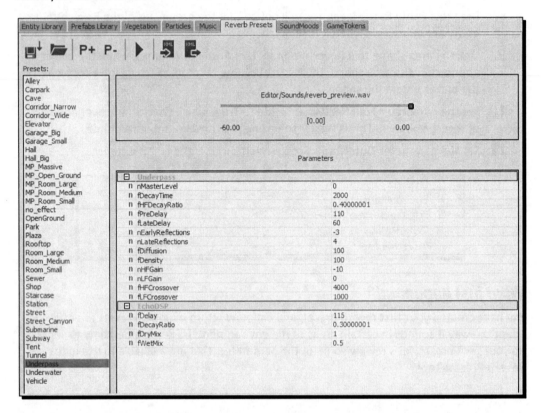

In the **Parameters** window, there are settings that can be adjusted. These **Parameters** are mainly derived from the I3DL2 specification, which can be found on `http://www.IASIG.org` or in the FMOD help menu. In some reverb implementations, few parameters are completely ignored. Numbers describe min, max, and default values. All intensity levels or relative attenuations are expressed in hundredths of decibels (**millibels, mB**). All times values are expressed in seconds.

Adding sounds to particle effects

In many cases, when there is a particle effect being triggered, you'd like to also trigger a sound. It wouldn't make sense to set up sound entities and trigger them at the same time as a particle effect; thus to make things easier, we can add sounds directly onto the particle effects.

Time for action - add a sound to a particle effect

Let's say we have an explosion sound and an explosion particle effect.

1. Select a particle effect of the subeffect in the **Particles** editor within Sandbox.

2. Browse and add a sound event. The sound event will start when the effect or subeffect starts. If you wish to delay the start of the sound, attach it to a subeffect and use spawn delay to delay the start time.

3. Sounds will stop when the particle effect stops. It is recommended that a fade out time be set in the sound event properties in the FMOD Designer project, to enable a smooth stopping of the sound.

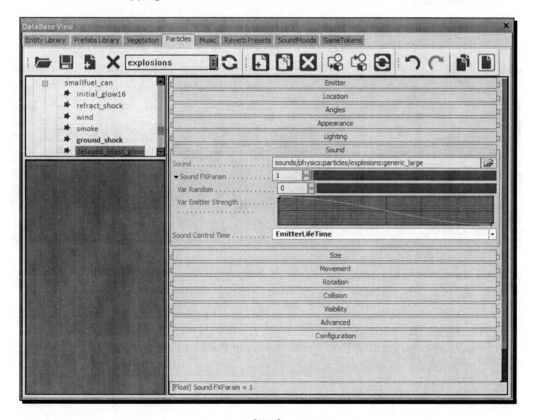

What just happened?

You've now added a sound to a particle effect: It will play every time this particle is triggered. This way we don't have to add secondary entities to play the sound in addition to explosions and other particle effects, which would have some obvious sound within it. There is, however, an exception to this as weapon particle effects do not usually have the sound assigned within the particle but rather in the weapon .xml file, which we will see in the next example.

Have a go hero - changing sound over time on particles

We have seen in previous examples that we have the ability to add parameters within FMOD on the sound event. When dealing with particles, one of the valuable sound parameters is the particlefx parameter.

1. Create a parameter called particlefx in a sound event.

2. Add that sound event to a particle effect.

3. Set the **Sound FXParam** to **1**.

   This defines the maximum value sent to the particlefx parameter of the sound event.

4. Draw a curve in the **Var Emitter Strength** graph. The x axis, horizontal, represents time; whereas the y axis, vertical, represents the value sent to the particlefx parameter in the FMOD **Sound** event.

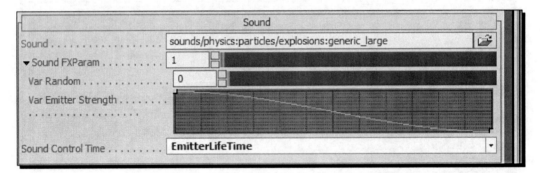

This graph is reversed from the graph you would see for the particlefx parameter in the sound event in FMOD Designer.

As seen in the previous screenshot, the curve will gradually move the value of particlefx from 0.0 to 1.0, over the life of the particle effect.

A typical use may be to have a **Volume** effect curve on the `particlefx` parameter in the sound event, which reduces the volume of the sound as the value of the parameter moves from 0.0 to 1.0.

Optionally, select a value for the **Var Random** value in the particle editor. A random amount from **0.0** to the maximum random value will be subtracted from the parameter each time the particle effect is played. This causes the value of the parameter to be lowered by a random amount.

For example, if the value of **Sound FXParam** is `1.0` and **Var Random** is set to `0.2`, then, each time the effect is played, the maximum value of **FXParam** would be set anywhere between `1.0` and `0.8`.

Using the three different sound control overtime functions

There is a property within the particle editor called **Sound Control Time**. This pull-down window offers three different choices and is designed to work in conjunction with the `particlefx` parameter within FMOD.

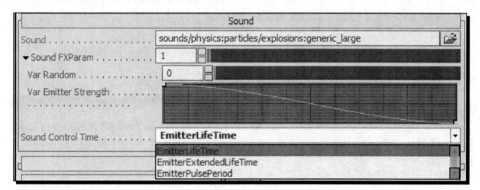

The three different choices and its uses are as follows:

◆ Use **EmitterLifeTime** to update the `particlefx` parameter according to the curve set in **Var Emitter Strength**.

◆ Use **EmitterExtendedLifetime** to update the `particlefx` parameter, while the emitter emits as long as the emitted particle is still alive.

◆ Use **EmitterPulsePeriod** to update the `particlefx` parameter over the entire emitter's pulse time.

 All of these functions apply to looping as well as one-shot sounds. Looping sounds will be stopped at the end of **EmitterLifeTime** and **EmitterExtendedLifeTime** but not **EmitterPulsePeriod**.

Sound events and weapons

A weapon without sound is not a very fun weapon at all. Weapon sounds are easily one of the most important aspects of any sound design within most games—at least the ones that use weapons.

Time for action - add sound to a weapon

The weapon system of CryENGINE 3 supports various actions, which are used to trigger actions such as animation, effects, and sounds. Within the weapon system, one-shot, tail, and looping sounds are the typical types of FMOD events used.

1. Open one of the weapon scripts within your game directory. Weapon scripts are stored under `\Game\Scripts\Entities\Items\XML\Weapons`.

For this example, we will open the `SCAR.xml` file in a text editor.

2. When looking through this file, you will see that there are many actions triggered by game code that have a sound event attached.

```
<action name="fire">
    <animation target="firstperson" name="fire_bullets_
right_%suffix%01" />
    <animation target="owner" name="shoot" />
    <sound target="firstperson" name="sounds/weapons:scar:fire_
single_fp" radius="200" static="1" />
    <sound target="thirdperson" name="sounds/weapons:scar:fire_
single_3p" radius="200" static="1" />
</action>
<action name="rapid_fire">
    <sound target="firstperson" name="Sounds/weapons:scar:fire_
loop_fp" radius="200" static="1" synched="1"/>
    <sound target="thirdperson" name="Sounds/weapons:scar:fire_
loop_3p" radius="200" static="1" synched="1"/>
</action>
<action name="spin_down">
    <sound target="firstperson" name="sounds/weapons:scar:fire_
tail_fp" radius="200" static="1" />
    <sound target="thirdperson" name="sounds/weapons:scar:fire_
tail_3p" radius="200" static="1" />
</action>
```

3. First, let's discuss some of the properties here:

   ❑ The `action name=` property specifies weapon action in conjunction with game code.

   ❑ The `sound target=` property specifies first person or third person sound in conjunction with game code.

   ❑ The `name=` property specifies the sound event name starting from the `sounds` root folder.

   ❑ The `radius=` property specifies the radius of the sound to which the AI entity reacts.

   ❑ The `static=` property specifies whether sound should stop immediately when switching the weapon.

   ❑ The `synched=` property specifies whether the sound should look for sync points within FMOD and plays until the next marker before stopping.

4. To use sync points, the asset and FMOD sound banks need to be set accordingly. The asset itself requires that sync points be defined by markers, as seen in the following screenshot:

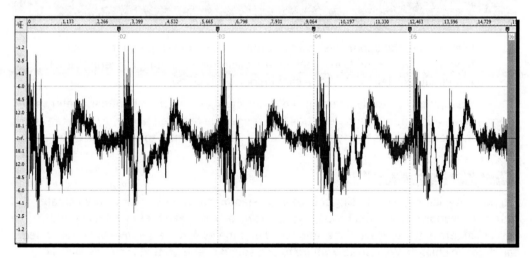

5. The sound bank must set the property **Enable Sync Points** to `YES`.

6. For multiple tail setup, the FMOD event requires the **environment** parameter.

   This directly connects with the **Reverb Presets** environment's setting. It enables different tail settings, depending on the environmental setup.

The following screenshot shows an example of such a setup:

In each case, the upper layer with just the attack of the single shot is being triggered. The second layer reacts to the environment setting triggering either a long outdoor tail (0 - 1.5) or a shot indoor tail (1.5 - 3).

This system can easily be enhanced by increasing the environment parameter values and adding more sound definitions. To trigger the required tail behavior in the game, the **ReverbVolume** entity requires the **environment** entry to be set correctly.

What just happened?

You have now learned about using sounds and weapons together so that you can create your own weapon sounds. You have also seen how you can make them interact with the **ReverbVolume** entity to make the sound blend into the level more seamlessly, as discussed earlier in the chapter. We also saw where to add sound events so that they are played on certain weapons. Additionally, we discussed the relevant properties used by the sound and weapon system to trigger sound events.

Weapon sound workflow tips

Creating one FMOD project per weapon has proven to be a good choice. It not only helps to keep an eye on the memory budget but also enables multiple designers to work with multiple weapons at the same time. Splitting the FMOD sound banks according to the sound target as well as a "shared" bank for elements, which both targets will use, will decrease the memory usage. It also enables the **Audio File Cache Manager (AFCM)** to only load the sound bank, which is needed via the gamehint system. Also, reusing the tails on single gunshot sound events does save some memory, since the actual attack of the gun is fairly short and thus requires less memory.

Also, using FMOD's granular functionality helps to save memory while avoiding repetition. By doing this, the original loop gets cut into small pieces of three to six shots and randomized via the **Sound Defs** property, as shown in the following screenshot:

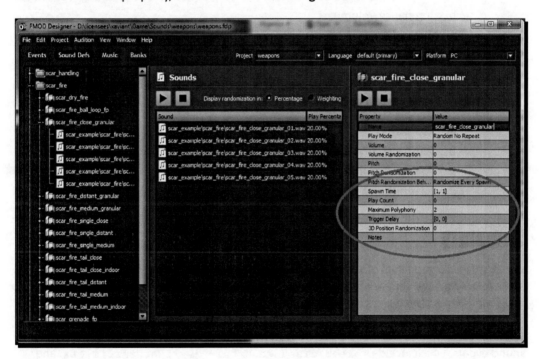

Pop quiz - creating sound for your game

1. What is the tool used, in conjunction with the CryENGINE game engine, for creating and compressing sound assets for ingame use?

   a. Soundguru

   b. Adobe Photoshop

   c. Fmod Designer

   d. Visual Studio

2. When using the various sound entities, to what are they targeted within a level to play them?

   a. Area Shapes

   b. Irradiance Volumes

   c. Time of Day

   d. Tag Points

3. What entity is best used, when creating a random sound asset using multiple sounds within a single sound definition?

   a. BasicEntity

   b. RandomSoundVolume

   c. AmbientVolume

   d. ReverbPreset

Summary

We've created a good deal of sound design examples ourselves throughout this chapter, and explored a huge variety of sound topics. Specifically, we covered how to get our first raw sound into a playable engine format, starting from creating an FMOD Designer project, all the way to assigning the event created within FMOD, to an **AmbientVolume** entity within a level. We also discussed some important FMOD parameters that we can assign to sound events, which include spread, distance, battle, daylight, particlefx, and environment. The sound browser was discussed briefly, which can preview the effects of these parameters.

We created events for other useful entities, such as **RandomSoundVolumes** and **ReverbVolumes**. Finally, we saw where to assign sound events to weapons, and discussed the SCAR.xml example and some specifics on its workflow and setup. Now that we've learned how to put the final touch on our player experience using sound, we are ready to share it with the world!

10
Preparing to Share Your Content

*"If you build it, they will come." One of the best feelings for any game developer is releasing their creations for their players. There are different routes that could be taken, be it releasing a game completely for free, making a **free-to-play (F2P)** game, releasing through digital distribution, and many others. When releasing your creation is the goal, success is all about being able to provide your users with a high performance, entertaining, and immersive experience.*

At long last, we are nearing the end of our journey, of the creation and distribution of our CryENGINE creations. There are many different scenarios that would require you to send your game/level or even assets to others for them to play, review, or even help. This chapter will take you through some of the important last steps, which you will need to take before sharing your content.

In this chapter, we will:

- Profile our level's performance in Sandbox
- Save Level Statistics
- Learn how to enable Debug Draw modes
- Optimize levels with VisAreas and Portals
- Use light boxes and light areas
- Activate and deactivate layers
- Register our project, team, and files on the CryDev database

Let's begin by discussing some of the profiling tools available within the Sandbox application.

Profiling performance in Sandbox

Before we unleash our creations to the world, it is very important to always be aware of our game's performance and how it will affect your player's experience. CryENGINE has a variety of different, built-in debugging and profiling tools. As you will soon find out, some of them are specific to certain subsystems and are useful for advanced users of the technology. Other tools, however, are very useful for most engine users in their regular, daily workflow. The next section lists the profiling CVARs and commands that each programmer, artist, and level designer working with CryENGINE should know.

Profiling with display info

The proverbial first line of defense for developers in terms of profiling and reading performance in Sandbox is the display info CVAR. This is activated and displayed in most cases by default; however, we will discuss how to enable it as well as explore some of the values it is communicating to you.

Time for action – enabling and reading display info

As mentioned previously, this is usually enabled in the CryENGINE Sandbox by default. For any real values to be displayed, however, you need to open a level, otherwise it will just display the values of rendering a blank image.

```
CamPos=708.29 316.15 180.59 Angl= 41  0  97 ZN=0.25 ZF=2500 FC=18.37 Zoom=1.00 Speed=9.99
                         DX9 Profile 64bit VeryHighSpec GI DevMode forest [9.3419]
                                        DP:   586 ( 586) ShadowGen:668 (669)
                             Polys: 307,379 (307,258) Shadow:287,358 (288,123)
                                        Streaming IO: ACT: 1885msec, Jobs: 0
                                        Mem=830 Peak=860 DLights=(1/1/1/0)
                                              FPS  44.0 ( 36.. 47)
```

1. Open the console within Sandbox using the **View** menu and selecting **Show Console**.

2. Type the `r_displayinfo = 1` command. This command displays important information concerning the engine's overall performance. Some of the major values, which you should be able to identify, are:

   ❑ CamPos

   ❑ Tris

   ❑ DP

   ❑ Mem

   ❑ DLights

   ❑ FPS

These values are important because entire projects set budgets around these values.

Other than the camera position, if you notice abnormal values or activity in any of these values, you can be sure that you are experiencing some sort of performance loss.

The *most effective* measurement of performance is the **frame time**. The reason for this is that **frames per second (FPS)** is defined as 1 / frame time and is hence a nonlinear measure. An increase of 2 FPS, for example, when the game is running at 20 FPS gives a profitable gain of 5 ms, while the same 2 FPS improvement on a game running at 60 FPS will just result in a gain of 0.5 ms.

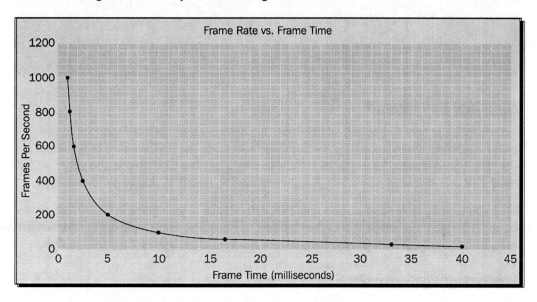

Frame time refers to the time that each frame takes from the beginning to the end and is usually expressed in **milliseconds (ms)**.

3. Type the r_displayinfo = 2 command. By setting r_DisplayInfo to 2 instead of 1, it is possible to see the frame time instead of FPS.

What just happened?

Performance can heavily depend on the execution environment, so it is important to use similar conditions when comparing performance numbers. The performance of systems with different hardware, for example, is likely to vary a lot. The GPU time is also very dependent on the screen resolution. A higher resolution results in slower performance.

Being able to accurately measure and read the performance of your game in CryENGINE allows you to set budgets and follow them when creating content. The display info command, in most cases, contains enough high-level information for this kind of general performance profiling.

Understanding draw calls

Every object with a different material has a separate draw call. This also means that every submaterial is a separate draw call.

Each draw call will mean setting material data and some other extra work on the CPU side plus fill rate costs on the GPU side (which varies depending on the screen area occupied by the draw call).

Draw call count can and will be affected depending on a certain number of conditions, which are discussed as follows:

◆ Opaque geometry has at least two draw calls (one for Zpass and one for general rendering)

◆ Shadows are extra draw calls, as are detail passes and some material layers as well

◆ The amount of nondeferred lights affecting geometry

Strive to maintain an acceptable draw call count—around 2,000 draw calls—on design and art side, at all times per frame.

Visualizing triangle count

One way to view just the triangles in CryENGINE is to enable wireframe.

You can do this using the `r_wireframe = 1` CVAR.

This visualizes the value seen in the display info for what the renderer is currently drawing in terms of triangles. This should be monitored and can usually identify faults in occlusion as well as view distance ratios.

Setting budgets

In most cases, it is impossible to define specific, per-object budgets for each art asset. The final makeup of each view in the game depends on too many variables (how many objects, how many characters, how much vegetation, and so on).

 In most cases, developers set per-view budgets.

For example, a good, overall budget comprises of:

- ◆ 2,000 to 2,500 draw calls
- ◆ 1 to 2 million triangles

These budgets represent final in-game maximums for any particular view, including all rendering features and effects (after the entire scene has been polished). These budgets do not give the environment or character artists a clear budget for how many triangles to put into a building or a character, or for the level artists, for how many white box buildings should go into a particular view (and still leave enough room for characters, vehicles, particles, and so on).

Saving a level's statistics

In this section, we will create an XML report with statistics for the currently loaded level. The report includes all assets that are loaded, their size, dependencies, and the number of instances in the scene.

Time for action – Save Level Statistics

The report that we will generate will be created as a .xml file and can be opened by using Microsoft Excel.

Save Level Statistics can be printed out and accessed in two ways:

1. The first way is to open the **Tools** menu in Sandbox and navigate to the **Save Level Statistics** option.

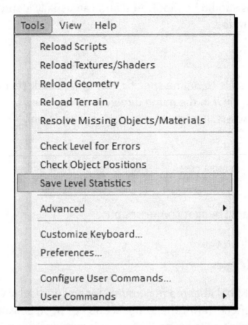

2. The second way is to output the level statistics by using a console command. Triggering the writing of the data from the console is quite useful when running in the launcher.

3. Open the console in Sandbox.

4. Type the command `savelevelstats`.

Performing this command through either of the two methods will create two `.xml` files under the `root directory\TestResults` folder.

The name of these files contains the name of the level from which they were saved. For example, the two files in the following screenshot were saved from the `forest.cry` level:

 These files are best opened with Microsoft Excel.

5. Open `Forest.xml` in Excel.

The first tab of the save level stats printout gives some important information.

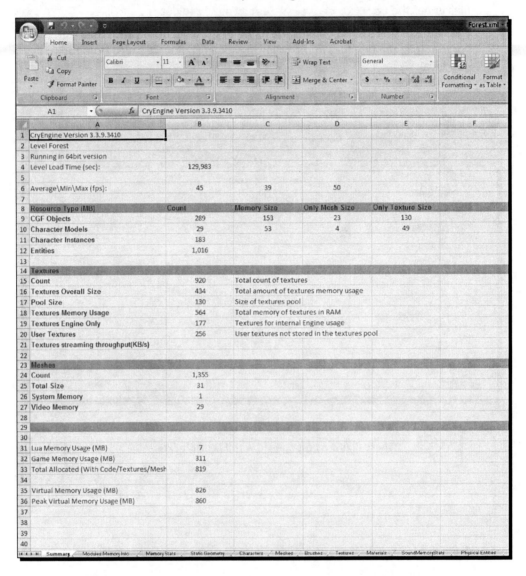

It describes the engine version, the level, and whether the engine is running in a 32- or 64-bit configuration. It also shows the average, min, and max frames per second.

The overall cost of a level can be quickly observed here, as the count for static `.cgf` geometry is printed as well as for character models, and finally entities. It even shows the memory consumption required for each type.

You can also get various profile information through the different pages generated. You can change these pages in Excel easily by clicking on the corresponding tab.

6. Click on the **Static Geometry** tab.

In this tab, you can see in-depth information for every static piece of geometry in the level.

You can arrange the worksheet by using Excel's arrange feature to display the rows in either descending or ascending format, doing so will allow you to spot assets that use high texture memory or that might have other performance problems.

In the following screenshot, you can easily see a performance issue where a hair object is taking up a much more texture memory than it should:

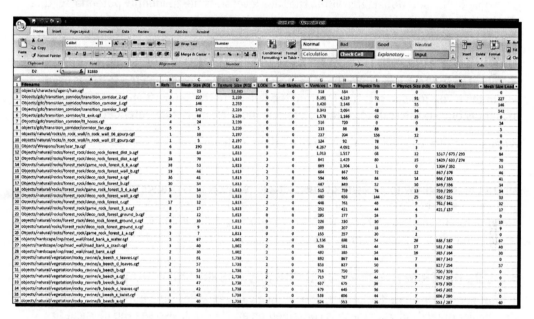

There are many more tabs and values associated with each tab. Some tabs will only be useful to people working on code, such as module memory, and others will be important for artists, such as static objects and characters.

7. Close the `Forest.xml` file.

8. Open the `depends_Forest.xml` file.

The entire file prints out the dependencies of certain files on other files. For example, it shows that a certain `.mtl` file might have six different textures depending on it.

In a lot of cases, this can be used to reduce build and distribution sizes as well as identify areas and objects, where textures might be able to be combined.

What just happened?

Save level stats print out a variety of information in regard to a level as well as the assets within certain levels. Being able to now print out this information into an Excel spreadsheet allows complex operations to take place, such as tracking the performance of a certain level over its development or even identifying problem assets.

As it is in an Excel sheet, further systems could be created within Excel to graph the improvement of the level's performance over time, as it is developed.

Have a go hero – view additional statistics in the save level stats file

Use some of the additional tabs within the save level stats file to identify potential texture, physics, and memory problems.

Viewing textures and render targets in the Textures tab

Switching to the **Textures** tab in the save level stats file will display all the textures used within the level. You can sort this list from the largest to the smallest memory consumption to identify quickly the textures that are utilizing more memory than intended.

When doing this, you will inevitably notice values with descriptions such as $HDRTarget or $SceneTarget.

Any of the textures with a $ symbol preceding it are known as **render targets**. These are not manually authored textures but are rather scene render targets, which are generated by the use of different shaders and post effects in real-time graphic engines. The texture size of the render target will depend, in most cases, on the current render window size.

Viewing physical triangle count and physics memory footprints

In most geometry-related printouts, you will see values for both the number of triangles a particular object's physics mesh is contained of, and you will also see the physical size in KB. It can be very easy to find problems with physics meshes and performance in this place, as almost all objects need a physics mesh, and it must be as small as possible. The other modifiers of physics size are the user-defined properties contained within the asset.

Reading the Detailed Dependencies tab

In the depends_Forest.xml file, you must have noticed the **Detailed Dependencies** tab. This tab is arguably one of the most useful, as it thoroughly breaks down asset interdependencies. For example, Object A uses Material B, which contains Texture C. It also simplifies the analysis further by adding a prefix for every object with or without dependencies.

Enabling Debug Draw modes

In this section, we will explore the different modes that you can enable in Sandbox to be able to track down and spot performance and some asset problems.

Time for action – enabling Debug Draw modes

This example will include extensive use of the console, and as in the previous examples of this chapter, you must have a populated level opened in the editor application for majority of these functions.

As our goal is to provide the best performance, we need to be visually able to observe the impact of using different features, especially in combination with each other.

1. The first debug view that we will use is the r_stats 1 view. Enable this view by typing in r_stats = 1 into the console within Sandbox.

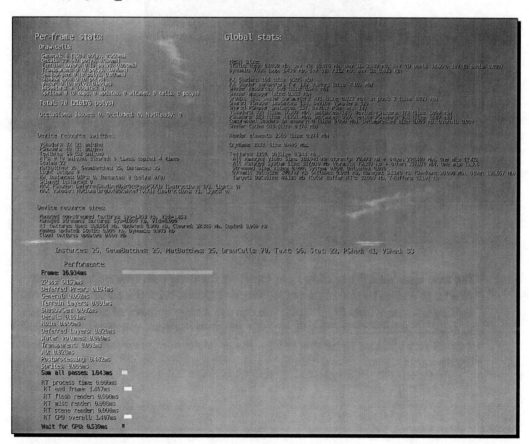

As you can see in the previous screenshot, this view breaks down the per-frame statistics of the renderer. This is extremely important as the render takes up the highest percentage, in most cases, of the frame time. It is also the most important view to use when following certain budget guidelines, as designers and artist have direct control over these variables by adjusting the number of lights in their viewable scenes or even by adjusting the decals.

Many artists and designers prefer to use a slimmed-down version of this view, which shows only frame-time costs of particular render passes.

2. Enable the slimmed-down render statistics view by typing `r_stats= 15` into the console.

The `r_stats 15` command is extremely valuable as it displays the frame-time cost per render pass. If the value appears in *red*, then it is over budget.

```
GPU Times
Scene                   7.50ms
    Shadows             0.01ms
    ZPass               0.21ms
    Deferred decals     0.00ms
    Deferred lighting   2.12ms
        Ambient         0.38ms
        Cubemaps        0.00ms
        SSAO+GI         0.06ms
        Lights          0.01ms
    Opaque              0.62ms
    Transparent         0.21ms
    HDR                 4.00ms
    PostFX              0.71ms
```

The next view we will use allows you to assess the draw calls created by different effects, as well as by materials and lighting on objects. With the advanced deferred lighting solution within CryENGINE, you can use a large number of deferred lights to achieve advanced effects with minimal affect on the draw call count. However, it is still very valuable to be able to view the breakdown of draw calls, by object, within a scene.

3. Enable this view by using `r_stats 6`.

This will show the draw call cost of each object on the screen. They are listed with Zpass calls, general calls, shadow calls, and finally, misc calls.

Each material equates to at least two draw calls. One for Zpass, which calls the geometry depth and normals, and one for the opaque pass, also known as the general pass.

Additional draw calls are then added as lighting, shadows, shader properties, and postprocesses change.

 Submaterials add to the draw call count if they are used as a render material.

Another important consideration here could be to omit normal maps for decals as they add to the depth pass (Zpass) calls.

4. Finally, we will explore overdraw.

5. Disable `r_Stats 6` by typing into the console `r_stats 0`.

6. Enable the overdraw render mode by typing `r_measureoverdraw 1`.

This view allows you to visualize the amount of pixel instructions performed on each pixel in a scene. Overdraw is caused by a number of things including alpha blending, where a pixel is calculated multiple times.

In the previous screenshot, you can see the selection of four decals that overlap each other and a road texture that is also alpha blended. The surrounding vegetation and terrain is relatively low cost, but the overlapping decals and road add greatly to the pixel cost.

Depending on your performance guidelines, you may have different budgets or need to view different scales of the `r_measureoverdraw` command.

7. Adjust the overdraw pixel cost scale using the `r_MeasureOverdrawScale` command. This will adjust the representation color of the number of instructions required in each pixel, as shown in the following screenshot:

```
-- >48 instructions --
-- >96 instructions --
-- >144 instructions --
-- >192 instructions --
-- >249 instructions --
-- >288 instructions --
-- >336 instructions --
-- >384 instructions --
```

The final debug view we will now explore is the entity Debug Draw. These enable a number of different debug draws, which, for the ease of writing, we will not cover.

8. Type `P_draw_helpers 1` into the console.

This view is one of the most useful Debug Draw commands that a developer can use when adjusting the physical properties of anything within the engine.

This view essentially shows the view the physics system has of the engine. Different levels of physical simulation are shown as different colors in this view. The following screenshot shows a mix of static and live physics as well as the character's collider:

What just happened?

Being able to enable the various debug views is essential! For designers, it is especially important as they are the ones that spend the most time in Sandbox putting all the assets together, and usually have a direct impact on the overall, per-view performance in a level.

Profiles

Profiles can be activated by typing `profile` followed by a specific number, to enable subsystem information on screen. This is extremely useful when identifying slowly performing functions and systems as they are measured in terms of a frame time and are broken down into various views.

Time for action – using profiles to break down frame-time performance

In this example, we will use some of the more useful profiles immediately available to us within the editor or launcher applications.

1. Type `profile 1` into the console.

    This view displays a per-function breakdown cost in frame time. This is especially useful for programmers when scripting and adding new game code.

    Note that it shows a descending list of the most expensive functions that are executed. If, for example, functions named particle and character are at the top of the list, it is likely that there is an element within the level negatively affecting performance.

2. Type `profile 6` into the console.

    This view shows the time in milliseconds and the percentage of the overall frame time that each system within the CryENGINE consumes.

3. Try some of the other profiles available by typing in `profile 1` through `profile 7`.

What just happened?

We have just seen how to visualize our performance and identify potential performance problems quickly using the `profile` console command. It is important to check these, should lag spikes and other frame rate problems manifest while you create your content. Identifying these problems early is the key to sharing a high performance experience.

Optimizing levels with VisAreas and Portals

The **VisArea** is used to define indoor areas, which have their own ambient color. You can also create indoor areas without this object; however, you will not be able to achieve completely dark or black lighting conditions. The bright, outdoor, ambient lighting affects indoor areas that do not contain a VisArea. Some important points to understand about VisAreas are as follows:

♦ Objects inside a VisArea won't be rendered from the outside

♦ VisAreas help to isolate lightning conditions inside rooms

♦ Using Portals, you can cut holes inside the VisAreas

- When using Portals they must be smaller than the VisArea shape
- You can enable/disable Portals via Flow Graph
- You can have multiple Portals in one VisArea

Time for action – set up a VisArea

Open any level and set up a small structure, as seen in the next screenshot examples.

1. On the Rollup Bar, go to **Area | VisArea**.
2. Place the VisArea shape around your room.
3. Set the height.
4. Try to stay on the grid.
5. Keep the shape of the VisArea as simple as possible.

Next, we must create a portal for our room.

Portals are used to add a visual "entrance" into the VisArea.

6. Create the portal shape according to the size of the entrance by creating the portal area with four points and aligning them to the outside and inside entrance points.

Keep the size as small as possible. (Also, the size of the portal can't be bigger than the VisArea itself.)

The portal has to be half inside the VisArea. (Being in the top and front view helps.)

If you leave the VisArea (indoor), everything behind you will disappear, including the walls that are located inside.

You will need a wall inside the VisArea and a wall outside the VisArea.

What just happened?

VisAreas and Portals allow for complex effects, such as achieving underwater rooms or expansive interiors, while rigidly controlling what is being rendered at the time. They are typically used to remove entire building interiors from rendering when the player views them from the outside. It also allows you to do the opposite, where all exterior rendering is disabled and only the objects within the VisArea are rendered. In either case, more control is given directly to the designer.

Ambient color of VisAreas and Portals

The ambient color parameter specifies which ambient color should be inside the VisArea or portal. This should be thoroughly considered, as the color difference between objects in a portal with a different ambient color than the attached VisArea will cause discontinuity in lighting and visual quality.

Blind spots

You may find when adjusting Portals and VisAreas that having any rotation outside of 90 degrees between their areas will cause blind spots and unpredictable behavior. This can be easily fixed by simply ensuring that the connection between the portal and VisArea is 90 degrees.

Using VisAreas and Portals vertically

To create VisAreas and Portals that work vertically, you must create them with their position in mind. They cannot be rotated from vertical to lateral, but rather must be drawn laterally instead.

Light clipping boxes and areas

Light clipping boxes and areas are used for the implementation of deferred light clipping in CryENGINE, a tool that will enable interior spaces to be lit far better and more accurately than they currently are.

 The use of light boxes and light areas is highly dependent on the situation.

Time for action – create a light clipping box

In this example, we will create a light clipping box that will restrict a light to a certain area. This is extremely useful when lighting interiors, as spherical lights tend to bleed through walls.

1. To test the process of using a light box, drag-and-drop **LightBox** from the **Area** tab in the Rollup Bar.

2. Next, add a light to your scene.

3. In the **Lights** entity link, add a link to the light box.

4. The light has the **DeferredClipBounds** property set to **True**. Once setting it to **True**, you will see that the light will be clipped to that volume.

A deferred light that is linked to either a light shape or a light box will be clipped to that volume regardless of whether it is inside the volume or not.

What just happened?

There is a common problem of light bleeding becoming apparent with the deferred approach—the boundaries of the lighting are not controllable. Deferred light, for example, placed in one room can bleed through the wall into another room. Thankfully, the light clip boxes and shapes are tools available for artists, which they can use to specify a custom stencil culling geometry for each light source in the scene.

Using a concave light shape

If a concave light shape has been created, the editor should warn the user and not clip the light.

Linking to multiple light shapes

If a light falls inside or is linked to more than one LightBox/LightShape, the editor will warn the user and clip the light to the first LightBox/LightShape in the list.

Activating and deactivating layers

In the next example, we will explore the use of an important Flow Graph node that allows designers to stream in and stream out entire layers of objects.

Time for action – use layer switching logic

The requirements for each level will be different, and thus, to begin with, you should have a populated level open that has entities organized onto different layers.

In this example, we will use layer activation and deactivation to show all the contents required for a particular gameplay section.

Typically when creating levels, they are split into unique sections named action bubbles.

It is a common practice to hide layers that contain action bubbles, which are not being played.

It is possible to activate and deactivate all the entities in a specific layer by using the **Engine:LayerSwitch** FlowNode.

 Even brushes and solids can be hidden/unhidden using this node.

1. Simply create a new Flow Graph and add the **Engine: LayerSwitch** FlowNode to the graph.

2. Next, double-click on the **Layer** property. This will present you with a pull-down window, allowing you to set what layer should be attached to this node.

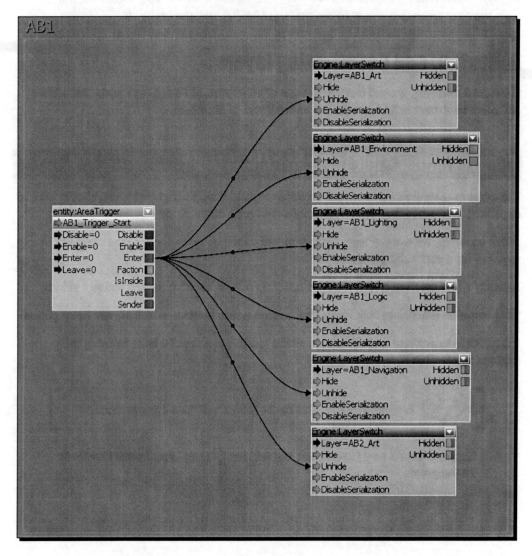

Layer switching needs to be globally enabled in order for the level to work.

3. In the Rollup Bar, switch to the **Terrain** tab, then select **Environment**, and set **UseLayersActivation** to **True**.

What just happened?

Being able to hide and show the different layers expands the control a designer has on the world while the player is playing in it. It is common that multiple triggers are used to hide certain layers or unhide other layers as the player progresses through a level. This can also save a massive amount of time when it comes to reworking entire areas for a player's revisit to the area after an event.

 It is important to know that, though it can immediately save performance, there is no core manipulation of the streaming system when performing layer switching.

Limitations of layer switching

Though layer switching is a simple technique, there are some limitations to what it can and cannot do.

◆ Entities that are set to be hidden in a game will not unhide if the **Unhide** input is triggered

◆ Picked up objects will disappear in the player's hands when their layer gets hidden

◆ Only entities, brushes, and solids are affected

◆ The layer switch has nothing to do with streaming

Cinematics

It is good workflow to always create a layer dedicated to cinematics. The cinematics layer will typically have to unhide and hide different entities within the game world to function, as well as be able to maintain a high standard of quality in the cutscene while saving performance on the rest of the level. Using the layer switch combined with the cinematics layer gives a lot of control over to the designer in terms of which objects are being shown when, and whether they remain in the level or not after the cinematic has finished.

Pop quiz – performance profiling

1. Which `r_stats` variable will display a per-object draw call count on screen?

    a. `r_stats = 1`

    b. `r_stats = 2`

    c. `r_stats =15`

    d. `r_stats = 6`

2. Which is the console command to display the physical information visually in the viewport?

   a. `p_draw_helper = 1`

   b. `e_debug_draw = 1`

   c. `ca_displayskeleton = 1`

   d. `physicsplz = 1`

3. Which editor construct is used to connect a VisArea to other VisAreas and outdoors?

   a. BasicEntity

   b. IrradianceVolume

   c. Portals

   d. LightBox

Packaging your content to share

The time has finally come for us to package up our levels and assets and unleash them on the gaming community! Sharing your creations can be a very educational and rewarding experience, as it allows others to critique as well as enjoy your work. It is very common for games to go through many releases and patching, and this can be considered when sharing your content for free.

CryDev project database

At the beginning of this book, we registered on `http://crydev.net` to get access to the Free SDK using a login and password. Using CryDev, we can give individual users access to our content using the project system. You can also save your level with a global share parameter, which will allow anyone with a CryDev username and password to access your levels.

Time for action – create a team, project, and share an upload

The CryDev project system is a nice system that we can easily use to share and store our projects! In this example, we will create a team and then we will register a project within that team. Next, we will upload some data to our project, to share with other CryDev users.

1. Open your favorite web browser and go to `http://crydev.net`.

2. Log in using your username and password. This is the same username and password used to log in to the CryENGINE Sandbox.

3. Click on the **Projects** link as shown in the following screenshot:

Upon clicking on **Projects**, you'll see a list of all the CryDev projects sorted by the latest update. As our final goal here is to create a project and upload our files, we must first create a team. Teams can be made up of one or many people, however, for this example, we will create one just for ourselves.

4. Click on the **Create Team** icon and then enter a team name.

In the following screenshot, I have named the team as **My Super Development Team**.

5. Now that we've created a team, you'll likely want to add a description for your team, or leave it blank if you like.

6. You can also change the default logo by clicking on it and uploading a new image. You can also enter the website that you might have for your game or team below this.

7. On the bottom right of your team page, you will see a **Members** list where you can add, kick, and manage the team members.

 When a team is deleted, everything from this team is deleted including member lists, files, and any descriptions.

Now let's create a project for our team.

8. Click on **Create a new Project**.

9. Enter a project name, platform, and the type of the project.

   When selecting a platform, understand that this means the selected platform is the SDK it was made for and/or with. If your project is made with the Crysis 2 Mod SDK, it's unlikely to work on the Crysis Wars platform without an extensive engineering effort. So choose whatever platform on which you've actually run and tested the project. As far as selecting the type goes, simply select one that fits your type of project best.

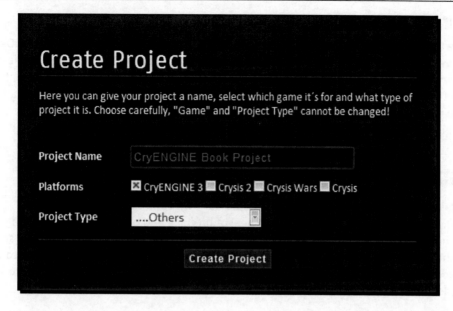

 Multiple platforms may be chosen at once, as many older projects functioned in both the Crysis and Crysis Wars platforms.

You will now be presented with the project page, which is very similar to the team page seen earlier. Dissimilar to the team page, project pages can have two associated images. The largest is called the project banner and is only displayed on the project page. The project logo is a smaller image, which is used on the main project's page list.

10. We can now add a download link to our project by using **Add a Download Link**.

11. Add a file that you wish to share; for this example, it is not actually required to upload a file.

 Currently, the file size is restricted to no greater than 1.5 gigabytes.

What just happened?

Before the file that you have uploaded is made public, it needs to be checked by the CryDev database staff. After the file has been uploaded and before it has been approved, team leaders will see that the file is awaiting approval; all the other users will see **No Download Available**. When the file has been approved by the CryDev staff, it will be published and a **Download** button will appear. Anyone can download this file, including guests. Team leaders will be able to delete the file and upload a new one, which will start the approval process again.

Summary

Well here we are, we've done it. We've created our own content with CryENGINE and have distributed it online. We saw a good deal of profiling and performance monitoring tools in this chapter, and now have the ability to improve our player's experience and spot potential performance issues. We have also created a project on the CryDev site and can now add more projects, as we go beyond this book and experiment with the various tools we've learned!

The theme throughout this book has been one of learning through experimentation, and because CryENGINE has been around for quite some time now, it contains a huge repertoire of tools to create anywhere from a AAA experience to a casual game. As the cliché goes, "practice makes perfect", and truly, the practice and knowledge of the tools available within your games technology is what separates those big AAA developments from the smaller, hobbyist developers. Should you want to build a project, start with what you enjoy doing! This book has gone over a huge variety of different disciplines, from programming, art, design, animation, and sound, and I sincerely hope you have enjoyed discovering some of the workflow and processes from each.

Pop Quiz Answers

Chapter 2, Breaking Ground with Sandbox

Pop quiz – level size and scale

1	c
2	c
3	a

Pop quiz – Terrain texture layers

1	a
2	a
3	d

Chapter 3, Playable Levels in No Time

Pop quiz – essential game objects

1	b
2	d
3	a

Chapter 4, I'm a Scripter Not a Coder

Pop quiz – scripting

1	d
2	b
3	c

Chapter 5, C++ and Compiling Your Own Game Code

Pop quiz – lua entities and scriptbind functions

1	b
2	a
3	c

Chapter 6, User Interface and HUD Creation with Flash

Pop quiz – UI Actions

1	b
2	c
3	b

Chapter 7, Creating Assets for the CryENGINE 3

Pop quiz - creating assets for your games

1	c
2	b
3	c

Chapter 8, Creating Real-time Cutscenes and Cinematic Events

Pop quiz – creating cinematics and cutscenes

1	d
2	a
3	d
4	b

Chapter 9, Immersion through Audio Design

Pop quiz – creating sound for your game

1	c
2	a
3	b

Chapter 10, Preparing to Share Your Content

Pop quiz – performance profiling

1	d
2	a
3	b

Index

About Packt Publishing

Packt, pronounced 'packed', published its first book "Mastering phpMyAdmin for Effective MySQL Management" in April 2004 and subsequently continued to specialize in publishing highly focused books on specific technologies and solutions.

Our books and publications share the experiences of your fellow IT professionals in adapting and customizing today's systems, applications, and frameworks. Our solution-based books give you the knowledge and power to customize the software and technologies you're using to get the job done. Packt books are more specific and less general than the IT books you have seen in the past. Our unique business model allows us to bring you more focused information, giving you more of what you need to know, and less of what you don't.

Packt is a modern, yet unique publishing company, which focuses on producing quality, cutting-edge books for communities of developers, administrators, and newbies alike. For more information, please visit our website: www.PacktPub.com.

Writing for Packt

We welcome all inquiries from people who are interested in authoring. Book proposals should be sent to author@packtpub.com. If your book idea is still at an early stage and you would like to discuss it first before writing a formal book proposal, contact us; one of our commissioning editors will get in touch with you.

We're not just looking for published authors; if you have strong technical skills but no writing experience, our experienced editors can help you develop a writing career, or simply get some additional reward for your expertise.

CryENGINE 3 Cookbook

ISBN: 978-1-84969-106-2   Paperback: 324 pages

Over 90 recipes written by Crytek developers for creating third-generation real-time games

1. Begin developing your AAA game or simulation by harnessing the power of the award winning CryENGINE3.

2. Create entire game worlds using the powerful CryENGINE 3 Sandbox.

3. Create your very own customized content for use within the CryENGINE3 with the multiple creation recipes in this book.

Google SketchUp for Game Design: Beginner's Guide

ISBN: 978-1-84969-134-5   Paperback: 270 pages

Create 3D game worlds complete with textures, levels, and props

1. Learn how to create realistic game worlds with Google's easy 3D modeling tool.

2. Populate your games with realistic terrain, buildings, vehicles and objects.

3. Import to game engines such as Unity 3D and create a first person 3D game simulation.

4. Learn the skills you need to sell low polygon 3D objects in game asset stores.

Please check **www.PacktPub.com** for information on our titles

Blender 3D Basics Beginner's Guide

ISBN: 978-1-84951-690-7   Paperback: 468 pages

The Complete novice's guide to 3D modeling and animation

1. The best starter guide for complete newcomers to 3D modeling and animation.

2. Easier learning curve than any other book on Blender.

3. You will learn all the important foundation skills ready to apply to any 3D software.

Unity 3D Game Development by Example Beginner's Guide

ISBN: 978-1-84969-054-6   Paperback: 384 pages

A seat-of-your-pants manual for building fun, groovy little games quickly

1. Build fun games using the free Unity 3D game engine even if you've never coded before.

2. Learn how to "skin" projects to make totally different games from the same file – more games, less effort!

3. Deploy your games to the Internet so that your friends and family can play them.

4. Packed with ideas, inspiration, and advice for your own game design and development.

Please check **www.PacktPub.com** for information on our titles

Lightning Source UK Ltd.
Milton Keynes UK
UKOW021356080313

207351UK00003B/94/P